L I B R A R Y   O F   C O N G R E S S

Law Library

A N   I L L U S T R A T E D   G U I D E

L I B R A R Y   O F   C O N G R E S S   W A S H I N G T O N   2 0 0 5

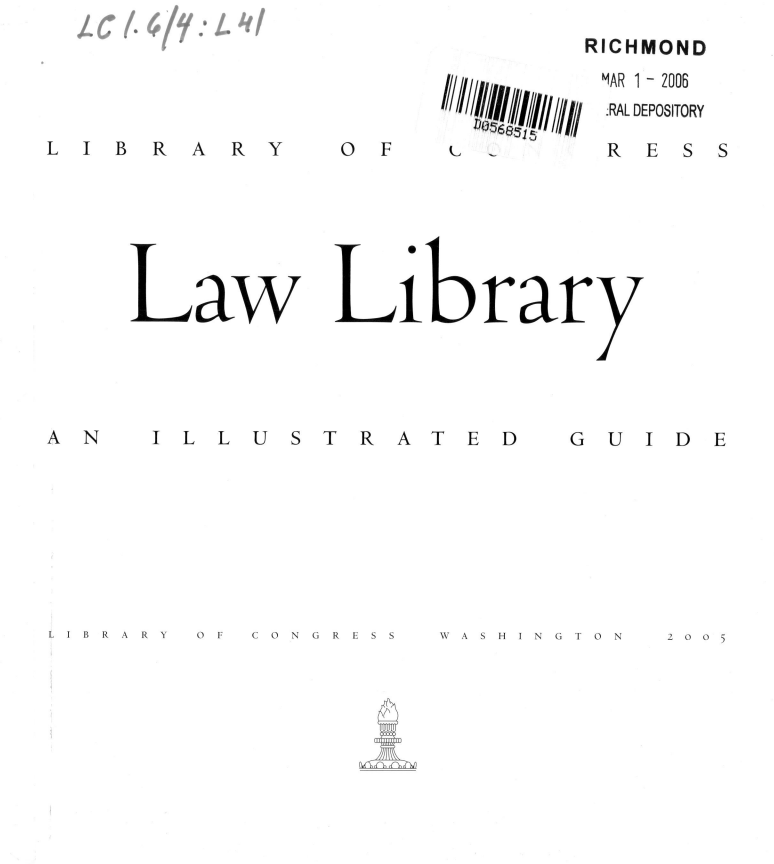

Law Library was co-authored by Jolande Goldberg of the Cataloging Policy and Support Office and Natalie Gawdiak of the Law Library, under the direction of Law Librarian Rubens Medina. Additional research and review were carried out by Law Library staff Kersi Shroff, James Martin, and Donald DeGlopper. Assistance was also provided by Law Library specialists Nicole Atwill, Marie-Louise Bernal, Emily Carr, Pamela Craig, Dario Ferreira, Ruth Levush, Krishan Nehra, the late David Rabasca, Peter Roudik, George Sfeir, Meredith Shedd-Driskell, Sayuri Umeda, and Pamela Wroten, as well as former staff or associates Andrei Pliguzov, Michael Shannon, and Jose Torres. The Law Library is also indebted to Library colleagues from other departments, including John Bertonaschi, Barbara Dash, Mark Dimunation, Clark Evans, Michael Grunberger, James Higgins, Allen Maberry, Rosemary Fry Plakas, Fawzi Tadros, the late Gerald Wager, and to Iris Newsom for her editorial expertise.

This publication was made possible by generous support from the James Madison Council, a national, private-sector advisory council dedicated to helping the Library of Congress share its unique resources with the nation and the world.

The text is composed in Centaur, a typeface designed by American typographer and book designer Bruce Rogers (1870–1957). The full type font was first used at The Montagne Press in 1915 for an edition of Maurice de Guérin's *The Centaur.*

This guide was designed by Robert L. Wiser of Silver Spring, Maryland, and directed by Gloria Baskerville-Holmes, Production Manager, Publishing Office.

COVER: One of the Law Library's treasures is an undated manuscript of *Les institutes de l'empereur Justinien.* This elegant manuscript on vellum is a translation into (Old) French of Justinian's *Institutes,* made ca. 1280. (*Law Library Rare Book Collection;* LCCN 98178271)

LIBRARY OF CONGRESS CATALOGING-IN-PUBLICATION DATA

Law Library of Congress (U.S.)
     Library of Congress Law Library : an illustrated guide.
        p.   cm.
     Co-authored by Jolande Goldberg and Natalie Gawdiak.
     ISBN 0-8444-1137-X
     1. Law—Bibliography. 2. Law Library of Congress (U.S.) 3. Law libraries—Washington (D.C.) I. Goldberg, Jolande E. II. Gawdiak, Natalie.
    Z663.5 L54 2005
    016'.34—dc22

                          2005044329

For sale by the U.S. Government Printing Office
Superintendent of Documents
Mail Stop: SSOP, Washington, D.C. 20402–9328

Contents

These examples, shown with their containers, from the Law Library's Miniature Law Book Collection include constitutions, codes, and *coutumes* (Customary Law) published in various cities in Continental Europe, Cuba, and Argentina from 1619 to 1989. (*Law Library Rare Book Collection*)

The smallest book of the collection, the *Constitución de la Republica de Cuba* (La Habana, 1986; LCCN 89181971) is only 2½ inches tall.

Preface

THE LAW COLLECTION found in the Library of Congress—most notably in the Law Library of Congress, the world's largest law library—constitutes a unique resource for Congress and the nation. Scholars, students, practitioners, and researchers in law and related disciplines will find the breadth of the law collection, and in many areas its depth, unparalleled. The Library's collections are a premier source for information on law, whether research is needed on current legislation or some aspect of the legal heritage of the United States or of other nations. Unknown to many is the fact that, beyond its role as national law library and curator of the written record of the world's legal systems, the Law Library of Congress is also a legal research center for the federal government, and its staff of foreign-trained attorneys from around the world and senior reference specialists are daily involved in the interpretation of complex and dynamic legal issues for government requesters, who include not only the members of Congress but judicial and executive branch authorities as well. The Law Library also assists state governments and international organizations to the extent that its congressional workload permits.

The situation of the Law Library and the challenges the staff face today seem infinitely different from those which confronted their predecessors in the early days of this Republic. After the establishment of the main Library of Congress in 1800 in the Capitol building, the Library became a fashionable gathering place for tourists and the local gentry. The crowded conditions that resulted hampered the Library in carrying out its first major mission: serving the legal information needs of the U.S. Congress. For this reason, the law books were ordered to be culled from the collection and set up in a separate room from the main Library by an Act of Congress in 1832. The primary function of the single "law custodian"—as the sole Law Library employee was then called—was to deliver law books from this collection, which numbered a little over two thousand volumes, to the Congress as well as to the Justices of the Supreme Court, also located in the Capitol building.

While the primary mission of the Library is still to serve the Congress, the task has become more varied with the growing intensity of the international legal-political and legal-economic relationships worldwide. In carrying out its mandate, the Law Library must meet the challenges of digital technology to ensure that the online law sources available in the Library are as comprehensive, up-to-date, and authentic as possible. Over half the collections in the Law Library are in foreign languages. Inasmuch as some nations have not been able to index their own laws, the Law Library has taken the lead in establishing online legal research aids,

AN
ABSTRACT
OR THE
LAWES
OF
NEVV ENGLAND,

As they are novv established.

LONDON,

Printed for *F. Coules*, and *W. Ley* at Paules Chain,

1641.

including an international cooperative among parliaments of the world to exchange authentic legal sources online under a partnership called GLIN, the Global Legal Information Network.

The degree to which the practice of law is a science or an art is open to debate, but certainly research in the legal field often requires an approach that is at once systematic and creative. Although the schematic arrangement and organization of the collections are being constantly refined for ease of access and retrieval, guidance in the use of the collection and in the interpretation of its substance provided by the staff of the Library often constitutes the crucial element necessary for a successful outcome in one's research. The Library has been fortunate in having been able to attract a unique staff whose expertise has been able to interpret so much of the vast store of information contained in the ever-expanding sources on law and its scholars-in-residence program has been a mutually beneficial undertaking for participants and staff.

Law holdings in the Library of Congress have been assigned by and large to the care of the Law Library of Congress in the Library's James Madison Memorial Building. Custody over some of the rarest of the law holdings, however, is shared by the Library's Rare Book and Special Collections Division in the Thomas Jefferson Building. Due to the wide-ranging nature of law, legal scholars and students of the law may also need to pursue their research in one or more of

Lunette with images of Law and Justice overlooking the Old Supreme Court Chamber, one of the original sites of the Law Library of Congress when it was located in the Capitol building. (*U.S. Senate Curator's Office*)

the nearly two dozen reading rooms in the Library, especially for such subjects as business, economics, government, political science, and the like. In some cases, earlier collections of a given law-related subject are maintained in the General Collections even though holdings of the same subject are housed in the Law Library. Books on income tax law, for example, were assigned due to past collection policies to the Business Reading Room, but later receipts are now in the Law Library. Much important material, especially related to colonial and U.S. law and lawmaking, may also be found in the Manuscript Division in the James Madison Building where papers of U.S. presidents, Supreme Court justices, and other principals involved in court cases, law making, treaty negotiations and the like are kept. Legal documents which contain maps may be located in the Geography and Map Reading Room in the same building. Certain law materials in non-Roman alphabets are contained in area studies collections of the Library in the Adams Building. General information about copyright law, both U.S. and foreign, may be studied in the Law Library, but actual research into copyright records must be carried out in the U.S. Registrar of Copyrights department, a separate entity from the Law Library, also located in the Madison Building.

Because of the vast reach of the law, legal and legislative research may require the need for broad subject expertise. Despite the ubiquitous presence and significance of law in interdisciplinary studies, however, the fact that the law holdings in the Library of Congress are still for the most part held separately from the main collection attests to the special requirements that the discipline of law imposes on those who collect its sources. The authenticity of legal sources, for example, is another requisite element of legal and legislative research, which exceeds the level required of sources in most other areas, hence the entire subdiscipline of legal citation. Law is dynamic and ever-changing, and thus timeliness and currency are vital aspects of retrieval and delivery. Such exigencies as are placed on those who need to maintain, retrieve, and analyze law sources and legislative collections are seldom demanded from those in other fields.

It is difficult to envision the law library of the future. One assumes that converting paper to digital collections is a logical and essential way to proceed. No matter what the future brings, as we move forward, the treasures depicted in these pages will remain timeless reminders of the richness and diversity of the world's legacy of law.

RUBENS MEDINA
LAW LIBRARIAN OF CONGRESS

Introduction

THE NEED for a law collection for the members of the U.S. Congress was the original rationale for the creation of the Library of Congress. An early proponent of establishing a legislative library, Representative Eldridge Gerry of Massachusetts, was appointed the head of the House committee to investigate purchasing books for the First Congress. In a 1790 report to the House, Gerry proposed that a congressional library be founded on the laws of the United States and several European nations and should include among other things "a collection of treaties and alliances from the earliest periods . . . sundry books on the civil and common law, etc. etc." Limited by budgetary concerns, the members did not act on Gerry's recommendation and made use instead of the New York Society Library and the Library Company of Philadelphia, when the capital was located in those cities. In 1800, faced with yet another move of the nation's capital—to Washington—and not wishing to have to transport "to the seat of the General Government a considerable part of their personal library," the members of Congress passed a bill to establish a congressional library in the Capitol building to be set up in 1801. A catalog of the period listed forty law-related titles in two hundred sixty-six volumes; of these only two were produced on American soil, *Swift's System of the Laws of Connecticut* (2 v.) and *Dallas's Reports.*

In 1814 when British troops attacked the U.S. Capitol in retaliation for the Americans' having previously torched public buildings in Toronto (then known as York), the resulting fire destroyed much of the Library. All one hundred seventy-four law titles it held by that time, including five indigenous works among which were Joseph Story's *Selections of Pleadings in Civil Actions* (1805) and the early issues of the first American legal periodical, *Hall's American Law Journal*, went up in smoke.

The young nation was fortunate in having the opportunity to replace the Library with the purchase of the personal collection of former President Thomas Jefferson. A successful lawyer before the Revolution, Jefferson had included in his library four hundred seventy-five law titles in six hundred thirty-nine volumes. Of these three hundred eighteen were English and sixty were American; the rest originated in Scotland, Ireland, or on the continent. English court reports were contained in one hundred volumes, but there were only four American reports, three from Virginia and the fourth was *Dallas's Pennsylvania Reports*. Despite the number of legal works in Jefferson's library, some debate ensued in Congress about the suitability of the contents of his library for congressional purposes. Jefferson knew that an informed populace was the best guarantor of democracy. "No one more sincerely wishes the spread of information among mankind than I do, and none has greater confidence in its effect towards supporting free and good government." Jefferson also firmly established the concept that a nation's legislators should have access to all disciplines, and with his vast erudition and catholic interests, he successfully argued the principle that there was "no subject to which a member of Congress may not have occasion to refer." The purchase of the Jefferson collection was concluded in 1815.

A year later, Representative Robert Goodloe Harper, a lawyer from Maryland, made the first move toward creating a separate law department within the Library. Although Jefferson's broad perspective established the foundation of the Library of Congress that we know today, the very particular demands of the legal and legislative work fueled this early, unsuccessful initiative. The attempt to introduce a bill to separate the law collection was made for the benefit not only of the Congress but of the Supreme Court and lawyers in the capital as well. Lawyer Charles Jared Ingersoll, the U.S. District Attorney for Pennsylvania, noted in his diary in 1823 that the absence of a law library in the capital was "deplorable."

Charles A. Wickliffe, a Representative from Kentucky and later Postmaster General, sought to put a measure through Congress to respond to the need for a separate law library in 1826, 1828, and again in 1830. Senators Felix Grundy and William Learned Marcy took up the challenge and on July 14, 1832, a separate law library was finally established when President Andrew Jackson signed into law an Act of Congress (currently cited as 2 U.S.C. 132, 134, 135, 137), directing that a separate "apartment near to" the main Library in the Capitol be set up to which the law books would be removed for the use of Congress and the Supreme Court. In 1833, Law Library privileges were extended to members of the bar with cases before the Supreme Court. Thus, the perseverance of several determined legislators saw to it that the Library of Congress's first separate department was devoted to law and to the business of providing the nation's legislators and judges with the legal resources they needed for their vital tasks of molding democracy and making it work.

The Library of Congress suffered a serious fire in 1851, but the law volumes, by virtue of the Law Library's separate locale, were saved. As its collections grew, the Law Library moved from its original room adjacent to the Library in the Capitol to a larger room opposite the Supreme Court chambers. In these early years, the Senate chamber was on the floor above the Supreme Court, but when the Senate wing was added to the Capitol, the Senate moved out to that wing, allowing the Supreme Court to move upstairs to occupy the former Senate chamber. The Law Library moved across the hall to the Supreme Court chamber thus vacated and occupied that room from 1860 to 1950. The room was eventually restored to what it looked like in the days of the Supreme Court. Now a prime tourist site in the Capitol building, this elegant space is known as the Old Supreme Court Chamber. The Law Library gradually transferred its collections to the Thomas Jefferson Building, after 1897, and then to the Madison Building in 1981. A Law Library satellite collection in the Capitol remained, however, only closing in 1989. Today's Law Library houses most of its collections on compact, mechanized shelving in the sub-basement of the James Madison Memorial Building. The largest such installation in the world, it covers about two acres and has sixty miles of shelving capacity.

The need for foreign legal research sources, especially in times of hostilities with other nations, intensified the Law Library's acquisition efforts over the years to such an extent that certain collections in the Law Library exceed those of the countries of origin. Superb rare acquisitions entered the collection from various sources donated or obtained by the Library of Congress, and many included rare law volumes. The Joseph Meredith Toner collection came to the Library in 1882; the John Boyd Thatcher collection in the 1910s and 1920s, the Otto Vollbehr collection and the Paul Krüger collection—with a great Roman law component—both in 1930. The Lessing J. Rosenwald collection gradually increased between 1943 and 1975 and in 1979 became part of the Rare Book and Special Collections Division. During the tenure of highly respected Law Librarian John C. Vance (1924–43) the Law Library collection doubled in size.

In building its collections, the Law Library seeks to obtain all possible primary sources and as many important secondary sources concerning the law of as many nations and legal systems in the world as it can; the number of jurisdictions represented is approximately two hundred sixty. Materials on colonial and historic regimes are also housed in the collection. Although some translations of certain foreign laws may be found in the Library's collections, one may assume that foreign law sources will, as a rule, exist only in the official language of the country of origin. In situations involving a court case, researchers may need to determine whether a translation will be deemed accurate enough to be accepted by the court.

Among the types of materials that the Law Library specifically collects are official law gazettes, constitutions, and the proceedings of constitutional conventions; codes, compilations, and consolidations of laws; law revisions; chronological publications of laws and session laws; hearings and various legislative materials; court decisions and reports; and decisions and rulings of administrative courts that have the effect of judicial decisions. Among the very important categories are the

"finding aids," such as citators; digests and noter-ups; and indexes to laws, rules, and regulations, as well as to the decisions and reports of courts and administrative courts and agencies. Next in importance after law and legislation are the learned commentaries and the monographic literature on all subjects of the law from all major national and many local jurisdictions. Another genre, assiduously collected, is that of legal periodicals, which are for legal discussion and development, conference proceedings, and generalia, such as legal bibliographies, legal encyclopedias, dictionaries of law and dictionaries of words and phrases, catalogs of law library collections, and finally, biographies of lawyers and jurists and directories of the legal profession.

The works featured in this Guide are of course merely indicative of the Library's rich collections, both modern and historic, and their vastness makes creating a representative sampling a daunting task.

The *Kormchaia Kniga* (Pilot Book) is a compilation of Ecclesiastical and Civil Laws made in Byzantium in about the ninth century and first printed in Russia in 1650. As a result of reforms that precipitated the schism in the Russian Church, the first printing was recalled and alterations were made to the first edition. The volume shown here is the 1650 printing with omissions and some additions made by Patriarch Nikon in 1653, and with further alterations. (*Law Library Rare Book Collection; LCCN 2004574704*)

GRATIA NVS

Quoniam nouis superuenientibus causis nouis est remedijs succurrendū. Idcirco ego Bartholomeus britiensis confidens de magnificentia creatoris apparatum decretorum duxi in melius resp̄mandi

non retrahendo alicui: nec attribuendo mihi glosas q̃ non feci sed supplendo sectus solūma do ubi correctio necessaria videret̄: vel p̄pter subtractionē decretaliū e dimunitionē earundem: vel p̄pter iura que superuenerunt de nouo. Interdum etiam solutiones interpositas que pretermisse fuerant a ioanne. hoc feci ad honorem dei e ecclesie romane: e ad cōmunem utilitatem omnium studentium in iure canonico. Bar.

Decretum vñi Gratiani in quo est discordantiū canonum cōcordia ac primi e iure viuēte e humane attōnis.
Auctor Gratianus. Distictio.j.
Humani genus duobus regitur. Interdum etiam etc.
Humani genus duo. Hec distinctio diuiditur in duas partes. In prima p̄ponit quattuor canones q̃ humanū genus regitur duobus s.iuribus e cōsuetudinibus. sed sib i est e alia. Jo. e san.
De. Casus iste sic ponitur. Dicitur b̄ q̃ duo sunt iustra per gentis humanum regitur e gubernat s.ius naturale e cōsuetudo siue mos. Jus naturale est quod in lege e euangelio continet̄: quo iubetur alij facere quod iuri sibi uult fieri e prohibetur alij inferre quod sibi nolit fieri: e hoc probatur auctoritate christi dicentis: Omnia quecunque etc.
Decretum.

a Humanum. Tractaturus diuus gratianus de iure canonico:primo incipit a simplicioribus in naturam.f.a iure naturali qᴅ antiquius e dignius est. Legit enim ab ipsa rationali institu.de reᵬ diuin e.comodius. Assignat ergo multas differentias iuris naturalis ad alia iura usᵹ ad.rv.di. in qua aggreditur pricipale p̄positum in iure canonico origi ne eius assignans.
b Duobus. Signatur contrarium.xx.ui.q.ij. sed alijs duobus regitur tanquã auctoritate istis tanᵹ instīs.
Mūi.i. diuino.

b Moribus.i.consuetudinario iure: vel etiam iure humano siue nō scripto.xv.d. q.j. instōnis.
Vull. Sed nonne ego volo qᴅ alter det mihi rem vulla.ꝑ hec exponit̄ ibi de charitate e ad quod vis.sic exponit̄ lex.ff.e solu.j. Uel expone iubetur.i.consilium. sic econuerso verbum rogandi pro verbo precipiendi ponit̄.xj.q.iij.rogo.
Prohibetur. Nunᵹ inueniet̄ expresse p̄hibitus in lege vel in euangelio nisi per quidam cōsequentias. Nam ubi unū contrariū precipitur per e̅s aliud,p̄hibet̄ sibi aliud iudicial meum e̅e pᵉ cōsequens iudicatiuū tuum non e̅e etc.nā pᵖpositis.S.j.
Inferre. Sed nonne idem vult mortem inferre reos:ed tamen non vult ut sibi mors inferatur e Sed ꝑ ꝯe iudex qᴅ infligit morte: sed lex.vt.xxiij.q.v.ho.

naturalic videlicet iure e moribus. Jus naturale est qᴅ in lege e euangelio continet̄: quo quisᵹ iubet̄ alij facere quod sibi uult fieri e prohibetur alij inferre quod sibi nolit fieri. Unde christus in euange

Uolo.id e̅ velle.etc

Precep tū p̄ti uni e̅ alteri p̄hibitio.

Iudex nō condēnat sed lex.

PHILOSOPHY OF LAW

The Library has a vast array of legal titles of broad scope. Overarching subjects and fields of learning include, for example, the history of law, philosophy of law, ethnological jurisprudence, comparative law, and international law. Many first and subsequent editions of books on jurisprudence, law and society, and lawmaking by eminent authors may be found in the Law Library and, in some instances, in the Rare Book and Special Collections Division. The first edition of John Locke's *Two Treatises on Government* (London, 1690) is found in the Rare Book and Special Collections Division. The works of Georg Wilhelm Friedrich Hegel, Baron de Montesquieu, Christian Thomasius, Jean-Jacques Rousseau, and Rudolf von Jhering may be consulted in the Library. Here, too, one finds works on global issues, tracking closely the work of international organizations and institutions. The titles span legal systems, languages, and time periods, and include remarkable and special collections of rare books dealing with Roman, Customary, or Religious Law. One example is the sixteenth-century *Tractatus universi juris* (Venice: Franciscus Zilettus, 1584–86), published in twenty volumes under the auspices of Pope Gregory XIII (1502–85) and including seven hundred fifteen treatises of the most prominent jurists of that period.

The subject of Natural Law may be found in the Library's numerous titles by famous European thinkers. The German jurist and historian, Samuel Pufendorf (1632–94), who was the first professor appointed to the Chair of Natural Law in 1616 at the University of Heidelberg, is best known for his *Elementorum jurisprudentiae universalis libri II* (Elements of universal law. Cambridge, 1672) and *De jure naturae et gentium libri octo* (Of the law of nature and of nations. Lund, Sweden, 1672); this work was written while he held the Chair of Natural Law at the University of Lund in Sweden. At the same time, Pufendorf published an excerpt entitled *De officio hominis et civis juxta legem natutralem libri duo* (Lund, 1673). The Library holds many French-language editions prepared by Jean Barbeyrac (1674–1744) and several English translations of this title. Among the one hundred four titles of Pufendorf's in the Library, the Law Library holds the first edition of those mentioned above; these works were widely studied and served as an inspiration for clergyman John Wise, who later was to champion civil and religious rights in the American colonies.

Pufendorf was in good company. His contemporaries were such philosophers and publicists as: Christian Thomasius (1655–1728), author of *Institutionum jurisprudentiae divinae libri tres: in quibus fundamenta juris naturalis secundum hypotheses illustris Pufendorffii perspicue demonstrantur* (Halle, 1717); Christian Freiherr von Wolff

OPPOSITE: The Library holds several incunabula of the *Decretum Gratiani.* This handsome edition was published in Venice in 1514. It also has illustrative woodcuts of the *Arbor consanguinitatis* and *Arbor affinitatis* (leaves 594b and 595a). (*Law Library Rare Book Collection*; LCCN 2002553408)

(1679–1754), *Jus naturae, methodo scientifica pertractatum* (Frankfurt/Leipzig, 1740–48); Gottfried Wilhelm Freiherr von Leibniz (1646–1716), *Codex juris gentium diplomaticus* (Hanover, 1693–1700); Jean Domat (1625–96), *Les loix civiles dans leur ordre naturel* (Luxembourg, 1702); and Jean Jacques Burlamaqui (1694–1748), *Principes du droit naturel* (Geneva, 1748–84) or the Latin-language title *Juris naturalis elementa* (Venice, 1757). In the ranks of the nineteenth-century philosophers and influential law reformers the name of the German Paul Johann Anselm von Feuerbach (1775–1833) stands out. He is considered one of Germany's most notable jurists of the nineteenth century, writing on Natural Law (*Kritik des natürlichen Rechts als Propadeutik zu einer Wissenschaft der natürlichen Reche.* Altona, 1796) and pioneering criminal law and criminology. Of course, the Law Library is an excellent source for holdings on twentieth-century philosophical schools and movements as well, such as the Free-law Movement, Neo-Thomism, and the "Positivists" of whom Hans Kelsen (1881–1973) with his *Reine Rechtslehre* (The Pure Theory of Law. Leipzig and Vienna, 1934) is probably the most renowned.

General Law collections include such specific subjects as crime and punishment, e.g., Cesare, marchese di Beccaria (1738–94), *Dei delitti e delle pene* (Of crime and punishment). The Library has all eighty-four editions of this title, beginning with a copy of the scarce first edition of 1764. At a young age Cesare was introduced to the harsh prison conditions in Milan. He protested the cruel and inhumane treatment of prisoners, particularly by torture, and the arbitrary power of judges when they allowed their discretionary powers to be swayed by political concerns or the social status of offenders. As a strong and successful advocate for the balance of crime and punishment and improvements of prisons, he greatly influenced the rulers of Europe and legislators of the eighteenth-century revolutions as well.

Another subject of the many in the realm of General Law is that of dueling. Dueling as a means of settling a dispute or avenging one's honor has a lengthy history and was resorted to by opponents in many eras under various legal systems. The Library has, for example, two copies of the record of a case concerning dueling in which Francis Bacon argued for the Crown, *The charge of Sir Francis Bacon knight, His Maiesties attourney generall, touching duells, upon an information in the Star-chamber against Priest and Wright* (London, 1614).

One set of rules of dueling, known as the *Code Duello* or the "26 Commandments," was codified by the Irish in 1777 at the Clonmel Summer Assizes, for application in Tipperary, Galway, Mayo, Sligo, and Roscommon. Generally, the right to legal duels was given by a king or a judge, who determined the rules for such confrontations, including the time, place, and weapons to be used. The Law Library also holds a work on dueling by John Selden (1584–1654), *The Duello* (London, 1711?).

Although those who took part in duels of honor in the United States were castigated by many, dueling was not outlawed until close to the 1890s, and participants and onlookers often included well-educated persons who held responsible positions in society. In the case of Burr and Hamilton, the duel was set in New Jersey, as dueling had already been outlawed in New York. The two antagonists, who were rowed in separate boats across the Hudson River, called their meeting for this reason an "interview." In some instances, before killing one's opponent in a duel became an act of murder, lesser punishments were enforced in various quarters, such as disqualification from office or the like (cf. *The Code Duello*, with special reference to the State of Virginia, by Archibald Williams Patterson. Richmond, 1927; LCCN 28002816).

One of the most famous duels in the United States occurred between two successful lawyers who shared a law practice in New York and also both served in high political offices. Vice President Aaron Burr, a Princeton alumnus, fatally wounded former Secretary of the Treasury Alexander Hamilton on July 11, 1804, on a cliff ledge below Weehawken, New Jersey, in revenge for Hamilton's having thwarted Burr's political aspirations at various points in Burr's career. (*Prints and Photographs Division*)

Quando facit separatõnē ⁊ qñ includit ⁊
q̄ndo excludit no·io·an·de p̄ben·c·statu
tum·li·vj·⁊ archi·de elec·c·j·e·li·Et
a ⁊ ab i sili no·archi·xxxj·di·alit·Et de
a in·c·potuit de do·⁊ contu·Etiā a ⁊ ab de
notāt sepatõnem·C·de nup·l·a caligato
et ibi p Cy·in glo·iij·l ordīata·ff·de duob⁹ re·⁊·l·si ex
duob⁹ v̄ tex·cum glo·ff·de actõ emp·l·iij·§·fi·Itē a vel
ab est dictõ significatia p̄mi termi a q̊/sic dictõ·vsq̧ ter
minū ad quē·Hūc aūt terminū a q̊ significat exclusiue vel
inclusiue·de q̄bar·in·l·patron⁹·ff·de le·iij·Vñ a vl' ab
sig̃t exclusiue dicēdo in statuto·a pulsu cāpane de sero nul
lus vadat p vicos sub pēa tli·Nā h̄ statutū intelligit' pul
sata cāpana·Ideo si q̄s vadat qñ pulsat' nō incidit penā
Inclusiue sig̃t ibi a pulsu cāpane de mane q̄sq̧ pōt domū
exire q̄ statuēs sic videt' intellexisse·⁊c̄·Et vide pleni⁹ de
istis dictõib⁹ per io·de fer·in sua practica in forma capi
tuli quando testes p̄ducunt' ad eternā rei memoriā·

¶ Abau⁹ est pr̄ ꝓaui vel ꝓauie sic ꝓau⁹ est pr̄ aui l' auie

¶ Abauia est mr̄ ꝓaui vel ꝓauie·sic ꝓauia est mr̄ aui vel
auie scd̄m ysi·ix·li·ethimo·Et plenius·ff·de gra·l·iu=
risconsult⁹·§·quarto gradu·⁊·§·tertõ·gradu·

¶ Abauunculus est frater abauie scd̄m ysi·

¶ Abamita est soror abaui·ff·de·g̃·l·pal'·§·auunculus

¶ Abmat'tera est soror abuie·De hijs terminis vi·insti·
de gra·§·tertõ gradu·

¶ Abnepos est filius nepotis sicut nepos filius filij vel fi
lie scd̄m ysi·li·ix·ethi·

¶ Abneptis est filia nepotis vel neptis sicut neptis filij
vel filie filia scd̄m ysi·v̄·supra·

¶ Abigē est a se expellē/l' crimē abigeatus exercē vt seq̄t

¶ Abactor scd̄m ysi·li·x·ethi·ē fur iumētoꝝ l' pecudū
quē vulgo vocam⁹ abigeū Nā abige⁹ ē q̄ crimē abigeat⁹
cōmittit ⁊ ꝓpe ille q̄ pecora alic⁹ a pascuis ⁊ alimētis vel

AUXILIARY, REFERENCE, AND POPULAR WORKS

Inasmuch as the legal profession is intimately and forever concerned with the definition of words and phrases and interpretation of their meanings, the fields of legal lexicography and legal semiotics have an ancient history. Legal dictionaries, commentaries on language in various legal contexts, and other reference aids abound in the Library's collections in many languages, including, for example, an Albanian-English legal dictionary. Some of the earliest of such works found in the Law Library come from the pens of Roman Law jurists and canonists, such as Albericus de Rosate (1290–1360) (*Dictionarium juris civilis et canonici*. Pavia, 1498 and Milan, 1485), Jean Juvénal des Ursins (1388–1473), Andrea Alciati (1492–1550) (*De verborvm significatione libri qvatvor. Eiusdem, in tractatum eius argumenti ueterum iureconsulton, commentaria.* Lyons, 1530), and Bartolo of Sassoferrato (1314–57) (*Repertorivm locvpletissimvm in omnes Bartoli a Saxoferrato lecturas.* Venice, 1580). The Library's Rare Book and Special Collections Division has several copies of one of the earliest works on the use of correct legal language in writing and speech by Friedrich Riederer (fl. 1493), *Spiegel der waren Rhetoric* (Mirror of proper Rhetoric. Freiburg, 1493).

Except for numerous incunabula of this work, the custody of which is shared between the Law Library and the Rare Book and Special Collections Division, the many subsequent editions through the seventeenth and eighteenth centuries are all found in the Law Library (e.g., by Alexander Scot, fl. 1591, and Béat Philippe Vicat, 1715–70?). Most of the sixteenth-century editions include the *Lexicon iuris civilis*, another widely used law dictionary, created by the Spanish lexicographer Antonio de Nebrija (1444?–1522). The latest edition of this popular reference work in the Law Library's holdings was published in 1805.

In the same category of legal auxiliary or reference literature fall such genres as the repertoria and indexes, the florilegia (e.g., *Flores legum.* Venice, ca. 1497 and subsequent editions), and the *margaritae, brocardica juris,* etc., which are usually extracts from individual or several works of Roman, Canon, and Civil Law provenance, cast into definitions or legal maxims. If the material lends itself to it, the arrangement is done by keyword in alphabetical order. One genre that stands out is the *Regulae juris* (Rules or principles of law and procedure). The 211 rules in the *Digest* of Emperor Justinian (*Digesta* book 50, 17, *De diversis regulis juris antiqui*) and the 88 rules formulated at the end of book 5, title 12, of the *Liber Sextus decretalium* (the decretal compilation of Pope Boniface VIII, 1294–1303, part of the *Corpus Iuris Canonici*) have attracted the best of Roman and Canon Law commentators and compilers up to recent times.

The numerous editions of Dinus de Mugello (1254–ca. 1300), *Commentarius mirabilis super titulo De regulis juris* (Canon Law); of Philippo Decio (1454–1536), *In*

OPPOSITE: *Vocabularius utriusque juris,* an encyclopedic dictionary of Roman and Canon Law, attributed to Jodocus Erfordensis (fl. ca. 1452), written probably in Erfurt around 1452, is one of the Library's earliest law books concerned with legal definitions. The presumed first printing dates from 1474 to 1475; the page pictured here with its elaborate initialing is from the Law Library's 1475 Basel edition. (*Law Library Rare Book Collection;* LCCN *81465504*)

titulum Digestorum De regulis iuris (Roman Law), and the entire line of other illustrious editions spanning four centuries, testify to their great popularity. The title, which appears prominently in the seventeenth-century *Regulae iuris utriusque*, covers compilations of earlier comparative studies and is another example of the integration of Roman and Canon Law. A recent important work in the collections of the Law Library is a historical comparative study by Vittorio Bartoccetti, *De regulis juris canonici: regularum in Libro VI Decretalium earumque praesertim cum Codice J.C. relationum brevis explanatio* (Rome, 1955), including the text of the *Regulae iuris canonici* compared to Roman Law and the *Codex Iuris Canonici* of 1917.

The field of law is notorious for its plethora of forms. Manuals such as form books or formularia for different courts and procedures, for trial lawyers and notaries, have been in use since the Middle Ages in various legal systems and jurisdictions and are present in the Law Library, both in its modern and rare book collections. One such title is the *Formularium instrumentorum necnon artis notariatus* in over twenty-five pre-1500 editions.

LEGAL SYMBOLISM AND ARS MEMORATIVA

The Library holds a host of literature, the classical "how to" books, as well as academic learning aids and guides (introductions) for law students. Early works in this field are exemplified by the *Modus studendi (in utroque jure) et vita doctorum* (The right way to study Roman and Canon Law. Bologna, 1499) by Giovanni Battista Caccialupi (d. 1496), or the work of Wernherus of Schussenried (fifteenth century), *Modus legendi abbreviaturas passim in iure tam civile quam pontifici* (Introduction to Latin abbreviations in Civil and Canon Law. Strasbourg, 1494). The Law Library has several incunabula and a number of sixteenth-century editions of this work. The *Ars dictandi* (ms., ca. 1500), a tabular manual on how to compose letters, salutations, etc., to clergy and nobles of high and low rank and to formulate letters for all occasions and the *Ars Dicendi siue perorandi* (Manual on textual composition for speeches or public addresses. Cologne, 1484) are other examples with a long tradition in the classroom.

The entire category is closely tied to the *Ars memorativa* (Art of memorizing)—the earliest dating back to the thirteenth century—the study that requires disciplined exercises in memorizing, writing, and (mental) composition. Although *memoria* in the Middle Ages address both the written and oral culture, mnemonic devices or systems for formulation, recollection, and retention of written thought appear as various schemes, including the order of numbers and text, location on the page, and so forth. They were applied particularly in the fields of law and theology as well as philosophy (cf. Mary J. Carruthers, *The Book of Memory*. Cambridge, 1990).

Visual aids and pictorial diagrams as mnemonic compositional aids have been major devices used in law books since the twelfth and thirteenth centuries. Such graphic explanations of textually presented legal concepts, institutes, or inter-relationship of "parts" have appeared commonly as genealogical charts, "ladder" diagrams, tree diagrams (*arbores*), or diagrams composed of circles or columns, with or without artistic elaborations. A favorite of the classroom, their common purpose has been to aid in memorizing and interpreting legal information and, subsequently, in application of the law.

The pictorial diagrams (line drawings) shown on page 23 are reproduced from thirty-nine woodcuts that illustrate two chapters in *De fluminibus seu Tiberiadis: De alluvione* (Of alluvium, i.e., deposits made by running water) and *De insula* (Of islands), both contained in *Consilia, quaestiones et tractatus* of Bartolo of Sassoferrato. These were graphic aids for Bartolo's discourse on land rights of riparian owners; the complex questions of private property rights on exposed land along the river vs. the use of land submerged under the river (public property); and, further, the equitable division of the alluvium between riverside land owners and ownership on islands in the middle of a river formed either by erosion or by silt deposited by the current. Included are notes on land surveying.

Probably the most interesting and varied technical didactic aids are the widely used stemmas and schemas in the form of trees (*arbores*). The arbor motif is present in a wide range of literature in the Library's collections, e.g., as a "genealogical tree" patterned like the theological *Compendium Historiae in Genealogia Christi* of Peter of Poitiers (ca. 1130–1205) or the *Arbor scientiae venerabilis* by Ramón Lull (d. 1315). However, appearing in the medieval and Renaissance literature of Roman or Canon Law provenance, they are akin to both symbolism in law and mnemonic aids. Their importance in the field of law and their rich representation in the Law Library's holdings deserve special attention. Family relationships determined by the degree (*gradus*) of closeness between individual members of a family posed a particular problem for the teaching of law.

One had to distinguish between the agnatic line (relating to members of the patriarchically defined household) and the cognatic line (relating to the mother's blood line), both of importance in law of inheritance and succession, depending upon whether the subject taught addressed Roman Law, Germanic, or Roman/ West Germanic Law (*Leges Romanae barbarorum*). In the latter group, the *Lex Romana Visigothorum* (Breviarium Alarici, 506 A.D.) or the *Lex Visigothorum* (seventh century A.D., translated in the thirteenth century from the original Latin text into vernacular Spanish as *Fuero juzgo*) are just two examples and appear in manuscripts from the sixth to the eleventh centuries.

On the other hand, the first simple tabular or schematic presentation of relationships is older still and can be traced to Mesopotamian/Babylonian antiquity and to Roman Law in the first century B.C. In the Jewish strain of ancient law, genealogical tables or schemas, however, do not delineate family relations to determine the string of succession and inheritance, but to aid in determining marriage impediments, i.e., a condition that leads to forbidden, incestuous marriages. The carryover of relationship schemas—together with the law governing marriages—into Canon Law may be based on the fact—as John Selden, the noted Oxford jurist, polyhistor, and Hebraist stated—that Judaism is the parent of Christianity.

In Canon Law, tree motifs, such as *arbor consanguinitatis* (tree of consanguinity or blood relationship) and the *arbor affinitatis* (tree of affinity), have appeared regularly since the eleventh and twelfth centuries. Among the most prominent and artistically elaborate are those found in Gratian's *Decretum* (1140). The tree with its organic structure of trunk and branches offers itself naturally for the "organic order" of systematic contents. It is up to speculation whether the highly symbolic and spiritual "tree of life in paradise" influenced since the fourteenth and fifteenth centuries the figurative *arbores* in legal treatises on family relationships as well. Examples of prominent works in the Library's collections are the *Somme rural* of Jean Boutiller (d. 1395 or 1396), representing family law of France and the Netherlands, or Nicasius de Voerda of the Netherlands (d. 1492), *Lectura arborum trium consanguinitatis, affinitatis, cognationisque spiritualis*, printed 1502 and in many subsequent editions. The 1566 Lyon edition has an interesting arbor diagram in the shape of a menorah growing out of strong roots.

The best-known treatise on consanguinity and affinity, always accompanied by artistic renderings of such *arbores*, was the *Lectura super arboribus consanguinitatis et affinitatis* by the canonist Giovanni d'Andrea (ca. 1270–1348).

The Latin text of the work, from which the illustration on the opposite page is reproduced, is an anonymously expanded version of Giovanni d'Andrea's *Lectura*, which also contains three "enigmata" exemplifying legal or spiritual relationships other than consanguinity and affinity (e.g., the relationship established at baptism between the child and the godparent). These diagrams are not in the shape of a tree but are rather simple line drawings. The arbor illustrations themselves are the same as those of the 1505 Nuremberg edition.

By mid-sixteenth century, the woodcut arbor diagram had developed into a fixed type that was used until the last authoritative Leipzig edition of the *Corpus Iuris Canonici* by Emil Friedberg in 1879.

OPPOSITE: Bartolo of Sassoferrato (1314–57) was probably the most illustrious commentator of his time on Justinian Law. The illustrations for the "Tiberiadis" are taken from the Venice 1495 edition of his *Consilia, quaestiones et tractatus*. The Law Library holds several sixteenth-century editions of this work. (*Law Library Rare Book Collection*; LCCN 77502720)

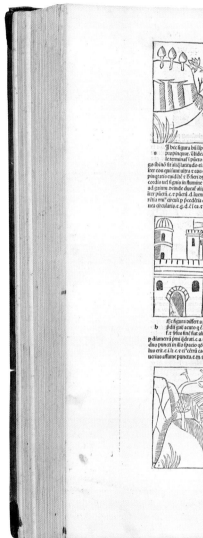

XXIX

Lucij

Gaij

Ihec figura bñ ñspiciaf. ppinus eft pũcto acuto a ripa pdii lucij e toti latitudini ripe gaij. Ad pdiiñ ff ricñi ef propinquiar. Eñideam ergo diuiñione iter gaiñ e feiiñ e lucijñ. vf e lucijñ nil debeaf. qñ ripa fua q appropinq̃ eñ le terminaf i pũcto ñdiuiñibili nõ hñi aliqua latitudine. lz ñfula bz diuidi p mõ latitudine. ut.l. iter eoñ. Eũ ñ go ibiñ ñt aliã latitudine õ ñul debet. Eñuñ dico. n̂ iter eoñ qñ ñut ab vna pte ñt diuiño. p mõ latitudine. ut.l. iter eoñ. Eñd iter eoñ qñ ñut vltra e eoñ qñ ñut i fit diuiño vrio ppinguatio ut dicu eñ. Eñdedũ e igif q ponamus vnã lineã iñ ipo pingiatio eiuñde e i̊z feñ oz e doctñ ñ ñpcedeñiñ figure. Eñ ñdeaf igif ñma cordula a pũcto pdii lucij vñq; añ ñgño in flumine vñã q̃drati.a.b.c.d. deiñ ñueniañ mediũ q̃drati p lineã.c.f.e.ñtat q; qcqd eñ.f. dicta lineñ ptinet ad gaiũ. deinde ducaf alia p diametrã q̃drati.b.d. e ñmiliter q id qd eñ.f. dictam lineñ ptinet ad pdiiñ iter pũcta.d. e.pucta.d. ñueniañ mediñ ño a pũcto pdii lucij ad ripã gaij e fit.g.f.ñic illi tree pũcti ñducunñ in pdeñ recta vrio e pñcta.d. deñ ducaf lineñ media.g.b. dico de eo qd eñ.g. eñ.ñ. dñ ñ ñbz ñe gaiũ: deñ ñ ducaf alñ iter duo pũcti in illo ñpacio qd eñ.f.ñ. eque diñ ño a pũcto gaij e lineñ pdii lucij.ut.l.t.q ñducaf i ñircumferētiã vñ ñircnlo̊ pñ hñ erit.c.i.l.e.e ñ ñcetñ cadit i pdio gaij i pũcto.m. qcqd eñ ñfra dictã lineñ circulñe ptinet ad gaiñ ut i pñdeñ puat ut vñiuñ añfume pñcta.e.m.e ñducañ ea in ñircumferēñã eiuñde ñircli e bebiñ. ppoñita qñ redit inde quod ñupa eñ.

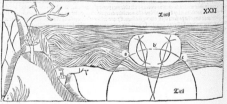

Lucij

XXX

d

Gaij

Ec figura differt a pñdeñi e i pñdeñi pũctñ magiñ ppinquñ erat i capite ñfule.h ño e i medio ut pñ pñdo pdii gaij acuto q e.b.e.ño i ñlumine vñã q̃drata.f.vñã.ñ.aliñ.f.ñat g̃ ñfune caput ñumiñ vñã q̃drati.a.b.c. e.f. ñrius ñat aliñ.a.b.c.d. deiñ ducaf lineñ media.g.b. dico de eo qd eñ.ñ.ñ. ñbz i̊ ñe gaiñ:deiñ ducaf alñ iter p diametrñ ñcidi.a.c.e ñmiliter de eo qd.ñ.ñ.ñ. nil ñz ñ ñbz i̊ ñe gaiñ:deiñ ñueniañ mediñ iter duo pũcti in illo ñpacio qd eñ.ñ.ñ. eque diñ ño a pũcto gaij e lineñ pdii lucij.ut.l.t.q ñducaf i ñircumferētiñ vñ ñircli qbo pñ hñ erit.c.i.l.e.e ñ ñcetñ cadit i pdio gaij i pũcto.m. qcqd eñ ñfra dictã lineñ circulñe ptinet ad gaiñ ut i pñdeñ puat ut vñiuñ añfume pñcta.e.m.e ñducañ ea in circumferēñã eiuñde ñircli e bebiñ. ppoñita qñ redit inde quod ñupa eñ.

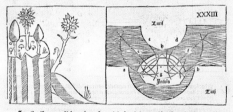

Lucij

XXXI

b

a

c

Gaij

Ticij

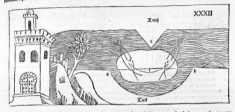

Ec figura differt a pñcedeñib̃ q̃ vel ab vtraq; pte eñ curua ab vna recta vel ab alia puñ ctuo acuto.bic vero eñ ab vna parte linea recta vel ab vtraq; pte eñ curua ab vna recta vel ab alia bz quidam rotundatem cuius caput côcaum eñ veriuñ inñulam. inueniañ ergo in principio inñule pñcedeñia e babebiñ medium.Eñquo collige regulam q̃ poñito trib̃ pñctis eque diñtā ñbus iter lineam rectam e lineam côcauam circulus in cuius circumferētia illi tree pñcti ñducunñ totum ñpaciũ iure p pñuitatis equaliter diuidit e hoc i̊ ñe figura demõñrabif.

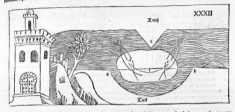

Lucij

XXXII

c

b

Ticij

Igura iñta differt a pñcedeñi q̃ i̊ bac ab vna ripe acute eñ pñctuo ab alia pte rotunda eñ côcauus veriuñ pñctuo cuius ñc faciñdñ eñ diuiño.Pñmo dicñ lineñ ab vna pte circuli vñq; añ aliñ.f.ñ.a.b.e i̊ô hoc ut ñciemus q̃ de eo qd ñupa dictñ lineñ nil pñ debeñi ripe côcauño ñomñillos pñctos qñ quilibet pñ eñ i̊fra e eñ magiñ i̊ pñe dinibus iter.a.e.c.erit mediuñ pñctñ.b.e iter.c.e.b.erit mediuñ.c. ut oñteñdũt lineñ ducte.deinde inuenia mediñ inter.e.e aliquñ pte dicte côcauitatis e ñit.f.deinde illa tria pñcta.d.f.c.ñducunñ i̊ circumferētias eiuñde circuli per pñcedeñia eñ cñ trum erit in pñcto.b.dico ergo q̃ qcqd eñ i̊fra circuliñ.d.f.c.ptinet ad ticium iure pñimitatis.qô i̊ño eñ i̊upa pertinet ad lucius.Et i̊quo collige regulam q̃ poñito vno pñcto i̊fra e alio i̊fra côcauitate e alio côcauitate i̊uenio trib̃ pñcto eque diñ ñtibus ab vtroq; latere linea circularis p quam illi tria pñcti in circumferētia ñducunñ p mediñ diuidat e.

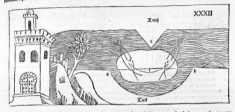

Lucij

XXXIII

d

a

e

b

Inñula

Tieij

Igura iñta differt a pñcedeñib̃ q̃ i̊upa eñ pñctñ ripe ñupiorie quam côñtat eñe propinquiore qualiter alia parte ipñius ripe.bic i̊ño ripa ñupiorie eñ rotunda e côñcaua veriuñ inñulam. e ideo q̃libet parñ illiuñ ripe ñit ppin quior pñctie ripe i̊feriorie côcauiñ. agif pñmo dicñ lineñ ab vno pñcto circuli i̊feriorie vñq; ad aliñ.e.ñit.a. b.ea rõne qua dictñ eñ i̊ pñcedeñi figura. deinde ponatur circulus i̊ pñcto.b.cui pñcto.b.ñit propinquior.a.e.eñdeaf vñq; ad ripam i̊uperiorñ e ibi ali quiñluñ ñoluñf circulariter oñteñdit lineñ curua crocea e ñle pñctuo vbi ripa i̊uperiorie tangif.ppinquiore eñ.e.c.e côdem modo ñoluñf ñircularitñ oñteñdit.b.cui pñcto.b.ppinquior eñ.a.c.inueniñf punctus mediuñ e ñit.e.e iter.b.ñit.ñ.deinde inuenia alius punctus mediñ e ñit.f.deinde iter ripam ñuperiorñ e i̊feriorñ e ñit .g.deinde illa tria pñcta.e.f.g.ñducañ i̊ circumferētia eiuñde circuli cuius centrum cadit i̊ pñctuo lucij i̊ pñcto. b.dico ergo q̃ qcqd eñ i̊fra illum circulñ.g.f.pertinet ad ticiuñ iure propñimitatis.qô i̊ño eñ i̊upa illum pertinet ad lucij e pñcedeñib̃ apparet e linee recte demõñrant e.

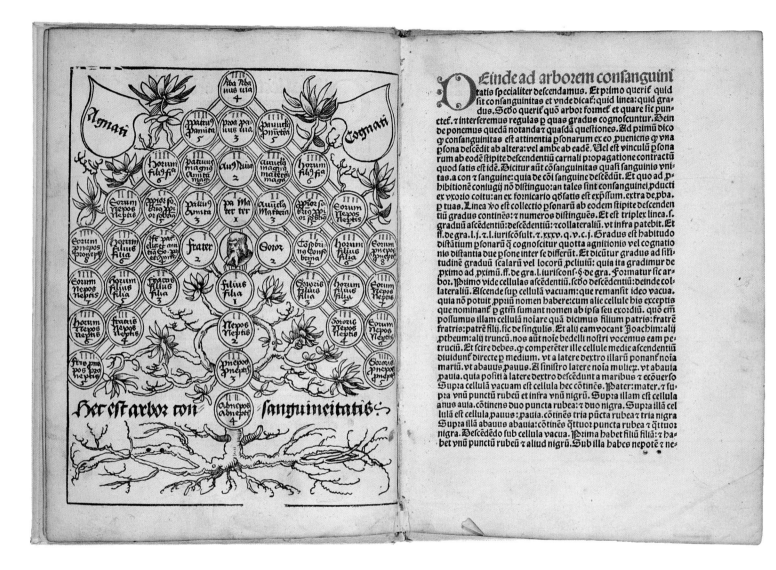

The reproduced arbor is from Giovanni d'Andrea, *Arborum consanguinitatis affinitatis, cognationis spiritualis et legalis textus . . . emendatus, ac bene correctus: enigmatibusque . . . additis* (Nuremberg, 1517). The art work is supposedly of Hans Baldung Grien, a contemporary of Albrecht Dürer (1471–1528) and an artist of equal standing. (Cf. Hermann Schadt, *Die Darstellungen der Arbores Consanguinitatis and der Arbores Affinitatis. Bildschemata in jurisatischen Handschriften.* Tübingen, 1982.) (*Law Library Rare Book Collection;* LCCN 2002554962)

Giovanni Crispo de' Monti, *Repetitio tituli de heredibus et de gradibus* (Venice, 1490). This arbor illustrating relationships with reference to inheritance (Roman Law) is very unusual in size and content. All three schemata for consanguinity, affinity, and succession grow as little trees out of the head and hands of a man, alluding to the "tree of life" symbolism and, to some extent, of the Greek myth in which Daphne escapes the attentions of Apollo when she is transformed by her mother into a laurel tree. (*Law Library Rare Book Collection; LCCN 77502714*)

Another example of this motif in the Law Library's collections is the *arbor bigamiae,* exemplifying the marriage impediment of bigamy in case of a successive marriage of one of the partners after dissolution of the marriage by death.

Variant forms of the arbor diagrams, often stripped of artistic elaborations, can be found in many German custumals, most importantly in the *Sachsenspiegel, Schwabenspiegel,* and the *Layenspiegel* of Ulrich Tengler (d. ca. 1511), and in other popular works such as Johannes Lindholz (d. 1535), *Arbores consanguinitatis, affinitatis, cognationis spiritualis atque legalis* (Strasbourg, 1516).

Numerous other arbor diagrams are present in the Law Library's collections. The *arbor patronatus* represents the canon doctrines of benefices and patronage, found in the *Clementinae,* i.e., the Constitutions of Clement V.

The *arbor actionum* was a type of flowchart used for the various kinds of actions and defenses and various stages of procedure in Roman Law.

A modern special format item in the Law Library is the packet of graphic and textual materials, published by the Centre for Structural Learning. It provides an innovative approach to the teaching of case law.

CONSILIA

Consilia form one of the core collections of the rare book holdings of the Law Library, but as a separate genre they are not widely studied in U.S. law schools. *Consilia,* i.e., expert opinions, emerged in Europe in the late 1200s. As a legal literature form, they remained essentially the same until the mid-eighteenth century. In their earliest and simplest form, *consilia* were formal analyses of points of law written by legal experts. Requests for these analyses often came from magistrates or itinerant judges who sought such local expertise in helping them decide a case. Other types of *consilia* were those provided to a party in a case and the *allegatio,* a more partisan form of *consilia,* similar to a defense brief. *Consilia* represent a fusion of influences, including Customary Law, Canon Law, Roman Law, the Scriptures, and even the works of some classical authors. Their growth contributed to the systematization of Civil Law in response to the growing complexity of European legal infrastructure and society. The content of most *consilia* includes much ancillary information, biographical and legal comparative material placed in local, national, or international historic context for the case at hand, which makes them a valuable source for social and intellectual as well as legal historians. Among the issues treated in *consilia* were some of the weightiest legal matters—the Investiture Controversy, the marriage of Henry VIII to Catherine of Aragon, and the status of women—and more mundane concerns, such as court procedures or local water and pasturing rights.

The Library's *Consilia* collection contains over twelve hundred separate volumes by approximately three hundred fifty authors of Italian, German, French, Dutch, Portuguese, and Spanish origin, and other continental legal scholars. It is the largest single collection in the United States and one of the foremost such collections in the world, with several incunabula *consilia* and a fourteenth-century manuscript. Most *consilia* are held in the Law Library and consist of printed volumes dating from the sixteenth century, including the edited works of fourteenth- and fifteenth-century jurists. Baldo degli Ubaldi (1327?–1400), an outstanding jurist of the Bolognese tradition, is probably best known for his *consilia* on Roman and Canon Law.

An extremely rare original manuscript *consilium* in the Law Library was rendered by Baldo in Perugia, ca. 1370, concerning certain disputed privileges and immunities which had been granted by Pope Urban V (1310–70) to the city of Recanati, Italy, in return for the city's assistance in restoring his power over the Papal States. It appears to be the earliest example of such a signed and sealed expert opinion in the Library's collection. Interestingly, both of Baldo's brothers, Angelo (1328–ca. 1407) and Pietro degli Ubaldi (d. ca. 1407?), signed the document in confirmation of Baldo's opinion. Neither had gained the same fame as Baldo, but they were counted among the noted "doctores" of the time. The Law Library holds incunabula and numerous other works on Roman or Canon Law by each of them. Other important, printed volumes in the collection include Baldo's five-volume *Consilia* (Venice, 1475). Library of Congress publications about *consilia* include Jolande Rummer Goldberg, "A Fourteenth-century Legal Opinion," *Library of Congress Quarterly Journal*, v. 25 (1968) pp. 179–91, and Peter R. Pazzaglini and Catharine A. Hawks, eds., *Consilia: A Bibliography of Holdings in the Library of Congress and Certain Other Collections in the United States* (Washington, D.C., Library of Congress, 1990).

LEGAL PERIODICALS

Law advances in numerous ways. One of the most important is through analysis and counter-analysis in the forum afforded by law reviews and journals. The Law Library's periodical collection, ca. forty-three thousand, includes English and foreign-language periodicals from all the major and many less well-known jurisdictions of the world, on general and on highly specific legal topics, including Year Books, and ca. three hundred Religious Law periodicals.

BALDVS VBALDVS PERVSINVS
Anno M·CCCLXV·

Portrait of the famous jurist Baldo degli Ubaldi taken from Marco Mantova Benevides, *Illustrium iureconsultorum imagines quae in eniri potuerunt ad vivam effigiem expressae* (Rome, 1566). (*Law Library Rare Book Collection*)

MANUSCRIPTS

As might be expected, the majority of the Library of Congress manuscripts are found in the Manuscript Division. The bulk of that collection with a legal content or related to matters of law focuses on papers relating to American constitutional history, or legal issues contained in the papers of U.S. presidents, federal justices, or members of Congress. The Law Library Rare Book Collection houses approximately two hundred fifty legal manuscripts or research papers (e.g., the Paul Krüger Collection). The manuscripts date from the thirteenth to the twentieth centuries and are mostly from Continental Europe. The collection is strongest in the Medieval and Renaissance eras, particularly in Roman, Canon, Feudal, and Customary Law. Some of the earliest manuscripts are among the Law Library's most treasured holdings.

Other splendid examples of the Law Library's manuscript holdings are the fourteenth-century *Ordenamiento de Alcalá* (also known as *Libro del ordenamjento real*) of King Alfonso XI (1312–50) of Castile (Spain), and the *Coutumes de Normandie*, an outstanding manuscript version of the *Grand Coutumier*, well worth being counted among the crown jewels of the Library of Congress.

INCUNABLES

The Law Library holds approximately two hundred and fifty law or law-related incunabula, i.e., pre-1500 printed books. Researchers will find such early printed legal materials in the vast Rare Book and Special Collections Division, especially in the Rosenwald, Vollbehr, and Thacher Collections, including different editions of the same works. The Law Library's discrete collection of incunabula is arranged according to the standard text incunabula in *American Libraries: A Third Census of Fifteenth-century Books Recorded in North American Collections*, compiled by Frederick Goff, former Chief of the Rare Book Division of the Library of Congress (New York, 1964) and its Third Supplement, in which the Law Library is designated as LC(L). The Law Library incunables include mainly *coutumes*—French Customary Laws—and Roman, Canon, and Feudal Law, and derive from incunabular presses in cities throughout Continental Europe and England. The variety of subjects and the number of the incunabula collections render it difficult to generalize about the collection. Suffice it to say that the holdings of the Law Library, both in Latin and national languages, offer scholars a wide range of subjects and jurisdictional sources. Examples of famous incunabular texts are given below in the sections discussing specific legal systems or topic areas.

This extremely rare original *consilium* (legal opinion) by the jurist of Bologna, Baldo degli Ubaldi (1327?–1400) is an example of a fourteenth-century Northern Italian manuscript. The document bears the only known Baldo seal. Judging by the still visible colored marks left behind, the seals of his two brothers, Pietro and Angelo degli Ubaldi, must originally have been affixed to this document as well. (*Law Library Rare Book Collection*; LCCN 2001554023)

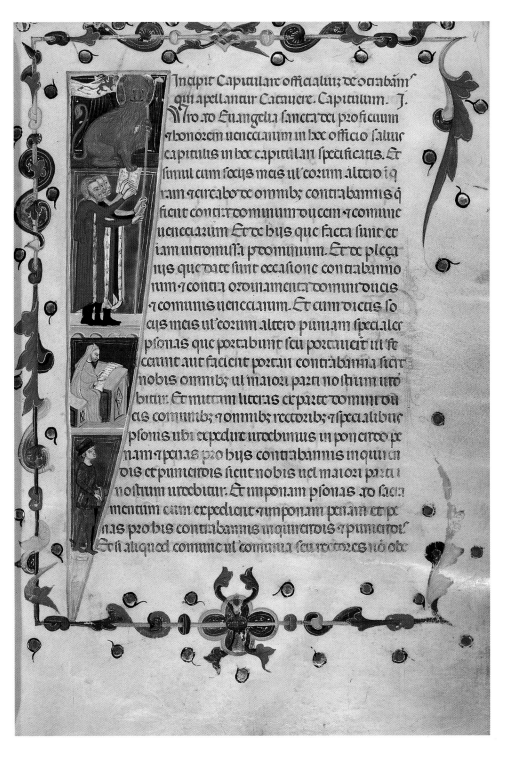

Capitulare officialium Urbis Venetiarum. This fourteenth-century manuscript book on vellum is a collection of legal measures on contraband issued by Venetian officials, known as *cattaveri,* who supervised all trade. (*Law Library Rare Book Collection;* LCCN *2004574701*)

This edition of the *Vocabularius utriusque juris* (Vincenza, 1482), apparently the sole known copy in the world, is bound in a manuscript of liturgical music written on vellum. (*Law Library Rare Book Collection*; LCCN 81455914)

MINIATURE LAW BOOKS

For the most part, books measuring ten centimeters or less in height are maintained in the Rare Book and Special Collections Division, but the Law Library Rare Book Collection has numerous miniature law books from around the world. Miniature book publishing in the field of law has had a specific relevance throughout history for several reasons. Law books or codes were produced in miniature in the era when judges and lawyers, riding their circuits, or sheriffs, overseeing their jurisdiction's law enforcement, rode on horseback and needed law books that would fit into saddlebags. Miniatures have also been published as deluxe celebratory editions to mark the adoption of an important law reform or a new code. A miniature edition of a country's constitution was also done for the same reason or simply to make a smaller, more affordable copy of a nation's basic law available for broad distribution.

JUVENILE LEGAL LITERATURE

In addition to its many august, historic legal treatises and treasures, the Law Library also collects juvenile legal literature from the United States and abroad.

Shh! We're Writing the Constitution (New York, Putnam's, 1987) is an illustrated history of the birth of our nation's Constitution for young readers. (*Law Library Collection; LCCN* 86022528)

This poster, concerning the issue of legalizing marijuana, is an example of graphic elements used in campaigns to sway public opinion concerning a headline legal issue. PLO Poster, ca. 1975 (Frankfurt, Germany, by Kakutti Burhan, 1932–2003). (*Prints and Photographs Division*)

POSTERS

Controversial legal topics are often the subject of high profile campaigns to sway public opinion and ultimately to gain the attention of the legislature. A graphic record of some of these kinds of campaigns as well as the popular portrayals of general legal themes may be traced in the poster collections in the Library's Prints and Photographs Division, especially in the Yanker Collection. This collection includes more than three thousand political propaganda and social issues posters and handbills, dating 1927 to 1980, from the United States and fifty-five other countries as well as from the United Nations.

Ad lectorē paruaꝝ decretaliū Sebastianus Brant.

Uos impssa (velim) q̄cunq volumīa iuris:
Cedite: nō par ē/ vr̄a ꝛ mea causa: locū q
Liberius ꝓdire queam date: cedite cūcta:
Et sinite huc iuuenū aspect⁹ q oc'os q venire
Judicio q graui: nr̄m pensare decorem.
Quid sim: q̄d ve ferā: q̄t cōmoda grandia:
Colligere ex nr̄o pot' ē q̄cū q libello. (ꝑuo
Si q̄d pōtifices: si q̄d suprema potestas
Ecclesie statuit: si quid decreuerit olim:
Seruari q suo iussu p̄ceperit vs q
Hoc decretalis liber h̄ tibi mōstrat habūde.
Quin tibi ꝯtinuat rubrū: casum q figurat:
Diuidit: ꝛ ptes capitū distinguit aptas:
Ordinis at q quote poteris repire registra

Huc ades o iuuenis cui pōtificalia forte
Jura placēt: pond⁹ facile ē tibi ferre minutū
Ferre in q manic': nec te labor ille grauabit.
In q scholis tecū potes hūc ſuare diurnis:
Cōmoda ꝛ ex illo cape haud taxāda libello.
Perlege cūcta velim: scio te/ me v̄a fateri/
Dictuꝝ: ꝛ grates habituꝝ ꝓinde decētes.
Queris habere parē: poter' decreta videre:
Que fraterna q̄dē: pariliq exacta labore:
Jam dudū in lucē nr̄a hec ꝓdire iubebat
Romani imperij specimen Basilea decus q.
Jam q vale lector studiose: ꝛ si tibi forte
Grādia ꝑua placēt: ꝑuo h̄ op⁹ emptor habeb̄
Nō (mihi crede) etiā grādi nū q ere repēdes.

a

Gregorius. ❡ In hui⁹ libri p̄ncipio q̄nq p̄cipue sunt p̄notāda: videlz q̄ sit intentio: que materia: q̄ vtilitas: cui parti ph̄ie supponat: q̄s modus agēdi: ꝛ q̄s libri titul⁹. ❡ Intētio dn̄i Gregorij in hac p̄nti cōpilatione fuit diuersas cōstitutiōes ꝛ decretales epistolas p̄decessorum suoꝝ in diuersa dispsas volumīa seu cōpilationes: q̄ difficultatez studentib⁹ ingerebāt: i vnā cōpilationem resecatis sup̄fluis ad vtilitatem legentiū ac studētiū reducere: ꝑ ut i eiusd... dn̄i gregorij ꝯstitutione euidentius declaratur. ❡ Materia in hoc opere: sunt ipse cōstitutiones ꝛ decretales ep̄le sub singulis titulis collocate. ❡ Utilitas ē: vt his lectis ꝛ intellectis sciamus discernere inter equū ꝛ iniquū: ꝛ vnicui q reddere q̄d suum ē: ꝛ in h̄ iusticia cōsistit: vt insti. d̄ iusti. ꝛ iur. in p̄n. ꝛ. xij. q. ij. cū deuotissimā. ❡ Supponitur ethice. i. morali sciētie: sicut ꝛ alij libri iuris: vnde etiā dicit imꝑator: legibus nr̄is hominū mores intendim⁹ corrigere. C. de secūd. nup. l. j. ❡ Modus agēdi talis est. Diuidit em̄ opus suū in q̄nq partes. In p̄ma pte tractat de sūma trinitate ꝛ fide catholica: ꝛ de ꝯstitutionib⁹: de rescriptis: de iudicib⁹ ꝛ coꝝ officijs. In scd̄a pte tractat de iudicijs ꝛ cooperātib⁹ ad iudicia. In tertia pte tractat de vita ꝛ honestate clericoꝝ ꝛ rebus coꝝ et eccl'iaꝝ. In q̄rta de spōsalib⁹ ꝛ matrimonijs ꝛ impedimētis coꝝ. In q̄nta de accusationib⁹ ꝛ criminibus ꝛ penis coꝝ. Et sic terminat tractatū suū: ipsum diuidēs in q̄nq ptes: ad similitudinē q̄nq sensuū corporis: q̄s quilibet q̄ iudicat h̄re debet: aliter nō est idoneus iudex. Sic em̄ oīs copula cōiugalis restricta ē vsq ad quartū gradū ad similitudinē q̄tuor humoꝝ vel elementoꝝ corꝑis humani: vt. j. de cōsan. ꝛ affi. nō debet. §. ꝓhibitio. ❡ Dicens: Gregorius ep̄s seruus seruoꝝ dei ꝛc. et hic est libri titulus. b ❡ Seruus. sic etiam imꝑator appellat se seruū. C. d̄ offi. pre. preto. aphrice. l. j. circa prin. Uel dic q̄ dicit ex humilitate: quia q̄ maior ē vestꝝ: fiat sicut minister vester. ix. q. iij. nullus primas. matth. xx. luce. xxij. ꝛ marc. ca. x. Uel seru⁹ d̄r: q̄r sicut ꝑ seruū acquirit̄ dn̄o. instit. ꝑ q̄s ꝑso. nobis acqui. circa prin. Ita etiā ꝑ dn̄m papā cuilibet ecclesie pōt acq̄ri. j. de censi. cū instantia: in p̄ticula q̄ decisa est de p̄n. j. vt li. pen. ecclesia. ij. Sic ꝑ iꝑatorē acquirit̄ hoīb⁹. in auc. cōsti. q̄ digni. fi. libe. a pa. po. §. illud quo q. col. vj. et noctes ducit insomnes: vt subiecti sub oī quiete consistant: in auc. vt iudi. sine quoquo suffra. in prin. col. ij. ꝛ dicit imꝑator volūtarios labores appetimus: vt quietem alijs preparemus: in auc. vt diui. iussi. sub scrip. habe. gloriosissi. q̄sto. in p̄n. col. viij. ꝛ. j. de resti. spo. c. freq̄es. c ❡ Filijs: benedicit filijs: q̄r solūmodo p̄triarchas: archiep̄os ꝛ ep̄os fratres appellat: omēs alios filios. j. de cri. fal. q̄ graui. d ❡ Bononie commorantib⁹. ꝛ ita nō in castris: q̄m si in castris studeāt: bn̄ficia ex p̄uilegio sibi cōcessa occasiōe studij h̄re nō debēt. j. de cle. nō resi. tue fraternitatis. Preterea ex quo dicit bononie: nō videt̄ q̄ alijs mittat̄ alibi studētib⁹: ꝛ sic nō tenēt̄ recipe hāc cōpilationē: q̄r l̄re pape nō extēdunt̄ ad alios q̄ ad eos q̄b⁹ mittunt̄ vel q̄ cōtinent̄ in eis. ar. j. de offi. dele. p. et. g. ꝛ. c. gratū. et c. cū olim. Sz nō ... oēs em̄ tenēt̄ ad obseruationē hui⁹ cōpilatiōis sz ꝓpter studiū q̄d ē bononie cōmuni⁹ ꝛ generali⁹ p̄cipue i vtro q iure: ꝛ ibi q̄si de oīb⁹ ptib⁹ mūdi sūt studētes: ideo poti⁹ bononie dirigūtur: et ita oēs tenentur hāc cōpilationē obseruare: q̄ nec possent nec debēt singuloꝝ auribus itimari. xvj. dis. q̄d dicitis c. j. de pos. prela. ad hec. ꝛ cōstitutio p̄ncipis post duos mēses a tp̄e publicationis oēs astrin... ... fa... cte noue consti. circa p̄n. ... noue... rit. e ❡ Salutem: ꝑ ... ... o collit̄ excōmunicatio: si aliqui sci... ... essent excōicati tp̄e publicatōis. j. ... ... q̄n: vbi d̄ h̄ Ber.

In noīe sancte trinitatis amen. Compilatio decretalium Gregorij pape. ix.

Gregorius Episcopus seruus seruorum dei: Dilect' filijs doctoribus et scholaribus vniuersis Bononie cōmorantibus: Salutē ꝛ apostolicam benedictionem.

Rex pacificus pia miseratione disposuit sibi subditos fore pudicos: pacificos et modestos: sed effrenata cupiditas: sui prodiga: pacis emula: mr̄ litiū: materia iurgioꝝ: tot q̄tidie

Rex pacific⁹ ... mo ponit exordiū in q̄ cōcludit finale int... iuris generalis. Scd̄o narrationē i q̄ ostēdit finale intētū hui⁹ cōpilationis seu iur' ꝑticular'. ibi. Sanc. Tertō ꝯcludit. ibi. Uolētes. Prima subdiuidit̄: q̄r p̄mo ponit finē viatoris. i. hoīs ad quē a deo disposit⁹ ē. Scd̄o causā deuiatiōis ab h̄ fine ibi: Sz effrenata. Tertio vt ad debitū finē viator deducat̄: ꝯcludit legē necessariā: ꝛ ostēdit tres ꝟtutes ac ꝓprietates legis. ibi: Ideo q lex ꝓdit̄. Scd̄a pars subdiuidit̄: q̄r Primo ponit euētū circa ꝯstitutiones eccl'iasticas correctiōi submittēdas: ꝛ ponit materiā ꝛ causā ipulsiuā hui⁹ co... ... ꝯcludit cām finalez. ibi. Ad cōem. ... cām coadiuuatiuā: ibi. Per dilectū. Quarto formalē. ibi. Resecat'. Et hec diuisio sufficit ꝑ sūmario. Abbas Si. f ❡ Rex. alibi appellat̄ iꝑator. xj. q. iij. iulian⁹. g ❡ Pacific⁹: q̄ vt pacē doceret venit i mūdum. xxiij. q. j. nisi bella. regnū tn̄ ei⁹ nō ē de h̄ mūdo. e. cā. q. iij. §. j. ꝛ i euangelio Joh. c. xviij. L. X. h ❡ Disposuit. s. ꝑ ꝓuidētiā ꝛ p̄destinationē nō necessitate: q̄r vasis ire ꝛc. xxiij. q. iiij. nabuchodonosor. de pe. di. iiij. §. sic ita q. ꝛ in p̄cedētib⁹ ꝛ sequētib⁹. §. i ❡ Subditos. i. p̄destinatos q̄ si etiā peccāt corā dn̄o dicūt̄ peccare. de pe. di. j. ꝛ venit: q̄ etiā si peccāt: nihilomin⁹ saluabūt̄. de pe. di. iiij. §. sic ita q. Cōtra p̄mū dictū ē. de pe. di. iiij. §. hāc societatē. k ❡ Pudicos. i. castos: sic ꝛ iꝑator subditos suos castitatē ſuare hortat̄. vn̄ d̄r castitas sola ē q̄ cū fiducia possibilis ē deo aīas p̄ntare. i auc. d̄ lenonib⁹. §. sancim⁹. col. iij. q̄ suaderi pōt: imꝑari vero nō pōt. xxxij. q. j. itegritas. vn̄ debem⁹ eē pudici: q̄r ipudic⁹ ocul⁹ ipudici cordis ē nūci⁹. xxxij. q. v. nec solo. l ❡ Pacificos. i. pacē custodiētes. vn̄ etiā d̄r: bt̄i pacifici q̄m filij dei vocabunt̄. xxiij. q. j. noli. ꝛ matth. c. v. L. X. m ❡ Modestos. i. tꝑatos: q̄r q̄libet d̄z h̄re i se tꝑātiā: vt sciat ſuare misc̄diaz ꝛ rigorē: vt' sit verū q. xlv. di. disciplia. Ber. n ❡ Cupiditas: q̄ ē radix oium maloꝝ. xlvij. di. bonoꝝ. in auc. vt iudi. sine q̄q suffra. §. cogitatio. col. ij. ꝛ h̄ idem innuit̄: de pe. di. ij. §. q̄r radix oim: p⁹ illū. §. ex p̄missis. Ber. o ❡ Pro-

Religious Law

WORKS ON RELIGION are found in many different collections of the Library of Congress. Works on the rules and "canons" governing the religious aspects of life and shaping religious institutions, such as Canon Law or Ecclesiastical Law, the manifestations of state and church interaction, as well as other Religious Law may be found in large part in the Law Library. For certain religions, such as Buddhism, the subject of "law," mainly ritual law and prescriptions, is so integral to the faith that works of a uniquely legal character—other than the rules for daily life encompassed in the major tenets of the creed—do not exist in the law collections. Materials for such faiths are more likely to be found in the Library's Area Studies reading rooms.

The basic text for the Judeo-Christian faiths is included in the Library's Gain Collections. On permanent public display in the Great Hall of the Thomas Jefferson Building are two of the Library's most valuable biblical treasures, a fifteenth-century manuscript, the *Great Bible of Mainz*, and the printed *Gutenberg Bible* of 1453. The latter, the first book printed with movable metal type, a process invented by Johann Gutenberg, is one of only three known perfect vellum copies in existence.

The reader interested in comparative studies on Religious Law, especially in the context of Ancient Law, may want to examine works in the collection of Comparative Religious Law which branches off into interdisciplinary studies. The discovery in 1901/1902 of the Hammurabi stele in the Acropolis of Susa, on which the *Code of Hammurabi* is engraved, generated tremendous excitement among Assyriologists and legal scholars and opened a window on Ancient Law in the Mesopotamian region. (Hammurabi was King of Babylonia, ca. 2250 B.C.) The first photographs and transliteration of the Akkadian cuneiform inscriptions on the stele and the translation were the work of Vincent Scheil (1858–1940): *Code des Lois (droit privé) de Hammurabi, roi de Babylon, vers l'an 2000 avant Jésus-Christ*, in *Textes élamites-sémetiques* (Délegation en Perse. Mémoires. t. IV. Paris, 1902–). Since then, the *Code of Hammurabi*, a legal source of timeless importance, has been the subject of numerous investigations comparing it with other Ancient Law, and especially with the Law of Moses. The Law Library holds leading works on these subjects, among them those of Robert Francis Harper (1864–1914), *The Code of Hammurabi, King of Babylon* (Chicago, 1904). This work was reprinted several times, most recently in 1999. One edition consists chiefly of illustrations, the *Codex Hammurabi: textus primigenius* by Eugen Bergmann (d. 1965), in *Scripta Pontificii Instituti Biblici*, v. 51 (Rome, 1953). The Law Library also holds the six-volume set *Hammurabi's Gesetz* (Leipzig, 1904–23) edited by Josef Kohler (1849–1919), Felix Ernst Peiser (1862–1921), Arthur Ungnad (b. 1879), and Paul Koschaker (1879–1951). Of the latter, the

OPPOSITE: *Decretalium D[omi]ni Pape Gregorij Noni co[m]pilatio accurata diligentia emendate su[m]moq[ue] studio elaborata et cu[m] Scripturis Sacris aptissime [con]cordata*, known as *Decretales Gregorii IX*. This incunabulum was issued in Basel by Johann Froben, on May 15, 1494. (*Law Library Rare Book Collection; LCCN 88167796*)

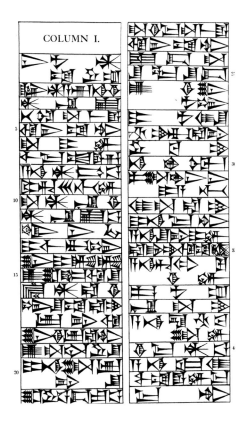

COLUMN I.

Plate I, from a set of eighty-two plates, of the *Code of Hammurabi, King of Babylon: about 2250 B.C: autographed text, transliteration, glossary index of subjects. . . .* (edited by Robert Francis Harper 1864–1914) (Chicago, 1904). The text of the eighty-two plates has been reconstructed and edited by Harper from the photographs published by Vincent Scheil. (*Law Library Rare Book Collection;* LCCN 99023953)

Law Library has *Rechtsvergleichende Studien zur Gesetzgebung Hammurapis* (Leipzig, 1917). Another work in the Law Library's collection is a comparison of Hammurabi, Mosaic Law, and Roman Law (*Lex duodecim tabularum*), *Die Gesetze Hammurabis und ihr Verhältnis zur Mosaischen Gesetzgebung sowie zu den XII Tafeln* (Amsterdam, 1975; repr. of Wien, 1903 and 1905 editions) by David Heinrich Müller (1846–1912), who establishes the similarity in content and form of Hammurabi's *Code* and the Mosaic Law found in the *Pentateuch,* the first part of the Bible. The *Mosaicarum et Romanrum legum collatio,* fragments of Roman and Jewish Law (Paris, 1573), is another famous compilation in the Law Library, also in many later editions.

JEWISH LAW

The Israeli and Jewish Law collections in the Library of Congress are among the best in the world. Whereas the Library's historic treasures offer unique sources in Jewish law observed by Jews in the diaspora for many centuries before the establishment of the State of Israel in 1948, the modern era collections enable jurists and practitioners to determine what is the applicable law in Israel today. As for most other developed nations, the Law Library maintains up-to-date collections of all Israeli official gazettes, primary and secondary legislation, court decisions, legal periodicals, and treatises in all areas of law.

Collections of sources of Judaism, including all of the traditional or ritual Jewish Law (*halakhah*), are found in the Hebraic Section of the Library's African and Middle Eastern Division; works on the Jewish Law corresponding to concepts of Civil Law and *halakhic* interpretations of contemporary legal concepts and rules for societal interactions are housed in the Law Library.

The Rare Book and Special Collections Division houses the incunabular edition (Bologna, 1482) of the *Humash* (i.e., *Torah* or *Pentateuch*). It includes the commentary of Rashi (1040–1105) and—side by side with the main text—the *Targum Onkeles,* which is the ancient and authoritative translation of the *Pentateuch* into Aramaic. Among the large collection of rabbinical literature in the Library of Congress, many historic editions of the Jewish compendium of laws, the *Talmud* (both the Babylon and the Jerusalem *Talmud*) may be found. Unlike the immutable law that makes up the *Torah,* the *Talmud* represents a collection of previously unwritten oral laws and traditions of the Jewish people that were modified to reflect societal needs as they historically evolved. An extremely rare edition of the Babylonian *Talmud* (*Talmud Bavli*) in the collections of the African and Middle Eastern Division's Hebraic Section was printed between 1520 and 1523 by Christian Daniel Bomberg

Displayed here is a page showing the format of the Bomberg edition (Venice, 1520–23) of the *Talmud Bavli* (Babylonian *Talmud*), housed in the African and Middle Eastern Division/Hebraic Section (LCCN 73951028; Jerusalem reprint edition of 1967–72). The Library also has a microfiche set, *The Talmud Editions of D. Bomberg*, edited by A. Rosenthal (Leiden, 1997–). (LCCN 98128083)

(1483–1553?) in Venice. His press became the foremost Hebrew press in sixteenth-century Europe. Among the most significant publications was the first complete edition of the *Talmud* in twenty-four volumes, which set the standard for layout and pagination of the *Talmud.*

For Judaic legal studies, the collections on the "restatement" of Jewish Law (*Posekim*), commonly treated, or referred to, as "codes," are extensive and important. They comprise works by Isaac ben Jacob Alfasi (1013–1103, his *Halakhot* editions), Jacob ben Asher (ca. 1269–ca. 1340), Moses Maimonides (1135–1204), and Joseph ben Ephraim Karo (1488–1575). Among the five hundred forty works covering Maimonides's *Mishneh Torah* are six incunabula. The Library has fifteen early sixteenth-century editions of the *Arba'ah Turim* by Jacob ben Asher and over two hundred ninety editions, including individual parts and selections, of the *Shulhan 'aruk* by Joseph ben Ephraim Karo, a leading rabbinical scholar born in Toledo, Spain, in 1488.

Noteworthy for its historical interest and currency is the rich and large collection of *Responsa*, the comprehensive treatises on many subjects of religion and law. Among many other objects of interest, a Hebrew translation of the *Qur'an* has been added to the collections.

Numerous sources are available for readers interested in Hebraic/legal studies. Among many others are those of Englishman John Selden (1584–1654), whose works are well represented in the Library's Renaissance and humanist treatise collections of the late sixteenth and early seventeenth centuries. A law student at Oxford, Selden was attracted early on by Judaic and Semitic studies already flourishing at that time. Self-taught in Hebrew and Aramaic and well trained in Roman and Common Law, Selden made important contributions to Christian Hebraism through his own comparative observations on the Bible vis-à-vis the Roman Twelve Tables, and on the *Talmud* (Babylonian or Jerusalem) compared with the Pandects (Digest) of Justinian, ultimately establishing the theory of the "civil" character of Jewish Law, in essence not different from other Civil Law. The sole exception was that it was given or set by God, the ultimate authority, in contrast to the law developed in the Christian Church. This is reflected in his first major treatise, *De successionibus in bona defuncti ad leges Ebraeorum* (Concerning succession according to Jewish Law), of which the Library holds several editions, including the enlarged 1638 Leiden edition. His most important work, *De jure naturali & gentium juxta disciplinam Ebraeorum* (Concerning Natural Law and Law of Nations according to Jewish Law. London, 1640), may be found in the Law Library. At first glance, this work contains much natural history rather than Natural Law. He describes in detail the lunar orbit on which the Jewish

JOANNIS SELDENI
UXOR
EBRAICA
ABSOLVENS
NUPTIAS ET DIVORTIA
Veterum Ebræorum
quibus accesserunt
DE SUCCESSIONIBUS IN BONA DEFUNCTORUM
& in
Pontificatum
LIBRI AD LEGES VETERUM ELABORATI.

VVITTENBERGÆ,
APUD GODOFREDUM ZIMMERMANNUM.
ANNO M. D. CC. XII.

JOHANNES SELDENUS *Armig.*

John Selden (1584–1654), *Uxor Ebraica: absolvens nuptias et divortia veterum Ebraeorum* (The Hebrew Wife: On marriage and divorce of the Ancient Hebrews. Frankfurt/Oder, 1712). (*Law Library Rare Book Collection*; LCCN 91229475)

calendar is based and the traditional holidays, such as the Jewish New Year (*Rosh ha-Shanah*). In fact, he outlines Natural Law as the "universal law" bestowed on the humans at creation, ordering the universe as well as inter-relationships between humans and among nations (*ius gentium*), either by custom or agreement. *De Synedriis Veterum Ebraeorum* (The Sanhedrin of the Ancient Hebrews. London, 1650–55), also in the holdings of the Law Library, is a treatise on the character and jurisdiction of the Great Sanhedrin to draw conclusions of what constitutes a court and jurisdiction in secular and ecclesiastical/religious matters.

Selden's oeuvre is important in the context of the Parliament/Westminster debate on religious issues and on the church and state relationship, still unresolved since the final break of England with Rome a century earlier. As a longtime lay delegate to the Westminster Assembly (the last time appointed in 1643 as one of thirty lay delegates), Selden was very much part of the debate on the future of the Church of England. His observations weigh in on questions of new organization, jurisdiction, and institutions of the Church, but also on controversial questions of reform, mainly of marriage and divorce, then still governed by Canon Law. Selden's work at the height of his career in Judaic-Christian scholarship, the *Uxor Hebraica, seu de Nuptiis et Divortiis ex Jure Civili, id est, Divino et Talmudico Veterum Ebraeorum* (The Jewish wife, or Marriage and divorce according to civil, i.e. divine and Talmudic Law; of the Ancient Hebrews. London, 1646; cf. supra, *Ars memorativa*) including later editions, was published during the controversy surrounding the legal formation of the Church of England. By itself, it is an outstanding piece of scholarship, uncovering similarities with other ancient legal systems and erudite parallels between doctrines of the "parent" religion (Judaism) and contemporary Christian/Canon Law doctrines.

The Law Library holds an English treatise *The Hebrew Wife: or, The law of marriage, examined in relation to the lawfulness of polygamy, and to the extent of the law of incest*, by Sereno Edwards Dwight (1786–1850), based on John Selden's *Uxor Ebraica* (New York, 1836; LCCN 99478303), and a more recent English-language edition by Jonathan R. Ziskind: *John Selden on Jewish Marriage Law: The Uxor Ebraica* (Leiden, 1991), based on the 1646 edition of the work and accompanied by an extensive essay on Selden (LCCN 90042392). All three works are held by the Law Library.

Selden's hidden agenda was to infuse the parliamentary debates on the divorce issue with the notion that—before Canon Law—marriages could be dissolved because marriage was a human contract and as such void of sacramentality. On the other hand, concerning marriage impediments, i.e., the law of consanguinity and affinity and the rules of incest, one can easily discern that the rules of the two religions are nearly congruent.

The Canon Law Collection is one of the better developed collections in the Law Library with an extensive and rare source component. The term *Canon Law* refers in general to the law of the Catholic Church in its entirety, both the Roman Catholic and the Eastern Churches. The Canon Law Collection in the Library of Congress contains primarily Roman Catholic Canon Law. Occupying the central position among the foremost Canon Law sources is the *Decretum Gratiani* (1140) and the subsequent decretal collections of Pope Gregory IX (1227–41), Pope Boniface VIII (1294–1303), and Pope Clement V (1305–15). These sources and the commentaries by the early *decretists* and *decretalists* tracking the *Decretum* or papal decretals, and all the works of post-Tridentine canonists, account for the richest part of the Law Library collection on canonical jurisprudence, although the wealth of pre-1501 prints is shared with the Rare Book and Special Collections Division. The Law Library holds numerous bullaries, forerunners of the official gazette of the Holy See containing papal legislation, as well as the official gazette, the *Acta Sanctae Sedis*, established in 1869—the year of the first Vatican Council— and in 1904 superseded by the *Acta Apostolicae Sedis.*

Compilations of the acts and decrees of ecumenical councils as well as provincial councils and synods are also found in the Law Library, among them sixteenth- and seventeenth-century editions. The Council of Constance, which opened on November 5, 1414, and closed on April 22, 1418, was an extremely important council, the purpose of which was to put an end to the Great Schism of the West and to institute certain reforms within the Church. It is reported that the Council was attended by more than a thousand persons. The eyewitness account of Ulrich von Richental provides important information for the history of both book illustration and heraldry in that he renders naturalistic illustrations of the arms and costumes of the participating clergy and nobility (including those of the Emperor and the Pope).

Two interesting incunabular editions of the decrees of the Council of Basel (1431–37) were edited by Sebastian Brant (1458–1521) and include the *Bulla super approbatione actorum et gestorum in Concilio Basiliensi* by Pope Nicholas V (1447–55). They are held by the Rare Book and Special Collections Division (LCCN 72207032). Works by the Portuguese canonist Augustinho Barbosa (1590–1649), including the 1643 edition of the *Collectanea doctorum, qui suis in operibus Concilii Tridentini loca referentes*, are among the Library's source materials relating to the famed Council of Trent.

Wie herczog Friderich võ österreich mit gra=
fen Herman von zilp stach auf dem Brül vō
Costencz als vornen stet am·lxxxii·blat·

Granff Herman von Zily·

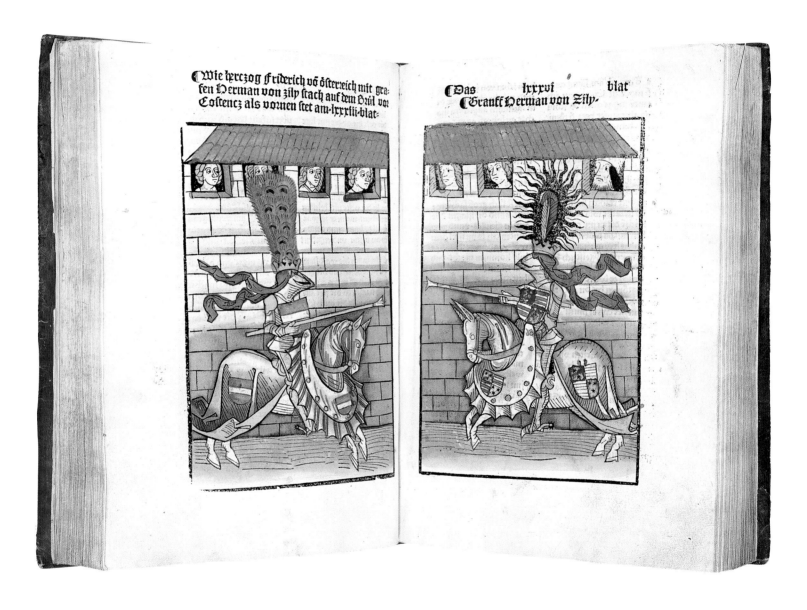

DECRETUM GRATIANI

Among the most significant works in the Law Library's Canon Law collection are those of Gratian, a Camaldolese monk who compiled some thirty-eight hundred texts of earlier Canon Law sources and harmonized them into a text formally known as the *Concordia discordantium canonum* (Concordance of discordant canons), customarily referred to as the *Decretum Gratiani* (the Decree of Gratian).

This text, completed in 1140, was for centuries thereafter the chief source of Canon Law. Important Law Library holdings by or related to Gratian include two manuscripts of the twelfth and thirteenth centuries (LCCN 2004574708 and LCCN 2004574709) and a manuscript epitome of the *Decretum, Flores sive Decretorum* (ca. 1260). The wealth of early print editions of the *Decretum* between 1471 and 1600 from printing houses in Mainz, Nuremberg, Strasbourg, Basel, Paris, and Lyon, and editions from 1600 on to 1879, in separate editions or as part of the *Corpus Iuris Canonici*, is shared between the Law Library and the Rare Book and Special Collections Division. The *Decretum* is among the earliest canonical compilations in the West, succeeding compilations such as the *Decretum* of Burchard, Bishop of Worms (965–1025) or the *Decretum* of Ivo, Bishop of Chartres (1040–1116). Composed of different texts, e.g., apostolic constitutions, canons of the councils, etc., accompanied by Gratian's systematic comments, the *Decretum* is considered the pivotal source for the development of Civil Law in Europe.

CORPUS IURIS CANONICI

Following the *Decretum,* new decrees issued by succeeding pontiffs resulted in the need for new compilations of laws. This work, undertaken first by Pope Gregory IX (1227–41), is represented in the Library by many editions of his *Decretales* (or *Liber Extra*). The Law Library holds two incunabular editions printed in Basel in 1494. *Liber Sextus decretalium* (or *Sext*) was subsequently compiled by Pope Boniface VIII, followed by *Constitutiones Clementinae* of Pope Clement V, the *Extravagantes Joannis* (Pope John XXII), and last the *Extravagantes communes* (late fifteenth century).

The first comprehensive edition, including the *Decretum* and subsequent *decretales* collections, was procured in Paris in 1500 and 1501 by the French jurist Jean Chappuis (fl. 1500). His original arrangement, adopted by Pope Gregory XIII in

OPPOSITE: This illustration is from the *Chronicle of the Council of Constance,* held from 1414 to 1418 (Augsburg, 1483), as described by Ulrich von Richental (ca. 1365–1437?). This volume, one of several incunabula editions in the Library, is illustrated with hand-painted woodcuts. The reproduced page depicts a jousting match—one of the rephrased entertainments in conjunction with the Council. (*Rare Book and Special Collections; LCCN 48042317*)

1582 and to be known as the *Corpus Iuris Canonici*, has set the standard for all subsequent editions. Now extremely rare and important incunabular editions, the *Constitutiones Clementinae* (1500), *Extravagantes Joannis XXII* (1500), and *Extravagantes communes* (1501), which were parts of Chappuis's original Paris edition, are held by the Rare Book and Special Collections Division (LCCN 68052952, 68052954, and 68052955).

The Law Library holds the *Decretum Gratiani: emendatum . . . Gregorii XIII Pont. Max. iussu editum* (Rome, 1582; LCCN 97126289), the first quasi-official Roman edition. The *Decretum* was never promulgated separately, but was part of the Church-controlled emendation of the *Corpus Iuris Canonici* of 1582 of which the Law Library holds a 1605 copy (*Corpus ivris canonici emendatum et notis illvstratvm Gregorii XIII Pont. Max. iussu editum*, Lvgduni, 1605). This compilation constitutes the pre-1918 law of the Catholic Church, until it was superseded in the twentieth century by the *Codex Iuris Canonici* (Code of Canon Law, 1917/18).

Apparatus super primo et secundo libro decretalium, an early fourteenth-century Italian manuscript of great authority in the Middle Ages and an indispensable source today in the interpretation of Medieval Canon Law, is another noteworthy Law Library Canon Law resource. Other books of interest to students of Canon Law are the Library's various editions of the *Speculum iudiciale* by the renowned canonist and French prelate Guillaume Durand (ca. 1230–96). Several incunabula and numerous sixteenth-century and subsequent editions of his encyclopedic treatise of Canon Law (and to some degree Civil Law) from the perspective of court procedure, as well as other related works, may be found in both the Law Library Rare Book Collection and the Rare Book and Special Collections Division.

One of the more popular canonists was Giovanni d'Andrea (ca. 1270–1348). He taught at Bologna during the second period of canonical jurisprudence, which coincided with the publication in 1298 of the *Liber Sextus decretalium* of Pope Boniface VIII, mentioned above. Of d'Andrea's eighty-six works in the Library of Congress's collections, fifteen (mostly incunabula) are editions of the *Lectura super arboribus consanguinitatis et affinitatis*, a commentary on the doctrine of family relationships with a view towards "allowed" and "disallowed" marriages. This particular work of d'Andrea, for the use of the clergy, local courts, notaries, etc., enjoyed tremendous popularity and had wide circulation throughout Europe. In short sequence, new editions, some with expanded text or commentaries, appeared in Latin or vernacular translations, such as Dutch or German. In

Nuremberg, the *Lectura* was printed six times in 1477 alone. About forty-six independent editions are known prior to 1500. The *Lectura* of d'Andrea with arbor diagram appears in the Library's incunabular edition of the *Coustumes du pais de Normandie* (Paris, 1483) and, beginning in 1465, was regularly included in subsequent editions of the *Liber Sextus*.

With the Reformation, hope for a uniform European Marriage Law had vanished. The reformers invoked "Mosaic Law," which they considered the law of God and Natural Law that affected the established canonical relationship degrees and the doctrine of marriage impediments. Marriage was stripped of the sacramental character and insolubility. As a consequence, the *Lectura* of d'Andrea, which was for so long a time the basic treatise on marriages in Europe, fell into oblivion.

From Roman Catholic England (to about 1559) the *Provinciale, seu Constitutiones Angliae* (short: *Provinciale*), an interesting compilation of the Canon Law, was enacted by some of the Legatine councils, i.e., English provincial councils under the Archbishop of Canterbury. Most of the editions the Law Library holds were collected, abridged, and commented on by the great English canonist William Lyndwood (ca. 1375–1446). The Law Library Rare Book Collection includes the 1679 Oxford edition in addition to an incunabulum and several sixteenth-century editions.

The Canon Law Collection is strongest in the works of seventeenth- and eighteenth-century Roman Catholic canonists, among them Cardinal Giovanni Battista De Luca (1614–83), at one time auditor at the Rota Romana, the papal court. De Luca, though not an academic teacher, ranks among the outstanding canonists of his times. His *Theatrum veritatis & Justitiae* is organized by subject and includes decisions, *consilia*, and systematic comparative treatises on Canon and Civil Law. The Law Library holds a beautifully embellished copy of the first (1669) printing of the sixteen-volume work and copies of each of the subsequent printings between 1706 and 1726, as well as the *Summa sive compendium Theatri veritatis* (Rome, 1679). These and other titles from De Luca's pen, such as the *Commentaria ad constitutionem sanctae mem. Innocentii XI. de statutariis successionibus* (in several printings between 1684 and 1758) and *Decisiones* from the time he served as auditor on the Rota Romana, form a collection of encyclopedic dimensions on comparative and early European Civil Law in the Law Library's holdings. De Luca's works in the Italian language also give evidence of the trend away from Latin towards the use of the vernacular in the scholarly community of his day.

Giovanni Battista DeLuca (1614–1683), *Theatrvm veritatis, Et ivstitae, sive Decisivi discvrsvs ad veritatem editi in forensibus controversijs canoniicis, & civilibus*, 16 vols. (Rome, 1669–78). (*Law Library Rare Book Collection*; LCCN 44023905)

N NOMINE DOMINI AMEN Anno a nati/
uitate eiusdem Millesimo Tricentesimo Septua/
gesimo sexto die Mercurii .xxx. mensis Ianuarii
Pontificatus domini Gregorii pape xi. Anno sexto
De mandato uoluntate et unanimi consensu omniuz
dominoz meoz coauditu sacri palacii Apostolici
protunc in Rota sedentiu uidelicz Roberti de stra/
cionen legu Arnoldi Terreni decretoru Galbardi
de noua ecclesia decreto Iohanis de Vayrolis le/
gum Nicolai & Creemona decreto Petri Chabonis
decretoru Egidii Bellemere utriusq iuris Beetrandi & alamo le/
gum et Iohannis de Amelia legum pcessor sedentiu etiaz tunc
in Rota cuz dictis dnis Auditorib9 Et cosentiete Reuerendo in
xpo patre dno Beetrando Epo Pampilonen legum doctore olim
predicti palacii causarum tunc uero Contradicta audiencie dni
nostri pape Auditore Ego Guilhelmus borbarch Alaman9 de/
creetorum doctac minim9 et inter dominos meos Auditores minores
conclusiones seu determinationes aut decisiones infrascriptas
quorundam dubioz in quibus simaliter oes aut uel maior pars dnoz
meoz predictoz cu et aliocum postea supeuenientiu remaserit ad
perpetuam rei memoriam cepi colligere et scribere cotinuando usq
ad anni dni. M.ccc.lxxxi. ad mesem Maii Et hoc sub correctoe
et emendatione omnium domino meoru predictorum et aliorum
supeuenientium et melius sentientium.

De constitutionibus Rica.

numero alias.ccxlvi.
Sequens decisio.h.d statutum capituli
potest pbari p testes .quia scriptura no
est de esse legis.h.d.
Vel sic.Constitutio pbatur per testes.
quia ad esse eioz non est necessaria scrip/
tura.h.d.de quo uide Bar.i.l.de quib9
ff.de legib9 per Ray.in.l.ssuetudinis
.C.que sit longa cosue. 2 per bar.in.c.i.
de constitut.li.vi.

ITEM qp cositutio siue
statutum canonicoru siue
capituli pot pbari p testes
quia scriptura no est de es
se siue substantia legis ut
stitutionis ut.xxv.q.ii.in
stitutionis.2 de iureiur.c.ii.in.li.i. Rn.
li.vi.2 de renun.c.i.e.li.Licet Io.an.in
mercui.in regula nemo pot ad impossi/
bile ptractando qones predictas 2 mul
tas solutioes ponendo 2 inter alias pe.
de bell. pg.dicentis non esse peccatum
dicere qp scriptura sit de esse legis p.l.
humani.C.de legi.dicat dcm qp habet
multum equitatis.2 dicit qp si princeps
esset necessitate scripture imponere co
stitutionibz inferiorz ita qp aliter facte
non ualerent nisi de scripto pmulgaren
tur 2 respondz ad iura primo itroducta
tamen aliqui dni dixerunt qp si statutu
esset antiquum 2 de longinquissimo te
ra difficaliter pbaretur. naz huiusmodi
antiqua facta melius pbatur p scriptu
ram q per testes ppter labilia hoim me
moriam put le.2 no.de pba. tertio loco
2.c.cum cam.de fide istru .nam Io.et
c.cum p.ad istam materiam uide archi.
i.di.lex scripta.

De rescriptis Rica.

alias.xxviii.
Sequens decisio.h.d qp cha quouis alio
modo respicit personas dumtaxat expl
sam. uel sic qp cha quouis aliomodo in
cludit dcm modum uacandi per psonaz
expsslam.h.b.uel qp impetrans cum
cha quouismodo sufficit p pb3 uniu
modum uacandi 2 quia expressum
per eandem personam non per diuersas
h.d.uel sic.qp impetrans exprimere de/
bet certus modus uacationis ex certa p
sona 2 tunc cha seu quouis alio modo cu
prebendit aliud modum ex dicta psoa
prouenientem.h.d.

ITEM si mandat alicui puide
ri de certo beneficio certo modo
uacante puta p stitutione exe
crabilis adiecta cha seu quouis
alio modo uacauerit si no uncet predco
sed alio modo.puta per stitutione de
multa uel per non pmotione ad ordines
psbiterat9 ut in.c.licet canon de cle.li.
vi.uel per ptractu meimorii ut in.c.i.
de cle.biuga.uel per ingresf religionis
de regula.beneficium.li.vi.fuit dubita
tum utz de dicto beneficio sic alio mo
qp expsso in gra uacante posset puideri
impetranti sup quo dni erant uarii ppi.
suceptum.de Rp.li.vi.p quod.c.aliq
dni declinabant in ptem negatiua.quia
uno modo expsso non uenit alius ut ibi
ar.c.nonne.de psump.hoc ueruz nisi ali
ud appareret de intentione mandantis
ut in.d.c.suceptum.i.Rn.puta quia pa
pa mandat alicui puideri de beneficio
uacan.per resignato 2 alio quocuq mo
uacauerit.tunc eni p9 Io.an.ibidem ue
nit omnis alius modo uacandi 2 hoc pp
ter cham antedictam in quo allegat ipe
.cum aliquibus.in fi 2.c.duobus.in fi.
e.ti.2.c.si motu pprio.de pben.e.li.uel
ius opinio indubitater uera 2 eandem p
sonaz.nam predicta cha seu quouis alio
modo respicit omne modu uacandi pe
eandem personaz.Secus si p diuersas se
cunduz lapus ibidem .licet dns Io.al.
in quadi sua qone.que incipit papa con
tulit tenueit disputando omne moduz
uacandi uenit etiam p alia psonam sub
cha antedicta.Ratio prima sua fuit bec
quia predicta cha omne modu includit
p9 charum intellectu 2 opetentem. p9
eum facit quia cha non addicta ad subie
ctum restrictuz 13 generaz 2 plus ipi
mit relatio generalis maxie cu bec dis/
iunctiua punctio termini pcedente no
repetat saltem restrictiue 2 uniuersal3
in uno solo supposito uerificat.Et quia
mens uerbis no repugnat que omnia co
priose fundat per iura multa 2 ad rones
omnes in ptracium alt.respondet.cuius
opinioe dns egi intellexit 2 uera puta
uit in beneficio iam uacan.de quo puta
det ut puideri mandatur per papa.nam
non potuit uidere qua rone hoc casu ve
cedendu foret a ppria significatioe ve
borum.qsentit tn bene qp opi.lapi.quam
seruat preallegz.locum sibi uendicat in
beneficio nondu uacan .de cui9 uacatio
ne certa sperat in certam persona puta
mandat puideri alicui d certo beneficio

The *Decisiones Rotae Romanae* represent a large special collection in the field of Canon Law composed of an uninterrupted line of important and well-known editions up to the twentieth century, commencing with *incunabula*. Included are contemporary commentaries and other secondary sources. Cases before the Rota Romana, originally the central court of the Roman Catholic Church with universal jurisdiction, were heard by the Rota auditors (traditionally cardinals) who prepared their legal opinions (*decisiones*) for the actual decisions by the court.

Modern Canon Law, the international collection of the definitive *Codex Iuris Canonici* (1917) superseded by the revised edition of 1983, and a mint collection of the works—precursors to the codification of Canon Law—by a slate of international noted jurists and canonists are also worth consulting. Equally interesting are collections on present-day, headline issues of concern.

In addition to the law of the Roman Catholic Church, Canon Law also encompasses the laws of the Eastern Catholic Churches, including those of Alexandria, Antioch, Armenia, Byzantium, and Chaldea—all of which recognize the Pope in Rome but are separate churches within the universal Roman Catholic Church. Within these various Catholic Churches there are numerous rites—I. Coptic and Ethiopian; II. Malankara, Maronite, and Syrian Orthodox; III. Armenian Catholic; IV. Albanian, Belarusian, Bulgarian, Georgian, Greek, Hungarian, Italo-Albanian, Melchite, Romanian, Russian, Ruthenian, Slovak, Ukrainian, and Yugoslav; as well as V. Chaldean, Syro-Malankarese, and Nestorian. Works concerning the law of Eastern Catholics represent about two percent of the Law Library's Canon Law holdings. A useful guide to distinguishing among these churches is included in *The Eastern Christian Churches: A Brief Survey*, by Ronald Roberson (5th ed., Rome, 1995). The laws of various Orthodox Christian Churches may be found in the Law Library (see the section on Russian Law below), Rare Book and Special Collections Division, and in various Area Studies reading rooms of the Library.

Overall, this collection holds an estimated thirty thousand titles predominantly in Latin and other European languages, among them important manuscripts and over one hundred Canon Law books printed before 1500, with many titles accounting for capacious multi-volume folio sets or serial publications. Complementing the Law Library's collections, notable Canon Law books may be found in the Rare Book and Special Collections Division, especially in the Thatcher, Vollbehr, and Rosenwald Collections.

OPPOSITE: Illustrating this incunabular edition of the *Decisiones Rotae Romanae* (Rome, 1475) are elegant initials on leaves 10b and 11a. This edition is the earliest printed instance of this group of fourteenth-century decisions (known as *novae, antiquae,* and *antiquiores decisiones,* compiled from Thomas Falstolus, the "Fastoli") being issued together. (*Law Library Rare Book Collection,* LCCN 76516271)

The various Protestant faiths and other creeds may be researched under the specific name of the faith about which information is sought. Early Church of England and Scottish Church Law materials and, of course, works on the German Protestant Church (*Augsburg Confession* and *Evangelische Kirche Deutschlands*) are the more numerous. Interesting literature published after the Peace of Westphalia in 1648 includes comparative works on both Catholic and Protestant denominations and religion and the state, i.e., Constitutional Law, or Religious Law and International Law. The Library's resources provide legal scholars and others with arresting material on how religious struggles and wars from the sixteenth century on deeply affected the development of law, and on the long-range effects the Reformation had on almost every branch of law. The Augsburg Religious Peace of 1555 (*Augsburger Religionsfrieden*) added yet another dimension to the century-old issue of "church and state," namely the issue of *freedom of religion* for the various classes. The territorial rulers, possessing now the *ius reformandi* (religious ban), could determine the religious faith in their territories—Catholicism, Augsburg Confession or, just maybe, both. For many a subject it meant freedom to leave, with or without possessions. Both the Augsburg Peace and, a hundred years later, the Peace of Westphalia 1648 (or: the Treaties of Münster and Osnabrück), concluding the Thirty Years War, were in fact considered imperial constitutions or fundamental laws. The treaty (*Friedens Schluss zwischen denen Röm. Kayser-vnd Königlichen Schwedischen Majestätten zu Osznabruck den 27 oder 26 August im Iahr MDCXLVIII deutlich verlesen. . . .* S.L., 1648; LCCN 92152875) and numerous, mostly European works on these subjects, including many works treating this war as a subject of International Law, can be researched in the Library's General Collections or Law Library.

Much interesting literature was produced by jurists who are known primarily through their works on Constitutional, Feudal, and Administrative Law, i.e., Public Law, such as Justus Henning Böhmer (1674–1749), *Jus ecclesiasticum protestantium usum modernum iuris canonici* (Halle, 1731–36); Johann Schilter (1632–1705), *De libertate ecclesiarum Germaniae libri septem* (Jena, 1683); Johann Brunnemann (1608–72), *De jure ecclesiastico; tractatus posthumus, in usum ecclesiarum evangel. & consistoriorum concinnatus* (Frankfurt, 1686); Samuel Stryk (1640–1710), *Consilia Hallensivm ivreconsvltorvm* (Halle, 1733–34); Johann Jacob Moser (1701–85), *Die Religionsfreyheiten und Beschwerden dere Evangelischen in gantz Europa, besonders in Teutschland* (Ebersdorff im Vogtland, 1741), or his *Corpus jvris evangelicorum ecclesiastici, oder Sammlung evangelisch- lutherisch- und reformirter Kirchen-Ordnungen, wie auch dergleichen*

Armen-, classical-, consistorial-, Ehe-, Gerichts-, Gymnasien-, Hochzeit-, Hospital-, Inspections, Leichen-, presbyterial-, Schul-, Superintendentz-, Tauf-, Visitations-, Universitäts-, Waisenhaus- und andere solche Ordnungen. . . . (Züllichau, 1737–38). The last is a collection of evangelical, reformed, and Lutheran church orders describing basically all the functions the church fulfilled in the social sector at that time.

The typically lengthy titles of early works relate much of the historical context surrounding their publication, such as this Church of England title printed in London in 1661: "A collection of articles, injunctions, canons, orders, ordinances, and constitutions ecclesiastical, with other publick records of the Church of England, chiefly in times of K. Edward VIth, Q. Elizabeth, and K. James; published to vindicate the Church of England and to promote uniformity and peace in the same, and humbly presented to the convocation." This volume was intended for "the convocation holden at London in the year 1562" (Law Library Rare Book Collection; LCCN 76366651).

Among the British titles published over a century later, this one concerning religion and law in the New World is equally descriptive: "A Draught of an act of Parliament for tolerating the Roman Catholick religion in the province of Lucbee [i.e., Luebeck, later Quebec] and for encouraging and introducing the Protestant religion into the said province, and for vesting the lands belonging to certain religious houses in the said province in the crown of this kingdom, for the support of the civil government of the said province, and for other purposes" (London, 1772; LCCN 10003716).

ISLAMIC LAW

Islam, originating in the seventh century, began as a system of religious beliefs and duties that regulate practically every aspect of a Muslim's daily life, with no distinction between matters of faith and of law. Its revealed source, the *Qur'an* (*Koran*), and its concrete source, the *hadith* or *sunna* (Tradition), remain the basic reference for both. The Law Library holds a significant number of materials on Islamic Law, i.e., on *shari'a* (the sacred law based on the *Qur'an*) and *fiqh* (the science of law, or more precisely, the science of *shari'a*) in Arabic, Persian, and Turkish. Among them are classical sources of Sunni and Shi'a jurisprudence, although the collection is richest in analytical and historic works by nineteenth- and twentieth-century scholars.

A large number of copies of the *Qur'an* may be found in the African and Middle Eastern Division, together with general works on Islam and the social conditions of Islamic society (cf. *The Holy Koran in the Library of Congress: A Bibliography*, compiled by Fawzi M. Tadros, Washington: Library of Congress, 1993).

The Law Library collection includes copies of the *Qur'an* as well to complement its holdings on Islamic Law. The main collection consists of legal treatises, commentaries and super-commentaries (i.e., commentaries on commentaries), and authoritative interpretations of *Qur'anic* and other revealed sources at the hands of Islamic jurists. They span centuries of Islamic scholarship and are of timeless importance. These works, which are housed exclusively in the Law Library, encompass a wide variety of what usually falls under the heading of Islamic Law: the rules concerning man's relation to God and the rules ordering the family of man and his relations and interactions in society.

An important treasure in the Law Library is Burhan al-Din ibn Muhammad ibn Ibrahim al-Halabi, *Multaqa al-abhur* (The Confluence of the currents. Rules for daily living), compiled in 1517 and written in Istanbul. Al-Halabi was one of the most learned legal scholars of the sixteenth-century Ottoman Empire and his text became an authoritative handbook of the *Hanafi* school of Islamic Law as practiced in the Ottoman Empire until the reforms that occurred in the nineteenth century. The manuscript contains rules covering practically every human activity: spiritual rites and prescriptions (*ibadat*) and the traditional civil aspects of persons, family, and inheritance (which form the core of Civil Law in all legal systems). It also treats contracts and commercial transactions (*mu'amalat*) and those rules governing the punishment of crimes (*hudud*).

The process of legal modernization, which began in the nineteenth century, saw simultaneous attempts at the codification of Islamic Law precepts and their incorporation into modern codes based on their European counterparts. These codes are found in the collection under the laws of a particular country, not among works of "Islamic Law" or *shari'a*.

Today, Islamic Law governs in varying degrees the life of almost a quarter of the world's population. While the national legal systems in most of these areas are today generally based on Civil or Common Law principles and practices, traditional Islamic Law remains an important component in the makeup of their legal culture and a principal source for their family and constitutional laws. The Law Library's collection, with its body of classical Islamic works, current codes, and legislation of Islamic countries, together with the large selection of topical monographs, periodicals, and official gazettes, constitutes a rich and important resource for both research scholars and practicing lawyers.

This manuscript copy of the *Qur'an* was penned in 1152 by Mustafa al-Khatib in Turkey (Sultaniyah Mosque) Ah/1739. It is one of many rare and valuable copies of the *Qur'an* in the collections of the Library's African and Middle Eastern Division. (*The Holy Koran in the Library of Congress: A Bibliography*, compiled by Fawzi M. Tadros, Washington: Library of Congress, 1993, no. 9)

Law of Indigenous Peoples

THE INDIGENOUS PEOPLES referred to in this section are limited to those present in the Western Hemisphere, as the previous sections of this guide have touched on the Customary Law of early peoples in other regions of the world.

INDIANS OF AMERICA

Research tracking the legal history of indigenous peoples of the Americas with roots deep in ancient customs, traditions, and rites—mostly without written record—faces the same challenges as research in peoples' early legal history in any given region of the world. Therefore, early sources of Customary Law of specific American indigenous peoples and the sources defining their legal organization are sparse.

The Library of Congress, however, offers quite a range of resources for the study of the encounters and legal relationships between the indigenous peoples of North and South America and the Europeans who came eventually to occupy the "New World" in the sixteenth and subsequent centuries, as well as for the study of colonial and American Indian treaty law, of U.S. Federal and State Law relating to American Indians, and of current Indian constitutions and charters.

For both areas of research on what has come to be called "American Indian Law," different collections have to be consulted. Early Customary Law may be ascertained in relevant anthropological, archeological, or ethnological sources, but is found mainly in the old and large collection on the history of the Americas (Native American Collection), all within the General Collections of the Library. An interesting work by Hugo Grotius (see below, Law of the Netherlands) concerns the origins of the American Indians (*De origine gentium americanarum dissertatio.* N.p., 1642, reprinted in Amsterdam and Paris in the same year), probably inspired by the excitement of that time over the reports on the explorations by the *Nederlandsche West-Indische Compagnie* (1621–75) and the Dutch colonization of what was to become New Netherlands (later New York). An Amsterdam and Paris edition of the same year, as well as a comment on it, *Notae ad dissertationum Hugonis Grotii De origine Gentium americanarum* (Amsterdam, 1643) by Johannes de Laet (1593–1649), and a translation *On the Origin of the Native Races of America* by Edmund Goldsmid (Edinburgh, 1884), are in the collections of the Library. Another example is *Omnium gentium mores, leges, et ritus* (Italian translation, Venice, 1564) by Joannes Boemus (ca. 1485–1535), a work on South American Indians' Customary Law in the anthropological collection (customs and manners).

The Native American Collection also contains some early and some current works on the Canadian Inuit, e.g., *Quebec Inuit Elders Conference* (Kangirsujuaq/

Quebec, 1983). The *Bulletin* (Smithsonian Institution, Bureau of American Ethnology. Washington: GPO, 1903–71) is another resource which is available in the General Collections of the Library. The user may also contact the American Folklife Center at the Library of Congress.

The reader seeking source materials with a bearing on the legal situation vis-á-vis various tribes in the earlier periods may find useful material in letters, reports, and diaries of individuals whose papers are held in the Library's Manuscript Division.

Inasmuch as maps are important for treaty research or border settlements, the Geography and Map Division is a significant repository of such cartographic information, e.g., on the westward expansion of the burgeoning white population and their military operations. Present-day maps of U.S. states show the current extent of Indian territory, which amounts to over fifty million acres, most within the borders of reservations.

Likewise, for certain tribes or nations, British, Dutch, French, and Spanish Colonial Law may need to be consulted and these sources may be found in the Law Library's Foreign Law collections. For example, Spanish (Royal ordinances) or early Mexican laws may offer glimpses of customs and Tribal Laws of the Pueblo or California tribes. One of the earliest legal cases in the New World is documented in the *Huexotzinco Codex of 1531* in the Library's Manuscript Division. The *Codex*—a document on pre-European paper called *amatl* and made in Centro-America—is part of the testimony in a case against representatives of the colonial government in Mexico, ten years after the Spanish Conquest in 1521. Additional documentation in the Library's collections shows that, in 1538, King Charles of Spain agreed with a judgment against the Spanish colonial administrators who had unfairly taxed the Nahua Indian people of the town of Huexotzinco, Mexico, and that two-thirds of all tributes taken from the people of Huexotzinco had to be returned, a rare turn of events in the history of indigenous people.

The library of Thomas Jefferson, whose collection was purchased by the Library of Congress in 1815, contained a significant source for historic Indian treaty research: *The Treaty Held with the Indians of the Six Nations, At Lancaster, in Pennsylvania in June 1744* (Williamsburg, Virginia, 1744). Although Jefferson's copy of this book is no longer extant, the text is available in several collections, such as the *Early American Indian Documents: Treaties and Laws, 1607–1789, Volume II* (1984), which is on the shelves of the Law Library Reading Room. It may be deduced from these materials that in 1744 the English colonists in North America did regard the Iroquois, for example, as a major foreign power to be negotiated with under the principles of International Law, as they would negotiate with the French or the Spanish. Other European colonial powers entertained the same view as evidenced by the history of treaty-making. This tradition was carried over and practiced—after independence—by the United States, but often with varying degrees of implementation.

With respect to Indian sovereignty, Benjamin Franklin and Thomas Jefferson were among the framers of the Constitution who respected the position of American Indian nations and regarded them as a foreign power. In the Constitution, the legal right to make treaties and regulate trade with the Indians, therefore, was federally preempted or, in other terms, reserved to the federal government and not left to the states. Less than a half century later, however, Justice John Marshall declared in a landmark Supreme Court case in 1831 that Indian polities, such as the Iroquois or the Cherokee, were not "foreign" powers and that an Indian nation was rather a "domestic dependent nation governing itself" within the sovereignty of the United States

The Rare Book Collection in the Law Library is important for research on Colonial and early American materials, including English acts of Parliament during the Colonial period. Of the early nineteenth century, the Law Library holds most of the laws and constitutions produced by the Cherokee, Choctaw, Chickasaw, Creek, and Seminole (often referred to as "the Five Civilized Tribes"), who were forced to leave the Southeast for the Indian Territory after passage of the Indian Removal Act in 1830. Several volumes of this rare collection deal with the Indian Territory, including the seven-volume *Indian Territory Reports 1900–1909*, as well as twentieth-century constitutions and corporate charters for some three hundred of the federally recognized nations, tribes, bands, and associated groups.

Three Seminole Wars between the United States and the Seminole Indians of Florida were waged at various times between 1817 and 1858. Andrew Jackson's forces attacked and burned Seminole villages and seized Spanish-held territory of Florida some thirty years after Congress issued the Northwest Ordinance of 1787, which set forth admission procedures for new states entering the Union and provided in its article 3 concerning Native Americans as follows:

The utmost good faith shall always be observed towards the Indians; their lands and property shall never be taken from them without their consent; and, in their property, rights, and liberty, they shall never be invaded or disturbed, unless in just and lawful wars authorized by Congress; but laws founded in justice and humanity, shall from time to time be made for preventing wrongs being done to them, and for preserving peace and friendship with them.

An important item in the Law Library's Rare Book Collection is the *Collected Laws of the Eastern and Western Cherokees* (Tahlequah, Cherokee Nation, Indian Territory, National Cherokee Printing Office, 1871). This is one of several nineteenth-century editions of the laws of the Cherokee Nation to be printed in the Cherokee language. It uses the syllabary invented by Sequoya (1770?–1843). From 1839 to 1906 the Cherokee in the Indian Territory (now Oklahoma) operated their own judicial system. The laws were drafted in English and later translated into Cherokee, for the use of those (including some judges) who were not literate in English.

The most extensive collections are the federal source collections which offer a broad spectrum on American Indian rights under U.S. Law and government relations. The Senate has ratified three hundred seventy-five treaties, and Congress has enacted over four thousand statutes concerning American Indians, a number which is surpassed only by the mass of regulations and guidelines implementing these laws, and by the number of reports on litigation over Indian rights and resources. Research in these areas has to negotiate subliminally present traces of old European precepts of Feudal Law and laws of war and conquest.

A classic work listing treaties, statutes, executive actions, and miscellaneous information on Indian affairs chronologically from 1778 to 1938 is the compilation by Charles J. Kappler, *Indian Affairs: Laws and Treaties*, 5 v. (Washington, D.C.: GPO, 1904–41. Reprint. New York: AMS Press, 1972. U.S. Department of the Interior). Volume 1 lists over two hundred seventy-five tribes and bands at the turn of the century; volume 2 consists of a thorough compilation of Indian treaties and has been separately reprinted (*Indian Treaties 1778–1883*. New York: Interland Publishing Inc., 1972; it is also available in the Law Library Microform Consortium's *Native American Legal Materials Collection* as Title 4228). The Kappler set also lists other useful materials, such as charts of population figures and tribal finances. Throughout the set, the texts of unratified treaties are listed as well. The original five Kappler volumes were issued as part of the *U.S. Congressional Serial Set* (see section 4.4.1 *Government Documents*). See also Kappler's *Indian Affairs: Laws and Treaties*, 2 v. (Washington, D.C.: GPO, 1979). These continuously paged volumes provide a thirty-year update (through 1970) on the original Kappler work.

English colonial treaties are listed by Henry Farr de Puy in his *A Bibliography of the English colonial treaties with the American Indians, including a synopsis of each treaty* (New York, 1917; reprinted by the Lawbook Exchange, 2001). The *Early American Indian documents: treaties and laws, 1607–1789*, by Alden T. Vaughan et al., is a compilation of (mostly) treaties in eighteen volumes. Another important North American treaty collection in the Library is *The treaties of Canada with the Indians of Manetoba and* the *North-West Territories* (Toronto, 1880) by Alexander Morris (1826–89). Extracted from this edition are *The treaties between her Majesty, Queen Victoria, and the Indians of British North America* (procured by the Provincial Committee on Minority-Groups . . . and the Federation of Saskatchewan Indians; Regina, 1961).

Other publications are the *American State Papers. Documents, Legislative and Executive, of the Congress of the United States* (1815–1827). *Class II: Indian Affairs*, 2 v. (Washington, 1834); and *Laws of the colonial and State governments, relating to Indians and Indian affairs, from 1633 to 1831, inclusive. . . .* (*American Indians at law series*) (Stanfordville, New York, 1979, a reprint of the 1832 Washington edition); or *Annotated acts of Congress*, edited by Clarence Lot Thomas (Columbia, Missouri, 1913).

After years of broken, often fraudulent treaties, the recognition of Indian nations or tribes by the federal government formally began with the *1934 Indian Reorganization Act*, providing for a mainstream legal framework for tribal governments subject to the U.S. Constitution, and an emphasis on a government-to-government relationship. Today, there are some five hundred sixty federally recognized sovereign Indian nations and tribes—under constitutions and charters—operating within the U.S. federal and state structure, although certain nations had constitutions much earlier than 1934. But only since the late 1960s (during the Johnson Administration) has Congress promoted the sovereignty and autonomy of tribal entities, and prohibited states' exercise of authority over Indian reservations and land deals. The constitutional organization of tribal entities is expressed in the corporate component, such as *Community, Association*, or *Community Association, Native Village, Traditional Council, Village of Council*, or *Corporation* added to the name of the tribe. The U.S. Bureau of Indian Affairs, Washington, D.C., maintains and publishes the list of federally recognized "tribal entities, eligible for funding and services from the Bureau by virtue of their status as Indian tribes" in the contiguous forty-eight states and in Alaska in the *Federal Register*.

These nations and tribes exercise constitutional and legislative powers; they exercise self-government which is inherent in tribal culture; and they have their own judicial system. The operations of these three branches of tribal government have produced a body of laws (e.g., codes), administrative regulations, and judgments by tribal courts that qualifies as primary law.

For a current evaluation and re-examination of Indians' legal/constitutional status within the United States, see *The Rights of Indians and Tribes: The Authoritative ACLU Guide to Indian Tribal Rights*, by Stephen L. Pevar, 3rd edition (Carbondale and Edwardsville, 2002); *Lessons from the Third Sovereign: Indian Tribal Courts*, by Justice Sandra Day O'Connor, in the *Tulsa Law Journal* (v. 33, 1, 1, 1997); or *American Indians*

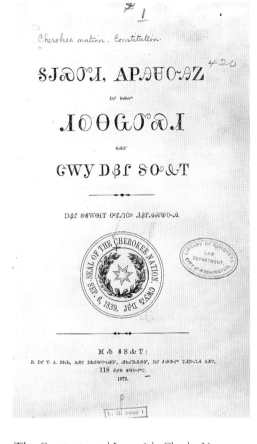

The *Constitution and Laws of the Cherokee Nation* was originally published by the authority of the National Council of the Cherokee Nation in 1839; the edition pictured dates from 1875. Written in the Cherokee language and displaying the Nation's seal, this document is witness to the advanced abilities of the Cherokee to meet legal standards foreign to their own heritage. Unfortunately, neither the Cherokees' political maturity nor their skillful adaptability in creating a legal culture based on European models worked to prevent their being deprived of the use of their original lands during the great push westward by white society. (*Prints and Photographs Division;* LC-USZ62-61141)

No. 3525. INDIAN CHIEFS
Who counciled with Gen. Miles and settled the
Indian War.
1 Standing Bull. 2 Bear who looks back running.
3 Has the Big   4 White Tail.   5 Liver Bear.
white horse.
6 Little Thunder. 7 Bull Dog. 8 High Hawk.
9 Lame. 10 Eagle Pipe.
Photo and copyright by Grabill. '91,
Deadwood, S. D.

"Indian Chiefs who counciled with Gen. Miles and setteled [sic] the Indian War. 1. Standing Bull, 2. Bear Who Looks Back Running, 3. Has The Big White Horse, 4. White Tail, 5. Liver [Living] Bear, 6. Little Thunder, 7. Bull Dog, 8. High Hawk, 9. Lame, 10. Eagle Pipe." (*Prints and Photographs Division*; LC-USZ62-46735)

and *Law Libraries: Acknowledging the Third Sovereign*, in *Law Library Journal* (v. 94, 1, 7) by Nancy Carol Carter; and a very recent work by Robert N. Clinton et al., *American Indian Law: Native Nations and the Federal System: Selected Federal Indian Law Provisions* (Newark, New Jersey, 2004).

Two current serial publications are: The *Native American Law Digest* (began to appear in 1991) and the *Indian Law Reporter* (Washington, 1974–).

The monographic legal literature offers a great wealth of topical discussion on many subjects of interest or urgency, such as rights to land and associated natural resources, environment, and revenue, for example, *Native American Natural Resources Law: Cases and Materials*, by Judith V. Royster et al. (Durham, 2002).

Among important standard reference works pertaining to Indian Law are two works of Felix Cohen (1907–53), who was at one point in his career the principal drafter of the *Indian Reorganization Act* of 1934, namely the *Handbook of Federal Indian Law*, 1982 edition (Charlottesville, Virginia), that can be consulted in conjunction with the *Statutory Compilation of the Indian Law Survey: A Compendium of Federal Laws and Treaties Relating to Indians*, 46 v. (Washington, 1940); and *Index of Interior Department Rulings on Indian Law* (Washington, 1940). In the bibliographic literature on North American Indian Law, the compilation *American Indian Legal Materials: A Union List*, by Laura N. Gasaway et al., (Stanfordville, New York, 1980) stands out and should be consulted.

A large-scale digital project of significant value, accessible to the public, is *Native American Constitutions and Law Digitization Project*, coordinated by the University of Oklahoma Law Library and the National Indian Law Library of the Native American Rights Fund (URL http://thorpe.ou.edu/). It provides access to current full-text tribal codes, constitutions, and charters and other legal documents of the federally recognized tribes. It also provides updates on the status of recent U.S. Supreme Court cases affecting Native Americans.

The *Guide to Law Online*, prepared by the Law Library of Congress Public Services Division, is an annotated guide to sources of information on government and law available online. The Indians of North America page (http://www.loc.gov/law/guide/indians.html) includes selected links to useful and reliable sites for legal information.

A Library of Congress reference work, *Many Nations: A Library of Congress Resource Guide for the Study of Indian and Alaska Native Peoples of the United States,* is a useful introduction for researchers wishing to have a survey of the wide-ranging materials in the Library's collections; one chapter of that work gives an overview of the Library's relevant law materials.

LAW OF HAWAI'I

Almost fifty years have passed since Hawai'i entered as the fiftieth state into the Union of American States (1959). More than one hundred years have passed since the 1893 overthrow of the Hawaiian monarchy and subsequent formal annexation of the islands by the United States in 1900. The Library of Congress holds an extensive collection that illustrates the history, anthropology, and ethnology of Hawai'i and its people. The collection includes works on the genealogy of the royal dynasty from before the discovery of the Islands by Captain James Cook in 1778 through the periods of the Kingdom until the forced abdication of the last royalty of Hawai'i, Queen Lili'uokalani, in 1894, and the history of the Territory of Hawai'i from annexation to its statehood in 1959. It is the story of the steady decline of a culture brought about by foreign economic and military interests.

The long record of civil injustices, humiliations, exploitations, and struggles of a people for preservation of their identity and cultural survival has preoccupied historians, politicians, legal scholars, and judges. The environment created by the Draft Declaration on the Rights of Indigenous Peoples of 1993 has attracted civil rights advocates as well (U.N. ESCOR, Comm'n on Hum. Rts . . . U.N. Doc. E/CN.4/Sub2/1993/29. 1993).

For the early, pre-1800 Customary Law of the Hawaiian people, written sources are lacking, since the culture of Hawai'i before the arrival of the early missionaries was a non-script culture, based on oral traditions and ancient observances. Therefore, the researcher in the field of legal history, legal symbolism, and legal archeology has to resort to works on anthropology, ethnology, and history in the Library's General Collections; works such as *History of the Hawaiian or Sandwich Islands: embracing their antiquity, mythology, legends, discovery by Europeans in the sixteenth century, rediscovery by Cook, with their civil, religious, and political history* (Boston, 1843) by James Jackson Jarves (1818–88); and *Colonizing Hawaii: The Cultural Power of Law* (Princeton, 2000) by Sally Engle Merry. Equally important is the literature on social life and customs, and civilization and ethnology, such as *Ancient Hawai'i: Words and Images* (Honolulu, 1997) by Herbert Kawainui Kane; *Feathered Gods and Fishhooks: An Introduction to Hawaiian Archeology and Prehistory* (Honolulu, 1985) by Patrick Vinton Kirch, and, by the same author an important work *Anahulu: The Anthropology of History in the Kingdom of Hawai'i* (Chicago, 1992). Other such works include: *Sacred Queens and Women of Consequence: Rank, Gender, and Colonialism in the Hawaiian Islands* (Ann Arbor, 1990) by Jocelyn Linnekin; *Symbols of Sovereignty: Feather Girdles of Tahiti and Hawai'i* (Honolulu, 1978) by Roger G. Rose; and *Rethinking the Native Hawaiian Past* (New York, 1998) by Kanalu G. Terry Young, including oral tradition. For the Hawaiian kings and ruling houses, and for dynastic rules, a sampling of works, some of a genealogical nature, may be considered, such as *Ruling Chiefs of Hawai'i* (Moolelo o Kamehameha I; Honolulu, 1992) by Samuel Manaiakalani Kamakau (1815–76); and *Hawaiian Royal Genealogies: Charts and Comments* (Dallas, 1988) by the Oukah, Emperor of Tsalagi, the Cherokee Nations. The Library also holds a *Catalog of Oral History Collections in Hawai'i* (Ethnic Studies Oral History Project, University of Hawaii at Manoa, 1982). Most works have illustrations and maps.

Printed law sources begin to flow in the nineteenth century roughly covering the periods of the Hawaiian Monarchy, from 1810 under Kamehameha I (1797–1818) to the abdication of Queen Lili'uokalani in 1894. The reader will find a fascinating view on constitution, government, and foreign relations of the indigenous society of Hawai'i, throughout the General Collections and the Law Library. Of the first printed works, the Library holds a facsimile of the first government document (Honolulu, 1972), issued in 1822 from the first printing press in Hawaii (Notice posted by order of King Kamehameha II, 1819–24, to preserve the peace of his dominions after disturbances on the shore and annoyance of the inhabitants by the crews of different foreign vessels; LCCN 98149513).

The compilations of *Treaties and conventions concluded between the Hawaiian Kingdom and other powers, since 1825* (Honolulu, 1875, and in an expanded edition of 1887 including all treaties since 1825 to 1885) and other official and diplomatic documents show the Kingdom of Hawai'i as an independent sovereign nation entertaining foreign relations with more than fifteen nations. Between 1826 and 1893, the United States—in diplomatic recognition of the Kingdom—concluded various treaties and conventions of friendship, commerce, and navigation. *The Annual reports of the King to the legislature* (Honolulu, 1852), *Reports on the King's personal accounts by the Commissioners of the King's privy purse* (Honolulu, 1853–55), the *Biannual report of the commissioner of Crown lands, with maps* (Honolulu, 18—), and the *Report of the Royal commission on the development of the resources of the kingdom* (Honolulu, 1877) are important sources to be consulted.

A translation of the first constitution of the monarchy (1840) and a compilation of Royal Session Laws, signed by King Kamehameha III (1824–54), are bound together and were published in 1842 as *Translation of the constitution and laws of the Hawaiian Islands, established in the reign of Kamehameha III, called now Hawai'i's "Blue Laws"* (Lahainaluna, Hawai'i, 1842; LCCN 37031612). This is a very important source since it illustrates the adaptation of Indigenous Law to Christian principles. As the introduction by the compiler states, in these Islands law was something like a system of Feudal Law and Common Law, consisting partly in their ancient taboos, and partly in the practices of their chiefs as handed down by tradition, but at the same time, the principles of the Bible were already fully adopted. Some of the laws were obviously proposed by foreign visitors, consuls, or ship commanders, but were materially modified by the House of Nobles and House of Representatives.

The constitution laid out the principles on which the dynasty was founded, i.e., the rights of the people and the chiefs, and the prerogatives of the king. Under the first king, Kamehameha I (1784–1819), all land belonged to the people and the chiefs in common; the king was only the head and administrator of the land. In contrast, Kamehameha III retained private land (called Crown lands). He had war and treaty powers, and was the supreme judge. The constitution also treats of the rights of governors, of the House of Nobles and House of Representatives and rules for their meetings, and of judges. Compiled statutes (mostly dating from 1841) offer a view on taxes (or tithes): a poll tax in money, and a land tax paid in swine. Laws on schools and education were extensive. The laws on marriage and divorce abrogated indigenous custom; marriages had to be concluded according to the word of God.

A large selection of criminal laws, dating from 1842, as well as court regulations and procedure laws, are also found in the collection. The reprints of the *Constitution* (1852 and 1868 during Kamehameha III's reign), a reprint of 1894 (after Queen Lili'uokalani's forced abdication) with the title: *Hawaiis "blue" laws: Constitution and laws of 1840. A practical illustration of the missionaries' love for the Hawaiians* (Honolulu, 1894), and a collection of laws (codes), *Ke Kuma kanawai, a me na kanawai, issued under Kamehameha III* (Honolulu, 1841; LCCN unk84241577), are in the Library's collection as well.

A volume of Session Laws dating from the year 1853 in the Law Library gives important insight into the country's progressing organization—although the Library falls short on earlier enactments for Kamehameha's government organization (between 1845–47): the *Act establishing a Supreme Court with a Chief Justice and two Associate Justices* (May 26, 1853), outlining the jurisdiction of the Court (Admiralty and maritime cases, and cases affecting ministers, ambassadors, and consuls); the 1853 Act on elections, election districts, and number of representatives for each district; and the 1853 Divorce Act introducing now Western Christian doctrine of marriage impediments and "the nullity of marriage within the fourth degree of consanguinity." In 1859, all Session Laws—including those not incorporated into the Penal Code of 1850—were compiled and enacted by the legislature as the "Civil Code." This Code and subsequent Session Laws, from 1860 to 1882, were compiled, edited in English, and published under the title *Compiled laws of the Hawaiian Kingdom: published by authority* (Honolulu, 1884; LCCN 32008619) by Lawrence McCully (1831–92).

The Civil Code formed Section I of the compilation on the laws governing particular subjects (e.g., Family Law, Criminal Law and Procedure, etc.), as well as on laws establishing and regulating government departments and their functions. As one would expect, the careful reader will discover in the area of Civil Law proper several prescriptions encompassing Customary Law, particularly on marital property and dower, or laws on inheritance of real and personal property. An Act of 1860 decrees that wives and their legal children have to bear the husband's name, and that such names are reported to the census agent. According to a statute of 1862, children have to be reported to the birth registrar of the district. To appreciate the developments on the area of real property (Land Law), one needs to know that in 1848 a new land division (the Mahele) was authorized by King Kamehameha III whereby the Islands' landmasses, originally divided among four high chiefs, were distributed now among the chiefs, the King, and the government and—for the first time in Hawaiian history—included private parties. The Act of 1850 with the Amendment of 1854, reproduced in the compilation, "abolished the disability of aliens to acquire and convey lands in fee-simple." This encouraged capital investment in land by all residents, native or foreign, but was, at the same time, responsible for the progressive loss of native land to foreign agricultural and business interests, especially to the sugar industry, introduced in 1830 and by then well established.

Maps are for study of the feudal land system and post-feudal development of real estate by foreign interests of particular importance. The Geography and Map Division may also be consulted for such cartographic information.

For the casual reader, this work portrays the organization of a modern, western-style government. At second glance, however, the Session Laws from the mid-1860s on begin to show the signs of internal erosion of the kingdom due to foreign political and economic pressures. The census around 1850 had already shown a significant decrease in native population. Acts of the years 1864 to 1868 decreed that natives were not allowed to leave the Islands, while a newly established Bureau of Immigration encouraged and regulated the flow of immigrants and took measures to attract Polynesians of both sexes to prevent the "depopulation of the Islands and diminution of the native race." At the same time, the Royal domains were relieved from encumbrances and rendered inalienable. In the 1870s, several acts dealt with licensing of firearms (for hunting), in order to prevent poaching and the destruction of native fowl and "useful insectivorous birds." An Act of 1872 established a National Museum of Archaeology, Literature, Botany, Geology, and Natural History. In 1880, the Boundary Commission's term was extended to facilitate the surveying and settlement of boundaries, evidence of the progressive privatization of Hawaiian lands.

An official visit from King Kalakaua (1874–91), immediate successor of King Lunalilo (1872–74), to the United States, was made from November 1874 to February 1875. Upon his return he gave an account of his visit in a speech delivered at Kawaiahao in February 1875 (Kawaiahao, 1875; broadside, English and Hawaiian in parallel columns; LCCN 98130692). He impressed his reflection on his people that the "vast wealth and prosperity of that Nation [United States] was the result of the industrious habits of these people . . . [and] created by the cultivators of the soil and by men who toil with their hands. . . . If we take a retrospect of the past, we shall plainly perceive that a failure to put our hands and our faculties to a popular use, has been one of the causes of the decline of our nation. . . ." An economically important treaty, the Reciprocity Treaty between Hawai'i and the United States, was concluded shortly after, in 1875. It granted to the contracting parties exemption from all duty on goods and lifting of the tariff on "Muscovado, brown, and all other unrefined sugar, known in the markets of San Francisco and Portland as Sandwich Island Sugar" (*Treaties and conventions concluded between the Hawaiian Kingdom and other powers, since 1825*. Honolulu, 1887; LCCN 01001042, copy 2).

This and the following events are described in the *Proclamation of a Provisional Government*, 1893 (Pamphlet, signed by the members of the "Committee of Safety" 1893; LCCN unk82088810. See also *The Hawaiian Kingdom*, 3 vols., Honolulu, 1938–67, and other works by Ralph S. Kuykendall, executive secretary of the Hawaiian Historical Commission). Because of a popular uprising and the desire of the American and European residents, mostly sugar planters and businessmen, to gain control of the government, Kalakaua was forced to make major changes to the Constitution in 1887, amounting to voting rights for Americans and Europeans regardless of citizenship and the exclusion of native Hawaiians from the reconstituted House of Nobles. In the same year, the revisited and expanded Reciprocity Treaty of 1875 was concluded between Hawai'i and the United States, ceding the exclusive right over Pearl Harbor to the United States.

Lili'uokalani (1838–1917), who succeeded King Kalakaua upon his death in 1891 as Queen of Hawai'i, attempted to revert this situation for her native subjects with a new constitution, which she tried to promulgate in January 1893. In opposition to the Queen, a "revolutionary" group of American and European settlers had formed the "Committee of Public Safety." Supported by the U.S. Minister in Hawai'i, John L. Stevens, and American troops already in the harbor, the "Committee" deposed the Queen without the consent of the Hawaiian people and the Hawaiian government. The Proclamation of January 16(?), 1893, signed by members of the "Committee," reads: "1. The Hawaiian Monarchical system of government is hereby abrogated. 2. A Provisional Government for control and management of public affairs and protection of the public peace is hereby established to exist until terms of union with the United States of America have been negotiated and agreed upon" (*Proclamation. Hawaiian Islands*. Provisional Government, 1893–94; LCCN unk82088810). Most offices continued their services, with

exception of the Queen and her Cabinet. The laws consistent with the new order remained in force until further notification. The Library holds the *Order no. 1. Provisional Government of the Hawaiian Islands of January 17th 1893* (LCCN 79305670), signed by the Executive Council and the Advisory Council with the request that supporters report with arms at the Government Building. There is also a small collection of *Rules and orders for conducting business by the Executive and Advisory councils of the Provisional Government* (Honolulu, 1893).

Despite President Grover Cleveland's appeal to Congress to restore the Queen to her position, the Provisional Government declared itself on July 4, 1894, as the "Republic of Hawai'i." The Library holds the *Constitution of the Republic of Hawai'i, 1894* (Rare Book and Special Collections Division; LCCN 06041096). Article 95 of the Constitution laid down that the Crown lands were to become the property of the Hawaiian Government. This constitutional proprietary land

Lili'uokalani, Queen of Hawai'i (1838–1917), who succeeded King Kalakaua upon his death in 1891 as Queen of Hawai'i, was an ardent advocate for her native subjects. Her attempts to promulgate a new constitution in January 1893 and her subsequent hesitancy in agreeing to grant an amnesty to her enemies (the annexationists) cost her the throne in 1894. (*Prints and Photographs Division*; LC-USZ62-105894)

right was the basis for the *Land Act* 1895 (LCCN 07039462) which sealed the ultimate breakup and disposal of the native land by the Department of the Interior in charge of public lands. When the United States in 1896, under President William McKinley, formally annexed Hawai'i as a Territory, the Republic of Hawai'i ceded authority and 1.8 million acres (almost half of the Hawaiian landmass) to the United States without the consent of the Hawaiian people.

The most intriguing aspect of the story is that, despite all these political and constitutional developments in the Islands, the early indigenous Civil Law, enacted in 1859 as Civil Code, has survived. The Library holds an edition of *The laws of Hawaii: comprising the civil law and the penal laws*, compiled by Sidney M. Ballou and published by authority in 1897, and the *Session laws of 1898: modified in conformity with the recommendations of the commission appointed by the President of the United States to recommend to Congress legislation concerning the Hawaiian Islands* (Washington, 1898; LCCN 77379252). The text was only revised to reflect current terminology (e.g., "Republic" changed to "Territory"; "minister of finance" to "treasurer"; "minister of the interior" to "superintendent of public works," etc.).

One could add on as a post-scriptum that the Hawaiian Homes Commission Act of 1921 that addressed Hawaiians' economic and social conditions had set aside two hundred thousand acres of Territory lands as homeland for "native" people of Hawaii with fifty or more percent of Hawaiian blood in their veins. This blood, i.e., "blood quantum," or race doctrine, as well as the legal status of the "Hawaiian people" in the State of Hawai'i (1959–), compared to other indigenous populations of the United States and their legal status, proved to be one of the most complex and contested questions with considerable moment. The combination of human rights, ethnological, and legal-ethical issues on the one hand, and geographic-physical realities on the other, have—as one might expect—generated a flood of literature, much of which is of a comparative nature concerning all indigenous peoples in the Americas, and often critical of the race consciousness and preoccupation with race in America of which the Polynesian race is no exception. A few select titles must suffice here for the wealth of literature on this subject: *Institutional Racism: The Case of Hawai'i* (Westport, Connecticut, 1992) by Michael Haas; *White by Law: The Legal Construction of Race* (New York, 1996) by Ian Haney-Lopez; *Hawaiian Americans: An Account of the Mingling of Japanese, Chinese, Polynesian, and American Cultures* (Hamden, Connecticut, 1970) by Edwin G. Burrows; *Hawai'i and Its Race Problem* (United States. Department of the Interior. (Washington, D.C., 1932); and *Native Hawaiian Data Book* (Office of Hawaiian Affairs, Planning and Research Office. Honolulu, 1994–).

In 1993, the centennial of the overthrow of the Kingdom of Hawai'i, President William Jefferson Clinton signed the historic apology to native Hawaiians on behalf of the United States. This document, the *Apology Resolution* (United States. Joint Resolution to Acknowledge the 100th Anniversary of the January 17, 1893, Overthrow of the Kingdom of Hawaii, and to Offer an Apology to Native Hawaiians on Behalf of the United States for the Overthrow of the Kingdom of Hawaii, signed by President William Jefferson Clinton. Honolulu, 1994; LCCN 94234729), is followed in the same year by the *Report on the Reconciliation Process between the Federal Government and Native Hawaiians of Oct. 23, 2000: From Mauka to Makai: The River of Justice Must Flow Freely* (U.S. Department of the Interior and U.S. Department of Justice; accessible at http://www.doi.gov/nativehawaiians/report/pdf.) Another very important document, recording the evolving doctrine of "blood quantum" and the prerogative "native," on which the legal status and important entitlements of Hawaiians are grounded, is *Reconciliation at a Crossroads: The Implications of the Apology Resolution and Rice v. Cayetano for the Federal and State Programs Benefiting Native Hawaiians. Summary Report of the August 1998 and September 2000 community forums in Honolulu, Hawai'i.* U.S. Commission on Civil Rights. Hawai'i Advisory Committee (Los Angeles, 2001; also accessible at http://purl.access.GPO.gov /LPS13586). The latter two documents demonstrate the problem of restitution to indigenous peoples for suffered wrongs when the legal outline is based on ethnicity as a prerogative in a multi-cultural society. All three documents can be accessed in the Law Library.

Well-researched works on nineteenth- and twentieth-century political and constitutional history, including the foreign economic endeavors and land deals, are recommended to be read together with the surviving laws for a better understanding of the evolution of Hawai'i from the Kingdom, Republic, and Territory to the modern U.S. State. As eyewitness reports could be considered *Hawaii's story by Hawaii's Queen, Lili'uokalani* (Boston, 1898) by Liliuokalani, Queen of Hawaii (1838–1917); *To Steal a Kingdom: Probing Hawaiian History* (Waimanalo, Hawai'i, 1992) by Michael Dougherty; *A Call for Hawaiian Sovereignty* (Honolulu, 1993) by Michael Kioni Dudley; *Annexation Hawaii, Fighting American Imperialism* (Waimanalo, 1998) by Thomas J. Osborne; *Hawaii, America's Sugar Territory, 1898–1959* (Lewiston, New York, 1999) by H. Brett Melendy; *The Island Edge of America: A Political History of Hawai'i* (Honolulu, 2003) by Tom Coffman; *Islands in Captivity: The International Tribunal on the Rights of Indigenous Hawaiians* (Cambridge, Massachusetts, 2004) compiled and edited by Ward Churchill and Sharon H. Venne; and *In the Name of Hawaiians: Native Identities and Cultural Politics* (Minneapolis, 2002) by Rona Tamiko Halualani.

In nomine domini. Incipit a deo vt infra de officio prefecti pretono Aphrice.l.in nomine domini.Accursius.

b ¶ Iustiniani quia Iustini filius vt Insti. de dona. §. est et aliud. et dicitur hoc ad differentiam trium codicuz de quibus.j. sit mentio.Accursius.

c ¶ Sacratissimi quia inunct?, vel quia sacras leges nobis tradidit.Ajo.

d ¶ Perpetui.i. generalis.vt insti. de satisda.tu. et cu.§.j.sic.j. de eden.l.edita.vn de illud erijt editum z cetera. j epistola omis anima z cetera. Ponitur et aliter vt dimus.ff. p socio.l.j.Ac.

e ¶ Augusti.ab augeo quod p politum vt z matrimonium dicitur res idiuidua: licet quandoq diuidatur.vt insti. de pa. po.in pn. et. L.d repu.l. consensu. vel dicitur ab octauiano augusto quod est dominare.Ac.

f ¶ Repetite. iussit eni fieri primo codice ex tribus z iterum iussit dissolui: vt ibi apponeret quasdā decisiones qs postea fecerat. et sic iterum iussit legari. et ideo dicit repetite. vt.j. de eme.l.co.per to. et.§. in antiquis eni z cetera. Item qd dicit p lectionis.i.lectionis z figura probebsis. sic ponit ff.d do.prele. per to.ti.Ac.

g ¶ De nouo.superior Rubrica est cōmunis ad totum librum sed quod sequitur.f. de nouo codice componendo ad constitutionem istam tātū.Ajo.

Ec.sez iam corrigenda vel melius id est corrigenda fin vos iudices.z dic q sez cōstitutio diuidit in quatuor partes. Prima vsq illuc. Ideoq z cetera. Secūda vsq illuc. Quibus specialiter z cetera. Tercia vsq illuc. Hoc igitur. Quarta et vltima abinde vsq in finem. dic ergo hec que corrigenda sez nunc.Ac.

i ¶ In presenti.hoc verbum in present determinat verbum donare:non verbum censuimus.quia contrarium asseuerat per preteritum censuimus.Ajo.

k ¶ Communibus.i. communi vtilitati que prouenit

In nomine dmini nostri Jesu christi. Codicis dmni Justiniani sacratissimi pricipis perpetui Augusti repetite prelectionis Incipit cōstitutio prima de nouo codice faciendo Rubrica.

I. Imperator Justinianº Augustus ad Senatum.

Ecque necessario corrigenda esse multis retroprincipib visa sunt interea tamen nullus eorū hoc ad effectū ducere ausus est: in presenti rebus vnare cōmunibus auxilio vel omni

potentis censuimus: z prolixitatem litium amputare. multitudine quidem constitutionuz que tribus codicibus Gregoriano: Hermogeniano atq Theodosiano continebantur. illarum etiam que post eosdem codices a Theodosio diuine recordationis: alijsq post eum retroprincipibus et a nostra etiam clemētia posite sunt resecanda. vno autem codice sub felici nostri nominis vocabulo componēdo in quem colligi tam memoratorum trium codicum qz nouellas post eos positas constitutiones oportet. ¶ Ideoq ad hoc maximum et ad ipsius reipublice sustentationez respicientes: opus efficiendū elegimus tanto fastigio laborum tātēq solicitudini sufficientes. Joannem viruz excellentissimum exquestorem nostri sacri palacij consularez atq patricium. Leontium virum sublimissimuz magistrū militum ex prefectum pretorio consularem atq patricium. Phocam virum eminentissimum magistrū militū consularem atq patricium. Basilidem virum excellentissimuz ex pfectū ptorio orientis atq patricium. Thomā virū gloriosissimuz questorē sacri nri palacij z excōsule. Tribunianū virū magnificū magisteria dignitate inter agētes decoratū

ex constitutionibus.Accursius.

l ¶ Litiū. que fiebāt in mortales etiā repete multitudine.

m ¶ Amputare.reddit attentum: et facit.ff.si cer.peta.l. quidam.

n ¶ Illarum.scilicet constitutionum.Accursius.

o ¶ Eum.s.theodosium.Ac.

p ¶ Retroprincipib, quo ad nos. id eante nos.Ac.

q ¶ Posite.vt extrauagantes constitutiones.Ac.

r ¶ Resecāda als resecando. et tunc habeas multitudinem, als resecanda z tunc multitudine.Ac.

s ¶ Nouellas.si vna sed vtiles.Ac.

t ¶ Post eos.tres codices.Ac.

v ¶ Republice. id ē imperij.Ac.

x ¶ Sustentationem, qz per leges sustentatur respublica: sicut z per arma.Ac.

y ¶ Respicies als respicientes. et tūc plana. als respiciens:et tunc sic cōstrue. ideoq elegimus viros ad hoc maximum op efficiendum.op dico respicientes ad sustentationem ipsius reipublice. id ē imperij.Ac.

z ¶ Elegimus.s. homines.Ac.

a ¶ Fastigio.id ē altitudini vel magnitudini.Ac.

b ¶ Exquestorez. nomen est dignitatis sicut dico iū expfector et cōsule.sm Jo. vt.j. de auo.diuer.iudici.l. petitionem.§. egredientem sicut exquestor. vt

ff. de officiis quest.l.j. in fi. Alij dicunt eum exquestorem qui questuram dimisit. et sic excōsul qui consulatum dimisit.Accursius.

c ¶ Consularem.consularis est qui insignia consulum beneficio principis consequit. sed consules sunt in ipso actu gerendi. vt.j.de cōsuli.l.iij. z.iiij.li.xij.Ac.

d ¶ Patricium.expone at institu.quibus modis ius patri.potes.solui.§. filiusfa.Ac.

e ¶ Pretorio.natum vel vocatum.Ac.

f ¶ Inter agentes.agentes dicunt qui sunt inter eos qui re imperiales administrant, vel qui agunt id est morantur circa latus principis.vnde habes.j. titu. de principib agentibus in rebus li. xij.Accursius.

Civil Law Systems

The complex phenomenon called "European legal culture" has its roots in the Roman Empire, Christianity, and the legal-ethical code of the corporate Germanic culture. The last contributed new ethical standards to early Medieval society, culminating in the feudal civilization and territorial-jurisdictional development in Europe, while the Justinian Roman—or Civil Law, expounded by the jurists of Bologna and adapted by Medieval canonists—laid the foundation for a universal jurisprudence in Europe.

COMPARATIVE AND UNIFORM LAW OF EUROPE

Besides specialized historic source collections, such as those on Roman, Byzantine, and Germanic Law, the Law Library has custody over the oldest and largest of the regional collections, the law of Europe, comprising comparative works on the law of two or more jurisdictions of the region Europe. Of course, comparative legal studies in Europe have always included comparisons of systems stemming from different historic periods, since such studies provide the links to modern comparative law. European philosophy and the theory of law, however, are not in the European collections but to a large extent in the General Law Collection because of their broad implications, although most of the works originated over many centuries in the European region. Mostly works on the techniques and methodology for regional law development, i.e., law integration and other unification processes, are retained in the regional collection.

EUROPEAN COMMUNITY LAW

The second component of the European collections comprises the record of the Treaty Law of the Conseil de l'Europe and other regional organizations, and the treaty system of the European Community, and the subsequent European Union (E.U.). The legislation of the European Union and the then European Community, established by two founding Treaties, the Treaty of Paris and the Treaty of Rome in the 1950s, contributes to the fast growth of the Modern European Collection. The European Union, brought into existence by the Treaty of Maestricht in 1992, is a transnational organization with a unique legal system composed of twenty-five Member States. Each of the four main institutions within the E.U. is assigned specific tasks by the Treaties. Its entire body of law, known as *acquis communataire*, comprises the Treaties that are considered primary legislation, along with the general principles of law common to all Members and

OPPOSITE: *Codex* (*Corpus iuris civilis*). This incunabulum of Justinian's *Codex* was printed by Anton Koberger in Nuremberg and is dated January 30, 1488. The text is surrounded by the *glossa in codicem* of Accursius. Woodcuts decorate the beginning of each book. Other incunabula of the *Codex* at the Library, printed in Venice in 1478 and 1496 (the latter with the gloss of the glossator Accursius), may be found in the Law Library Rare Book Collection (LCCN 92896663 and LCCN 78414529). (*Law Library Rare Book Collection*; LCCN 2004563817)

a vast body of secondary legislation enacted by the institutions in the form of regulations, directives, and decisions. The *acquis* also includes international agreements entered into by the E.U. institutions and the jurisprudence of the European Courts. The Law Library of Congress includes in its collections the E.U. body of law in hard copy and also has access to E.U. legal websites, including CELEX, Europa, and Eur-lex.

LAWS OF THE INDIVIDUAL EUROPEAN COUNTRIES

The third component of the body of Modern European Law consists of the large collections of the national laws of the countries of Europe. These national collections vary in size, age, and rarity from jurisdiction to jurisdiction, and they also contain—to varying degrees—legislation and regulatory material from governing bodies at the provincial (cantonal, state, land, etc.) level.

The concepts and doctrines of European Civil Law have traveled the globe where they have been widely adopted or superimposed on existing original law in the Americas as well as in Asia and Africa, as a result of occupation or colonization by the incursion of Civil Law powers. European Union (E.U.) Law has set the pattern for international organizations in all regions of the world. Differences in the world's legal systems are lessening to some extent, and certain legal traditions are of mixed heritage—such as those in Israel, Scotland, Sweden, and Turkey.

The following overviews focus mainly on the body of historic sources in the Law Library that formed the foundation of the Civil Law system, and further, on the law collections of those two countries which have individually, or together, set the pattern and course of adoption for Civil Law systems beyond Western Europe, i.e., France and Germany.

ROMAN LAW

Roman Law was a significant component of the original law collection of the Library of Congress and of Thomas Jefferson's law books. In the first decades of the nineteenth century, the books for the Library of Congress were selected by the Congressional Joint Committee on the Library. In 1826, the Honorable Edward Everett, a member of the Joint Committee and former professor of Greek at Harvard, discussed purchasing additional works on Roman Law with Joseph Story, Associate Justice of the U.S. Supreme Court from 1812 to 1845.

Justice Story wrote: "I entirely agree with you respecting the civil-law books to be placed in the Congress Library. It would be a sad dishonor of a national library not to contain the works of Cujacius, Vinnius, Heineccius . . . etc. They are often useful for reference and sometimes indispensable for a common lawyer. How could one be sure of some nice doctrine in the civil law of Louisiana without possessing and consulting them."

The Roman Law collection contains more than sixteen thousand volumes, including manuscripts, and over one hundred twenty-five incunabula. It includes extensive holdings of every type of Roman Law source and literature, from the over two hundred fifty editions of the most prominent source, Justinian's *Corpus Iuris Civilis* (the complete work or its constituent parts), published between the sixteenth and nineteenth centuries, to the most recent publications of scholars, to such rarities as the first printed edition (1553) of the sixth-century Florentine parchment manuscript of Justinian's *Digest*, the oldest and most valuable manuscript of the *Digest*.

Pre-Justinian Law or *jus Romanum antejustinianum* is treated in histories of Roman Law and in various compilations from the Western Roman Empire. The first history of Roman Law, *Civilis historiae juris*, which includes such early sources as the law of the Twelve Tables, was written by Aymar Du Rivail (ca. 1490–1557). The Law Library has the first edition of this work, printed 1515 in Valence, as well as five subsequent editions dating from 1527 to 1551. Among the many editions and reprints of collected sources on early Roman Law are the 1860 edition of the *Fontes juris Romani antiqui* by Carl Georg Bruns (1816–60) with several later editions; the three-volume *Fontes juris Romani* (1968–69) by Salvatore Riccobono (1864–1958); and the three-volume *Jurisprudentiae antejustinianae reliquias*. . . . (1908–27) by Ph. Eduard Huschke (1801–86) for which the Law Library also holds an earlier Leipzig edition (1874).

The elementary textbook of the pre-Justinian period, the *Institutes* of Gaius, from the second century A.D., is represented by numerous editions and translations. These include the famous edition of the Verona Codex by Wilhelm Friedrich Adolf Studemund (1843–89), published six times between 1874 and 1923 with slightly varying titles as *Gaii institutionum commentarii quattuor: codicis Veronensis denvo collati apographum confecit.*

Compilations of pre-Justinian Imperial legislation appear in many editions of the unofficial *Codex Gregorianus* (A.D. 291) and its continuation, the *Codex Hermogenianus*. There are also many editions of the *Codex Theodosianus*, the official codification of statutes from A.D. 312 to A.D. 438. The collection includes the valuable 1528 edition by Johannes Sichardt (1499–1552) and several editions by Jacques Cujas (1522–90) between 1566 and 1586, as well as standard nineteenth-century editions by Gustav Friedrich Haenel (1792–1878) and particularly by Theodor Mommsen (1817–1903) and Paul Krüger (1840–1926); editions of these codices are often included in the editions of the *Fragmenta Vaticana* prepared by Mommsen and Krüger. The private library of Krüger was acquired by the Law Library in 1930. A prominent professor of Roman Law at various German universities from 1888 to his death in 1926, he collaborated with the eminent German Romanist Theodor Mommsen in editing the texts of the *Corpus Iuris Civilis* as well. His library included forty-seven hundred volumes, pamphlets, and manuscripts, dating from the early sixteenth century to the 1920s. Apart from Krüger's own manuscripts relating to editing Roman Law texts and his lecture notes in a distinctive microscopic hand, the collection includes the manuscript of Friedrich Ludwig von Keller (1799–1860) on the Pandects, which was published posthumously in 1861. It also contains facsimiles of codices and papyri along with Krüger's notes on them. In 1934 the Law Library prepared a list of all the items in this collection. This list, although a comprehensive account, needs further arrangement and cross-referencing to serve as a more convenient finding aid.

At the center of the study of Roman Law is the monumental compilation made at the order of Justinian, Emperor of the East (483?–565), which brought together the results of nearly a thousand years of legal development. The earliest legislation is the Twelve Tables, traditionally dated to 451 to 450 B.C. and surviving only in fragments included in later texts. Justinian's comprehensive compilation consists of five parts: *Digestum vetus, Infortiatum, Digestum novum, Codex, Volumen parvum* (or *Volumen*). The *Volumen* includes the *Tres libri codicis, Institutiones,* and the *Authenticum.* Justinian's work was lost for centuries in the tides of war, conquest, and ruin. The discovery of a complete copy of Justinian's Digest in Pisa in the late twelfth century led to a revival of the study of Roman Law in the universities of Western Europe.

The compilation or its various parts were the subject of scholarly comments of the jurists of the school of Bologna between the twelfth and thirteenth centuries and have continued to attract the most erudite minds of Europe. The ancient texts were supplemented by interlinear or marginal notes, known as glosses. The scholars, known as glossators, produced a substantial body of work, which was itself compiled by the great Medieval jurist and glossator Accursius (ca. 1182–ca. 1260) into a "collection of glosses," the *glossa ordinaria,* which is regularly included in the editions of the *Corpus Iuris Civilis.* Interpretation, harmonization, and approximation have become key terms in modern jurisprudence. They are, however, the basic techniques already applied by the generations of glossators and "post-glossators" (commentators) in the effort to adapt the rules stemming from different sources, such as Classical and Justinian Roman Law, local observances, and Canon Law, to contemporary twelfth- to fourteenth-century societies. In this context, the *consilia*, "or expert opinions," form a significant and rare collection. The Law Library holds over eighty-five commentaries and *consilia* by Bartolo of Sassoferrato (1313–57). He is considered the most important jurist at the height of the legistic jurisprudence towards the end of the Middle Ages. His broad exegetic works and *consilia* were a critical influence on European scholarship for centuries to come. His collected works, the *Opera*, were published in a twelve-volume set in 1570 to 1571. The collection also includes several of the nearly forty editions of this work to be published by 1615.

A contemporary of Bartolo was Baldo degli Ubaldi (1327?–1400), who was of equal repute both in his fame and production. The sheer mass of titles by so many other outstanding authors residing in the Law Library and the Rare Book and Special Collections Division collections is testimony to the caliber of European scholarship that was to lay the foundation for European Civil Law.

The entire body of Justinian's compilations was first designated *Corpus Iuris Civilis* by Denis Godefroy (1549–1621) in his *Corpus ivris civilis in IIII partes distinctvm* (Frankfurt, 1587), published several times up to 1628. The Law Library holds many other printed editions of the complete *Corpus Iuris Civilis* and of its separate parts. The *Institutiones* are of particular interest since they take the place of the *Institutiones* of Gaius. There are, for instance, nine incunabula of the *Institutiones* alone, including the first printing at Mainz in 1468 with the gloss attributed to the glossator Accursius, followed by more than sixty *Institutiones* editions from the sixteenth to the nineteenth centuries, among them the sixteenth-century editions of the *Institutiones iuris civilis*, edited and annotated by Silvestro Aldobrandini (1499–1558), printed with the all-around gloss. The earliest Roman Law manuscript in the collection is a copy of the *Institutiones* made in Milan in 1482. This text is surrounded by a gloss attributed to Accursius as well.

In the Byzantine Empire, the *Corpus Iuris Civilis* was translated into Greek, and became the core of a body of abridgments, abstracts, and compilations intended to make the complex and rather poorly organized text more accessible to legal practitioners and students. This body of scholarship culminated in 1345 in the *Hexabiblos* of Constantinos Harmenopoulos (d. 1380?), a work characterized as "an epitome of epitomes of epitomes." In Western Europe, Roman Law survived after

BARTOLVS SAXOFERRATENSIS
Anno M · CCCXLVII ·

Bartolo of Sassoferrato (1313–57) is considered the most important of the commentators. This portrait, along with those of other famous *consilia* authors, appears in *Illustrium iureconsultorum imagines quae inveniri poterunt ad vivam effigiem expressae* (Rome, 1566). (*Law Library Rare Book Collection; LCCN unk84226165*). It is also in the Law Library in an 1831 Russian edition; and the Law Library also has his *Procheiron nomon* in a 1587 edition. The portrait is available from the Library of Congress Photoduplication Service. (*LC-USZ62-61145*)

Arbor omniū actionum tam pretoriarū q̄ ciuilium: et incipit a pretorijs tanq̄ a maiori parte: p̄ iuris vtriusq̄ doctorē: dnm̄ Johannē Crispum de montibus ciuem aquilanū.

the collapse of the Empire, but was simplified and adapted to the Customary Law of the new populations, such as the Visigoths. Three codes—the *Lex Romana Visig-othorum* (Breviarium Alarici, A.D. 506), the *Lex Romana Burgundionum* (before A.D. 516), and *Edictum Theoderici* (ca. A.D. 512)—are known collectively as the *Leges Romanae Barbarorum* (Roman Law of the Germanic Nations). The Law Library holds various separate editions and compilations of these texts, most of them done by eighteenth- and nineteenth-century scholars.

Histories and interpretations ranging from the 1518 edition of *Annotationes in quatuor et viginti pandectum libros* (Annotations to the LIV books of the Pandects) to recent publications by modern scholars are in the Roman Law collection, which also houses many early and rare works on the Roman process, among them two editions of Giovanni Crispo de' Monti's (d. fifteenth century) work *Termini omnium actionum, cum arbore* (List of terms for court actions according to civil and praetorian law) that are accompanied by an "arbor" diagram. The *arbor actionum* itself dates back to Johannes Bassianus and was printed with commentaries several times, particularly by Pontius de Ylerda (after 1213), *La Summa Arboris actionum* (ed. Guido Rossi; Milan, 1951); and Dinus de Mugello (1254–ca. 1300), *Lectura super arbore actionum* (Frankfurt a/Main, 1569). Other sixteenth- and seventeenth-century treatises on court actions are related works, such as Giasone dal Maino (1435–1519), *De actionibus . . . : locantur insuper in calce libri huius Termini actionum omnium cum arbore elegantissima . . . per . . . Ioannem Crispum de Montibus* (Lyon/France, 1543); and Nicasius de Voerda (d. 1492), *Arbor actionum omnium tam praetoriarum quam civilium* (with diagrams) (Lyon/France, 1566, and Venice, 1606). Most of the editions, however, although referring to Crispo de' Monti's work, are without the diagram.

GERMANIC LAW AND LAW OF THE HOLY ROMAN EMPIRE

Voltaire's statement that the Holy Roman Empire was "neither holy, Roman, nor an empire" notwithstanding, the numerous law books in the Library's collections commonly associated with its historic period by this term provide researchers with an insight into the early development of law in Central Europe, particularly of Germany and Austria, France, Italy, Spain, and other jurisdictions.

The collections related to early Central European law were developed at the Law Library along a historic divide. Charlemagne's *divisio imperii* of A.D. 806 among his sons had laid the ground for the division of the Frankish Empire by the Treaty of Verdun 843 into a West, Middle, and East Empire, which eventually resulted in the territorial division of Europe. The Eastern Empire (including the

OPPOSITE: Reproduced here is the incunabular edition of Giovanni Crispo de' Monti's *Termini omnium actionum, cum arbore* (Venice, 1490). The schematic presentation (arbor diagram) of the praetorian as well as the civil actions is followed by an alphabetical index of all terms related to the actions graphically cast into the *arbor actionum*. (*Law Library Rare Book Collection*; LCCN 77502719)

territories today known as Austria, Switzerland, the northeast *départments* of France, Belgium, the Netherlands, Luxembourg, and Germany) was known thenceforth as the Holy Roman Empire and was ruled by the German Emperor until its dissolution in 1806. It was based on the dogma that the German kings were the successors of the Roman emperors. Thus, what could be considered "German Law" consisted not only of "Imperial Law" or the "Emperor's Written Law," but also of Justinian's *Corpus Iuris Civilis*.

Therefore, all materials on the ancient Germanic period (to ca. A.D. 500) and on the Frankish period roughly from Chlodowech (481–511) to Charles III (885–87), including the Feudal Law of Europe, form the historic European collection. The Library holds the major sources of these periods, mostly in modern authoritative editions, and a wealth of secondary sources. Modern monographic literature authored by noted scholars, the critical and comparative evaluation of legal institutes and institutions as they evolved over the course of history, has always been an important part of European legal science. Materials from about the tenth century on, such as regional or local Customary Law, are to be found in the collections as "legal history" of a particular European country. Thus, only broad collections of sources relating to the North Germanic/Scandinavian group of nations are in the European collection, while sources pertaining to the individual Scandinavian countries are in the classes for those countries.

Among these sources are the *Leges Barbarorum* (Folk Laws), such as the *Leges Visigothorum* (i.e., collections of the laws for West Goths and for Roman Gothic subjects), of which group the Law Library has only the *Lex Romana Visigothorum.* The *Lex Burgundionum* (Burgundian Code, or *Liber constitutionum sive Lex Gundobada*) is represented in the Law Library by an English translation (Katherine Fisher, Philadelphia, 1949/1972). There is more on the Law of the Franks; in the collection are six nineteenth-century editions of the *Lex salica* (Law Code of the Salic Franks), the best by J. F. Behrend (Weimar, 1897), as well as analytical studies, such as the work by Georg Waitz (*Das alte Recht der Salischen Franken*. Kiel, 1846) and *Die Franken und ihr Recht* (Weimar, 1881) by Richard Schröder (1838–1917). The Law Library holds numerous translations, e.g., the English translation by J. H. Hessels and H. Kern (*Lex salica: the ten texts with the glosses, and the lex emendata.* London, 1880); further, the *Lex Ripuaria* (Code of the Salic and Ripuarian Franks), translated by Theodore John Rivers (New York, 1986), and a commented edition of the *Lex Francorum Chamavorum* (Breslau, 1855) by Ernst Theodor Gaupp (1796–1859). Of the Lombard Law, the Law Library holds two early sixteenth-century editions, *Leges Langobardorum seu Capitulare diui ac sacratissimi*

Carolimagni imperatoris et Francie regis. . . . annotated by Nicolas de Bohier (1469–1539) (Lyon, 1512?, and Venice, 1537). A comprehensive edition of the laws of the Germanic nations (Latin text and German translation on opposite pages) was prepared by Karl August Eckhardt (*Die Gesetze des Karolingerreiches, 714–911.* Weimar, 1934) and an edition of Saxon Law (*Recht und Verfassung der alten Sachsen.* Breslau, 1837) by Ernst Theodor Gaupp.

FEUDAL LAW

The principles of Feudal Law have long been understood as a synthesis of vassalage or clientage and land grants (*precaria* or *beneficia*) by a landlord to his vassal in return for military, political, or economic services. One can argue how much of the origins of feudalism is rooted in Roman and German antecedents. Both systems fostered the practice of loyalty and service in exchange for a plot of land, which practice culminated in the feudal system in the eighth and ninth centuries. The *Libri feudorum*, a private compilation of diverse Lombard/Italian Feudal Law sources, include the Imperial Feudal Laws of the Salic Emperor, Conrad II (1024–39; *lex* of 1034), the Welf Lothair II (1125–37; *lex* of 1136), and the Staufer Frederick I "Barbarossa" (1152–90; *lex* of 1158). The Medieval manuscripts or early incunabula present the *Libri feudorum*, often as a supplement or adjunct of the *Corpus Iuris Civilis*, such as in the 1476 Rome edition of the *Volumen parvum* (*Corpus Iuris Civilis*) in the collection of the Law Library. This explains why the *Libri* joined the fate of the *Corpus Iuris Civilis* at the *Reception* of the Roman Law— they became the "Common Law" (*Gemeines Recht*) of the Empire, but were subsidiary to the Local Law. The *Libri* are at the base of an extensive source collection of Feudal Law at the Library, the line of editions starting with two incunabula editions by Jacopo Alvarotti (1385–1453); followed by a German translation with the title *Keyserliche lehenrecht* by Jodokus Planzmann (Augsburg, 1494); and a commentary by Giantonio da Sangiorgio (1439–1509) *Lectura super usibus feudorum* (Pavia, 1490); as well as François Hotman (1524–1590) *Tractatus. De verbis feudalibus commentarius* (Frankfurt, 1587); an extremely interesting edition of *De feudis libri V* (Lyons, 1566) by Jacques Cujas (1522–90); and about twenty other sixteenth-century editions.

Among the numerous works published from the seventeenth to the nineteenth centuries on the subject, the work by Johann Schilter (1632–1705), *Codex juris Alemannici feudalis* (1697), and two works of the German publicist Johann Christian Lünig (1662–1740) are noteworthy: *Corpus juris feudalis Germanici* (Frankfurt, 1727)

IN nomine sancte et
indiuidue trinitatis
patris et filij z spus sancti glo
riosecp virginis marie vtriuscp
Jacobi apostoli · tociuscp curie
celestis Amen

Enerande vniuersitati
iuristaruz Padue Jacobus de Al
uarotis patau9 salute z opus plens·

Nimaduerti et se
pe mecum cogitaui Specta
biles Rector reuerendi Fra
tres dilectissimi Et vniuer
sitas veneranda vos no pa
rum admirari cp ego prese
ti opere necp officio lecture
opus nos fungi· visus sum necp vestris scolasti
cis disputacionibus multum frequens· tot la
boribus·tot vigilijs·totcp curijs z solicitudibus
ad hec studia vestra nedu visitanda veru z plu
rimum coadiuuanda atcp exornanda· hijs prese
tibus meis comentarijs accesserim Sed profe
cto vestra caritas z beniuolencia mordinata at
cp scribencium ta antiquoz cp modernoz cura
atcp diligecia me ad tam arduu tacp graue op9
mducat· Dum enim post sufice ptas doctorales in
sultis annis sedecim continuis lecture officio
operam cedissem peragrassem que omniu iudi
ces atcp scripta que in vtrocp iure in vsu haben
tur z a maioribus nostris ad nostram doctrina
tradita z relicta fuerunt omia alia nostri iuris
ciuilis volumina plane z copiose ac suo debito
ordine z elegancia laudabilem finem assecuta
Sed cum in has feudoru cosuetudines diuer
tissem in hijs que pro ipsaru magnitudme sub
tilitate atcp difficultate materie diucius sedis
sem animaduerti comentatores earum in plu
ribus defecisse ita vt nedu vtile sed necessarium

fore existimauerim huic tali morbo succurren
dum·Quis em ad hec vscp tempora continuaco
nes rubricarum vt congruum fuerat ad plenu
mducit que tamen profecto non minus lauda
biliter prout in alijs nostri iuris ciuilibus pacti
bus fieri consueuit in presenti opere z adduci
z declarari potuerunt·Quis scribecium adduc
in textualibus ad itegritatem mhesit· Nullus
preter ea glosarum expecaionem atcp declara
cionem suo debito ordme prosecutus est verum
eas vt in totum suo loco vel pro parte omitten
do vel salte vt docens fuerat eas no nobis pla
nas sed confusus relinquendo· Quis om
aliozum doctorum sentencias atcp dicta suo vo
lumie cophendit·Quis materias feudales vbi
cp alibi vagas z dispersas vna simul congene
collocauit· Quis omia capitula extra ordi
naria alterius copilacionis huic nostro feudoz
operi mteruit que tamen frequenter a non
nullis doctoribus suis in voluminibus allegan
tur· Quis msup post cuiuslibet tituli vel
comentum vbi de eadem materia in vtrocp
iure habeatur z p glo· z doc·copiosas remissio
nes adducit· Quis postremo repertorij tabu
lam supaddidit quo facile quid quod capit re
perire querat· Docemi sume necessarium
existimaui·Cum plerumcp ipsi studentes z pre
sertim scolastica has nostras leges z cosuetudi
nes feudales no multum familiares habere co
sueuerunt omnia ista deo propicio no tam ele
ganter quam vtiliter in hoc nostro preseu ope
consumauimus z ne dum quis doctus sed scola
sticus possit· Valeat in hac feudali sciencia
studere legere intelligere z quicquid cupit de
facili abscp labore repire nihil boni quid scri
benti tactum fuit omii omnia eozu scripta cui
sceraui p huic vni operi accomodaui in quacu
cp determinacione auctoritates ipsozu semper
adduxi z allegaui· Vt autem ipsorum docto
rum tam antiquoz cp modernozu qui sup has
feudoz consuetudines scripsere noticia ac lau
dabilis memoria non lateret eorum nomia hic
inserere curaui· Et si Johannes Andree iu
ris lume in suis addicionibus titulo de feudis

and the *Collectia nova, worinn der mittelbahren/oder landsässigen ritterschaft in Teutschland, welche untern dem käyser/auch chur-fürsten und herren angesessen, und von der unmittelbahren freyen käyserlichen reichsritterschaft . . . unterschieden ist, sonderbahre praerogativen und gerechtsame/auch privilegia und freyheiten, enthalten sind. . . .* (Frankfurt und Leipzig, 1730). Of course, Feudal Law continued to exist as a legal institute until the nineteenth century, as, for example, in France until the Napoleonic codification, or even longer, whereas in Germany it existed until the demise of the Empire in 1918.

IMPERIAL LAW AND LEGISLATION

Most important among the extensive imperial legislation were treaties and concordats which acquired the status of fundamental laws for the Empire, among them the law *licet iuris* issued at the Diet of Frankfurt 1338, which decreed the independence of the Emperors from Rome, followed by the Golden Bull (*Bulla aurea*) of 1356, issued by Charles IV (1347–78). The *bulla* laid down the rights of the electorate and rules for the election of the Emperor. The elections—and coronations—were held thenceforth during the *Reichstag* (Imperial diet) at Frankfurt. The Library holds, besides two incunabula, many editions from the seventeenth to nineteenth centuries, as well as the most recent 1908 edition, including other pertinent documents, a commentary, and historic introduction by Karl Zeumer (1849–1914). This work was reprinted in 1972.

Two other very important documents in the Library's collection belong to the long line of imperial *Landfrieden* legislation between the twelfth and sixteenth centuries: *Teütscher Nation Notturfft: die Ordnung vnd Reformation aller Stendt ym Römischen Reych* (Zwickau, 1523), the so-called *Reformatio Frederici*, decreed by emperor Frederick III (1440–93); and the *Römischer kayserlicher Maiestet Ordnungen . . . wie allenthalben im Hailigen Reich vnd sunderlich teütscher Nation wider die . . . des Hayligen Reichs Landtfridens Versprecher . . . gehandelt werden soll,* the decree signed at Nuremberg, February 10, 1522 (and published in Nuremberg, 1522). These laws were to secure or restore peace (*pax*—in modern terms, "law and order") in the Empire, thus outlawing feuds and self help, and instituting public prosecution of the breach of peace on the local level as well as addressing transgressions by territorial powers.

A group of treaties considered early fundamental laws of the Empire were the Augsburg Religious Peace of 1555 (*Augsburger Religionsfrieden*), which granted the territorial rulers the *ius reformandi* and, with this, the power to determine the religious faith in their territories. The two most important documents, the Treaty of Osnabrück of July 27 or August 6, 1648 (one of the treaties in the Peace of

OPPOSITE: *Super Feudis* by Jacopo Alvarotti (1385–1453), published in Lyons 1478 and bound with the *Corpus iuris civilis* (*Volumen parvum*), is an example of an early work on Feudal Law in the Law Library. (*Law Library Rare Book Collection;* LCCN 72203795). A 1477 Venice edition of the same work is in the Rare Book and Special Collections Division. (*Rare Book and Special Collections Division;* LCCN 72206237)

Westphalia); and the so-called *Friedens-Executions-Haubt-Recess* of June 26/27, 1650, are held by the Law Library.

The *Jüngste Reichsabschied of 1654* (final act of the Imperial Diet 1654) recognized the Peace of Westphalia 1648, or the Treaties of Münster and Osnabrück, as Imperial Constitutional Law, granting sovereignty to the larger territories, such as Austria, Saxony, Brandenburg, Hanover, and Bavaria. The text of this important imperial act is included in the collection of all acts between 1356 and 1654 of the Imperial Diet: *Aller des Heiligen Römis. Reichs gehaltenen Reich-Täge, Abschiede und Satzungen . . . nunmehr von Neuem collationiert* (Frankfurt, 1720); and in a modern edition prepared by Adolf Laufs (Bern and Frankfurt, 1975) in the Library's collections. Another collection in eighteen volumes (and one index volume) is *Der Römischen Käyserlichen Majestät und dess Heiligen Römischen Reichs geist- und weltlicher Stände . . . Acta publica und schrifftliche Handlungen,* compiled by Michael Caspar Lundorp (1580–1629) and published between 1668 and 1721 in Frankfurt.

Eminent collections of Imperial Fundamental Laws are those of Melchior Goldast (1578–1635), *Collectio constitutionum imperialium . . . ad d. n. imp. caes. Matthiam* (Frankfurt, 1673) and of Johann Jacob Schmauss (1690–1757), *Corpus juris publici S. R. Imperii academicum, enthaltend des Heil. Röm. Reichs Grundgesetze. . . .* (Leipzig, 1745). The Law Library holds several editions between 1745 and 1794 of this work. Imperial substantive legislation had gained momentum under Maximilian I (1475–1519) and Charles V (1500–56), attested to in the successive line of the *Reichsabschiede* (final acts of the Imperial Diets) and retrievable from registers, such as *Loci communes: aller des Heiligen Römischen Reichs Ordnungen, gehaltenen Reichstäge und Abschied gemeine Titel. . . .* (Mainz, 1578) by the noted jurist Noe Meurer. Of highest importance was the *Reichskammergerichtsordnung,* the constitution and procedure before the Imperial Chamber (*Camera Imperialis Judicii; Reichskammergericht*), first issued in 1495. During its several revisions or *Reformations* (until 1603), the Roman-Canonical process was introduced. The Library holds copies, either included in the final acts of the Imperial Diets (1532, 1548, and 1555) or separate editions between 1542 and 1584 by Noe Meurer. Mint regulations during the sixteenth century held an important position, particularly that of Ferdinand I (1558–64) *Keyser's Ferdinandi Newe Müntzordnung* (Diet of Augsburg, 1559), which was intended as a uniform law for the Empire. The Library of Congress holds the 1559 Mainz edition and other sixteenth-century editions. Major legislation dealt with criminal law and public administration (*Reichspolizeiordnungen*) during the Diets of 1530, 1548, and 1577. The most important law was the *Constitutio Criminalis Carolina* (Code of criminal procedure of Charles V), promulgated at the Diet of Regensburg 1532, which eventually would become the

OPPOSITE: Noe Meurer (sixteenth century), *Jag vnd Forstrecht, das ist, Vndericht chur- vnd fürstlicher Land- auch Graff vnd Herrschafften . . . Gebiet . . . wie die nach keyserlichen vnd fürstlichen gemeinen Rechten . . . in guter Ordnung zuhalten . . .* (Frankfurt, 1582), with its quaint illustrations, set forth Imperial Game and Forestry Laws. (*Law Library Rare Book Collection;* LCCN 89211038)

Das Schwein wirdt von den Hunden gestelle.

Die Hundt kriegend sie/oder das Schwein.

Das Schwein laufft.

Das Schwein hat scharpffe Waffen vnd Getwerff.

Das Schwein frißt oder erschlegt viel Hund oder Leut.

Das Schwein wirdt gestochen/oder ein fang geben.

Alte Sauw heißt ein hauwend Schwein.

Zweyjärig Schwein ein Backer.

Schweinmutter ein Leen oder Bach.

Junge Sauw ein Frischling.

Von Füchsen.

Der Fuchß billt/trabt/reyet.

Der Fuchß wirdt gehetzt.

Der Fuchß wirdt erschlagen.

Der Fuchß wirdt gestreifft.

Der Fuchß hat ein Balg an/kein Haut.Klauwen/vnd nicht Füß.

Der Fuchß wirt mit den Schlieffern auß einem Bauw gefangen.
Vom

Vom Hasen.

Der Haß schreyet.

Der Haß färt.

Der Haß wirt gehetzt.

Der Haß wirt erwürgt.

Der Haß wirt zerrissen.

Der Haß wirt gestreifft.

Der Haß hat ein Balg/vnd kein Haut.

Der Haß hat Läuff/vnd nicht Füß.

Der Haß hat zween Sprüng.

Von Bern.

Etliche werden genannt Ammeysen Bern/essen kein Aaß.

N

Etliche

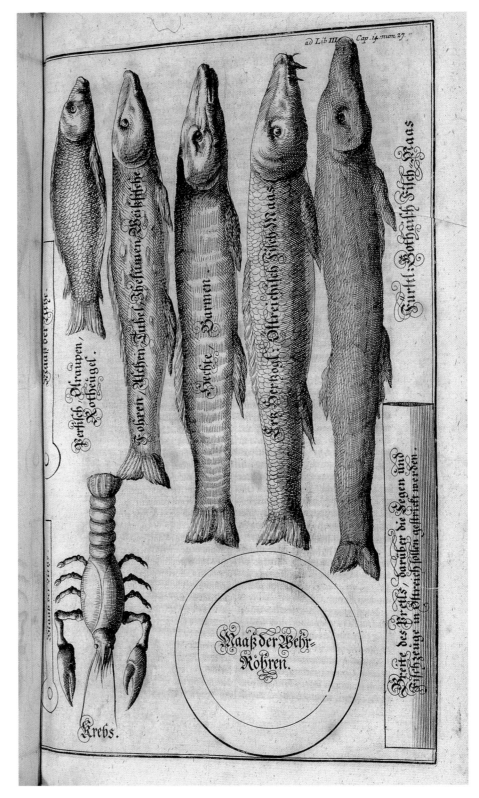

Jus georgicum by Christian Gottfried Leiser (fl. 1680–98). This late seventeenth-century illustrated treatise on laws pertaining to agriculture includes fishery laws in great detail, although one may wonder at the accuracy of the depiction of these fish (Leipzig and Frankfurt, 1698). (*Law Library Rare Book Collection*; LCCN 2004572401)

primary law of the Empire and its territories. The Law Library has numerous editions and reprints between 1548 and 1978 of this law. Roderich von Stintzing's *Geschichte der populären Literatur des römisch-kanonischen Rechts in Deutschland* (Leipzig, 1876) is an excellent overview of the period and literature.

Territorial losses and changes of the Empire as a consequence of historical events—such as the Revolutionary War (Peace of Luneville of 1801) and pending change of voting rights in the *Reichstag*—made the creation of the so-called *Deputation* necessary. The final act of the *Deputation*, called the *Reichs-Deputationshauptschluss* of 1803, and related documents are published in *Das Ende des Alten Reiches,* edited by Ernst Walder (Bern, 1975). It was the basis for territorial restructuring of the Empire and the first step towards its dissolution, finalized by resignation of Francis II in 1806.

Partikularrecht is the term referring to the body of regional and local laws and customs found throughout the realm of the Holy Roman Empire, including Italy. These legal historical materials from about the year A.D. 1000 on are included in the collections on the law of individual European countries and municipalities. They add up to a significant portion of the Law Library's Foreign Law Collection.

Manuscript document on parchment in German. Certificate awarded 1727 to Johann Georg Elsas for exemplary service as assistant game warden in Hanau, Germany. (*Law Library Rare Book Collection; LCCN 2004572903*)

The German Collection, with over ninety thousand titles, is not only the largest in the Foreign Law Collection, but also one of the best developed. Its breadth and depth of original sources and learned commentary document a thousand years of legal, socio-economic, religious, and constitutional developments, which culminated in the centennial event of the uniform Civil Law for Germany, the *Bürgerliches Gesetzbuch* (Civil Code), entering into force on New Year's Day, 1900.

Legal History and Sources. The treatises published by German legal scholars from the second half of the nineteenth century on, coinciding chiefly with the period of the *Historische Schule*, are exhaustive studies and interpretations of the early sources of law. These works form significant collections in their own right and should be used as authoritative reference works to related sources, especially Germanic sources. Only a small sampling of names and works in this collection can be provided here, such as the two works by Hermann Conring (1606–81), who was considered by many the "father" of German legal history, *De origine juris Germanici* and *De Germanorvm imperio romano liber vnus* (Helmstad, 1644 and 1694); *Geschichte der deutschen Rechtsquellen* (Leipzig, 1860–64) by Otto Stobbe (1831–87); *Grundriss des Germanischen Rechts* (Strassburg, 1913) and *Rechtsarchäologie* (Berlin-Dahlem, 1943–) by Karl von Amira (1848–1930), the eminent authority on Germanic law; *Deutsche Rechtsalterthümer* (Göttingen, 1854) by Jacob Grimm (1785–1863); *Deutsche Rechtsgeschichte* (Leipzig, 1887–92) and *Forschungen zur Geschichte des deutschen und französischen Rechts* (Stuttgart, 1840) by Heinrich Brunner (1840–1915); *Urkunden zur Geschichte des deutschen Privatrechts* (Bonn, 1881), edited by Richard Schröder (1838–1917) and Hugo Loersch (1840–1907); and Schröder's *Lehrbuch der deutschen Rechtsgeschichte*, the seventh edition (Leipzig, 1932), prepared by Eberhard von Künssberg (1881–1941). There is an abundance of older legal historical works with a focus on State—or Constitutional—Law since the mid-eighteenth century, such as the *Institvtiones ivris pvblici Germanici* (Goettingen, 1770 and 1792) and *Literatur des teutschen Staatsrechts* (1776–91) of Johann Stephan Pütter (1725–1807); and *Lehrbuch der deutschen Reichs- und Rechtsgeschichte* by Johann Friedrich von Schulte (1827–1914) in the Law Library's collections in several editions between 1861 and 1892. The dissolution of the Holy Roman Empire in 1806 and the following federal/constitutional developments in Germany—the *Rheinbund* (to 1815), *Deutscher Bund* (1815–66), and *Norddeutscher Bund* (1866–70)—contributed a wealth of elegant constructs to the literature on Public Law. Among the Library's important monographic collections or series are those produced under the editorship of Otto Friedrich von Gierke (1841–1921) *Untersuchungen zur deutschen Staats- und Rechtsgeschichte* (Breslau, 1878–1911), and Konrad Beyerle, *Deutschrechtliche Beiträge* (Heidelberg, 1907–11). Two significant periodical publications out of the many held by the Law Library include the *Zeitschrift der Savignystiftung für Rechtsgeschichte*, founded 1861 and published in two separate parts, *Romanistische Abteilung* and *Germanistische Abteilung;* and the *Deutsche Rechtswörterbuch (Wörterbuch der älteren deutschen Rechtssprache)*, originated and edited by the Preussische Akademie der Wissenschaften, Berlin, and continued by the Akademie der Wissenschaften, Heidelberg (Weimar, 1914–), the last an encyclopedic law dictionary based on the terminology of historic sources that may now be accessed over the Internet.

Another category of legal-historical writing is the history of legal science, or history of legal theory. On the eve of the national codification, such works are often re-examinations and analyses of accepted concepts rooted in the Germanic and particularly Roman Law traditions. The *Geschichte der deutschen Rechtswissenschaft* (Munich, 1884) of Roderich von Stintzing (1825–83) and *Enzyklopädie und Methologie der Rechtswissenschaft* (Giessen, 1905) by Karl Gareis (1844–1923), translated into English as the *Introduction to the Science of Law* by Albert Kocourek (Boston, 1911), are two examples.

The sources component is equally rich. The group of Germanic sources (Folk Laws) have been discussed earlier in connection with the Holy Roman Empire. The Medieval Regional or Local Law compilations in Germany, the *Rechtsbücher*, form a very special collection. They are early systematic works on Imperial Law prevalent in Statutory Law and in Customs Law. Although private publications, over time these *Rechtsbücher* had gained official appeal or authority, adding largely to the development and furthering of the law. The *Sachsenspiegel* stands out as the most significant among the Medieval German *custumals*. It was originally written in Latin, probably between 1215 and 1233, by Eike von Repgow (ca. 1180–ca. 1233). The German translation here of the Latin *speculum as* "Spiegel," a term applied to a particular genre of Medieval legal literature, means "reflection" or "mirror" of the prevailing law of the (Holy Roman) Empire.

A fabulously illuminated manuscript on vellum of the *Sachsenspiegel,* the best-known German law *custumal (Rechtsbuch)*, is maintained in the Rare Book and Special Collections Division. This work was probably executed for an Austrian, possibly a member of the Hapsburg family (Germany, ca. 1500). The manuscript contains thirty-six coats of arms. An illumination possibly shows the author, Eike von Repgow, presenting his work to Count Hoyer von Falkenstein at whose request the work was translated from its original Latin to Low German (Rare Book and Special Collections; LCCN 73213231).

A page from the illuminated manuscript *Der Sachsenspiegel* (Germany, ca. 1500), one of the oldest and most influential law codes written in German during the Holy Roman Empire. The original *Sachsenspiegel* dates from 1230. (*Rare Book and Special Collections Division; LCCN 73213231*)

The *Sachsenspiegel* treats of a wide range of legal topics, including Administrative Law, Penal Law, Property and Inheritance Law, dowries and marriage; and includes a book on the Feudal Law of the times. It also includes material on herding and the keeping and hunting of animals. The Library has four incunables and many later editions. Among early works in the Law Library, a 1581 Polish translation of the German *Sachsenspiegel* (The mirror of Saxon law) contains Hebrew text inside the book's binding. The *Schwabenspiegel: Spiegel keyserlicher und gemayner Landrecht* (ca. 1274–75), a "mirror" of the Emperor's and the prevailing Common Law of Germany that is based on the *Sachsenspiegel*, is represented by two incunabula, both printed in Augsburg, 1475 and 1480. Other noteworthy works are the *Magdeburgisch Weichbild* and the *Sächsische Weichbild* (in sixteenth-century editions); several sixteenth-century editions of the *Layenspiegel* by Ulrich Tengler (d. ca. 1511), one of 1509; and three early editions of the *Richterlich Klagspiegel* by the illustrious Sebastian Brant (1485–1521), a form book for civil, criminal, and canon court procedures.

Another type of *custumal*, an important collection for historic legal research, are the law books for medieval towns (*Stadtrechte*), such as those for Magdeburg, Görlitz, Mühlhausen, and the early laws of Munich, Bamberg, Nuremberg, Augsburg, Freiberg, and Zwickau, to name just a few.

The principal bodies of law of sovereign states or *Länder* within Germany make up a significant part of the German law collections, beginning in the sixteenth century with *Landrechte* and *Landsordnungen* to the present time. The most voluminous are those of Prussia, Saxony, Bavaria, Hesse, and Baden, including many constitutional changes. Examples are the Bavarian *Landrecht Policey* (Munich, 1616 and 1657–59) and the *Codex juris bavarici judiciarii* of 1753 (revised edition, Ulm, 1804); *Repertorium juris Saxonici copiosissimum* (Dresden, 1668) and the *Codex saxonicus, chronologische Sammlung . . . vom jahre 1255 bis 1840* for Saxony, compiled and edited by Wilhelm Michael Schaffrath (Leipzig, 1842–43); the *Landrecht* of the Duchy of Prussia (1620); and *Des Hertzogthumbs Württemberg ernewert gemein LandtRecht* (Stuttgart, 1626).

Among the notable achievements preluding the broad European codification movement of the nineteenth century is the *Allgemeine Landrecht für die Preussischen Staaten* of 1794, which exists in the Library in about twenty editions between 1817 and 1970; and Samuel Cocceji's (1679–1755) *Project des Codicis Fridericiani marchici*, the code he drafted as High Chancellor of Prussia under Frederick the Great. Of particular interest are the works relating to the Public and Constitutional Law in the individual states during the constitutional movement of the nineteenth century.

The literature produced on the eve of the German civil codification, in an atmosphere of the nineteenth-century revival of classical studies and antiquity, focused again on the "Modern" Roman Law, the so-called *Pandektenwissenschaft*. Names connected with the *Historische Schule*, and in particular with *Pandektenrecht*, are those of Georg Friedrich Puchta (1798–1846), Friedrich Carl von Savigny (1779–1861), Heinrich Dernburg (1820–1907), Bernhard Windscheid (1817–92), and Rudolf von Jhering (1818–92). The works of these authorities in the company of other noted jurists form a quite significant collection. Some of those names re-appear in connection with the drafting of the Civil Code; Bernhard Windscheid, for example, was a member of the commission involved in drafting the Civil Code.

The political movement uniting German States under the Constitution of 1871 as an Empire was also the force for uniform legislation of all branches of law for the Empire (*Reichsjustizgesetze*), adding the *Burgerliche Gesetzbuch* (Civil Code) as the crowning event at the fin de siécle. The Law Library has a large collection of different drafts, including the authoritative criticism of the members of the profession (such as Otto Friedrich von Gierke, *Der Entwurf eines bürgerlichen Gesetz-buches und das deutsche Recht*); papers of drafting committees and legislative commissions (e.g., *Die gesammelten Materialien zu den Reichs-Justizgesetzen*, and the *Bürgerliche Gesetzbuch*, edited by Carl Hahn and Benno Mugdan, respectively, between 1881 and 1899); and editions of the Code (*Bürgerliches Gesetzbuch. BGB*). Soon after the promulgation, the commentaries and another type of criticism followed, the *BGB* as the code for the moneyed bourgeoisie—cf. Anton Menger (1841–1906), *Das Bürgerliche Recht und die besitzlosen Volksklassen* (Tübingen, 1908).

The legal literature traces the demise of the Weimar Republic and the establishment of the Third Reich in great detail. While most of the collections on the Third Reich are in the General Collections under History and Political Science, or in the Third Reich Collection, the bulk of the Weimar and Third Reich legislation is in the Law Library. The German government was set on its most disastrous course by the pivotal new Marriage Law, which in due time developed into legislation on marital and hereditary health (*Ehe- oder Erbgesundheitsrecht*) and on protection of German blood and honor (*Schutz des deutschen Blutes und der deutschen Ehre*)—later referred to as *Rassegesetzgebung* or *Judengesetzgebung*—that promulgated the National-Socialist race hygiene and population policies. The *Reichsbürgergesetz* (citizenship and alien legislation barring unwanted elements from mixing into Aryan German society) and the *Reichsflaggengesetz* (the law concerning rituals and privileges of the flag) complete the foursome of the *Nürnberger Gesetze*, often referred to as the "fundamental Nürnberg laws." The laws dealing with the peasantry, land use, and entail (*Bodenrecht und Erbhofrecht*); the new organization of the German and annexed territories (*Deutscher Raum und Boden*); the National-Socialist labor, artisanship, and the intelligentsia (*Arbeiter der Stirn und der Faust*); the manpower orders for work, and on war or defense of the homeland, complete the picture. There are also, of course, in-depth holdings of works in the collection on the "pure blood" theory, and historic studies on the Aryan race and caste dogma, laying the foundation for the race policies that permeated the cultural, social, and economic fabric of the nation and criminalized all inter-racial relations (e.g., *Entjudung* or *Arisierung*, i.e., *Aryanization*, were very common terms). The Law Library also has a collection of indexes and guides to the entire legislation throughout the era of the Weimar Republic and the Third Reich, kept up-to-date until 1944 (*Das Recht der Neuzeit; ein Führer*), and transcripts of the *Volksgerichtshof* (Peoples Court, a court of special jurisdiction) of trials of participants in the attempted Hitler assassination in 1944.

A very good collection on modern constitutional developments in Germany in general is available for the patrons of the Law Library, which houses all the constitutions of Germany, i.e., the Imperial of 1871, the Constitution of the Weimar Republic 1919, and the two post–World War II Constitutions of West and East Germany 1949, then Territory under Allied Occupation (1945–55). This is a particularly arresting component of the constitutional collection. The political-legal problems following the breakup of Germany into East and West were almost insurmountable, which is documented in the flood of contemporary legal literature. There was never a peace treaty with the Allies. In West Germany, the complex co-existence of German Law and Occupation Law, formulated first in the *Occupation Statute* (*Besatzungsstatut*) of August 6, 1949, together with a control organ of the three Western Allies, the Allied High Commission, was a seedbed of competing theories and interests during the evolution of the new Constitutional Law. In the Law Library, there are many annotated and unannotated editions, foreign-language editions, and commentaries, usually published with the *Occupation Statute*, to be found. Of particular interest is the large set of *Acts and Protocols of the Parlamentarische Rat* (Boppard, 1975–2002), chronicling the drafting of the Constitution under the keen eye of the Allies, especially the Americans. One of the works written on the heels of this process was *Deutsches Staatsrecht* by Theodor Maunz, which has since been published twenty-eight times.

There are also decisions of the various Military Government Courts; decisions of the Supreme Restitution Court (British Zone) pursuant to Law 59 (*Restitutions of identifiable property to victims of Nazi oppression*); the fifty volumes of the *Monthly report of the Military Governor of Germany; the Military government gazette* (U.S. Zone); and a list of about seventy-five thousand Nazi Party members in foreign countries on microfilm.

East Germany—as part of the "Ostblock" (i.e., territories in the sphere of Soviet influence)—liquidated the federal states (*Länder*) beginning in 1952 in a concerted effort to centralize the power of the state and to create a central state apparatus. The Law Library holds copies of all East German Constitutions (1949, 1968, and 1974) reflecting these changes. During the same period of time, East Germany completed the phase-by-phase nationalization of natural and industrial resources and property. These events—evidenced by the rapidly changing legal concepts, institutions, and nomenclature—are manifest in the East German codes and legal literature on the shelves of the Law Library.

FRENCH LAW

The French Law collection, second in size only to the German collection in the Law Library, is another stellar collection, in particular in the holdings of the *droit coutumier*. The Library's *Coutume* collection includes approximately seven hundred volumes. It is one of the outstanding and extensive collections of historic legal sources in a given jurisdiction in the Law Library and is of particular interest for the history of the private law of France.

The *coutumes*, basically Frankish law, were unwritten local Customary Law observed in eastern and northern France, the region of the *droit coutumier*. Coinciding with the rise of feudalism in thirteenth-century France, *coutumes* began to appear in written form and were observed by the provincial *parlements*, acting as sovereign bodies independent of each other and claiming independence from the king. The systematic transcription was started with a decree of Charles VII in 1454, mostly concluded by 1580, and influenced more by observances of the *parlement de Paris* than by Roman Law. The Midi, the South of France, was the region of the *droit écrit*, applied by the *parlements*—the law here was based on royal decrees and showed a greater influence from Roman Law.

Overall, the *coutumes* allow one to trace the development of French legal doctrine as well as influences from other legal systems. The *coutumes* of Normandy, for example, provide a window on elements shared between British Common Law and the customary usages in Northern France. The first written compilation of Norman *coutumes* was the *Statuta et consuetudines Normannie*, produced in two parts between 1199 to 1204 and 1218 to 1223. The *Grand Coutumier*, a translation from the Latin work *Summa de legibus in curia laicali*, was the second compilation of Norman law, written between 1254 and 1258. Two incunabula of 1483 of *Coustumes du pais de Normandie* include the charter given to the Normans by

ois par la grace de dieu
roy de france et de na

Louis X, other statutes, and Giovanni d'Andrea's *Tractatus super arboribus consan-guineitatis, affinitatis, necnon spritualis cognationis*, with arbor diagrams.

The *Coutume de Paris* is an especially valuable source as it is a compilation of French Customary Law that served as a national model for the codification of provincial *coutumes*, which exerted a major influence on the drafters of the Napoleonic codes as well. One may trace the laws of the French colony of Louisiana and the Louisiana *Digest of 1808* to this *coutume*. Further information about the Law Library's French *Coutumes* Collection may be ascertained from *The Coutumes of France in the Library of Congress: An Annotated Bibliography,* by Jean Casewell and Ivan Sipkov (Library of Congress, Washington, D.C., 1977).

The Legist Era of the Sixteenth to the Eighteenth Centuries. France and the Netherlands were for two centuries (from about mid-sixteenth century on) the leading centers of the European humanist (or "elegant") jurisprudence with a superb body of scholarly literature in both theory and interpretive terminology. The Law Library holds an outstanding collection of French legal thought. Two names closely associated with the *coutumes* are of primary importance, Charles Du Moulin (1500–66) and Antoine Loisel (1536–1617). The Calvinist Du Moulin's work was probably even more valued as one of the earliest scholarly studies on the text and gloss of the *Decretum Gratiani.* Another important figure in this context is Jean Chappuis (fl. 1500), whose unified edition of the *Decretum* with the subsequent *decretal* collections would become the model for editions of Canon Law, henceforth to be known as the *Corpus Iuris Canonici.* For the historic-philological approach of sixteenth-century jurists, the Library's collections include the works of numerous scholars, such as Pierre Rebuffi (1487–1557), with his treatises on royal ordinances, constitutions, and Feudal Law; Andrea Alciati (1492–1550); François Hotman (1524–90); and Jacques Cujas (1522–90); all with notable treatises on the significance and precise meaning of legal terms and phrases. Jean Bodin (1530–96) is represented in the collections by about fifty titles, among them his *Exposé du droit universel* and his *Six livres de la Repvbliqve* in numerous editions. François Douaren (1509–69) and Hugues Doneau (1527–91) have many titles in the collections. Hugues Doneau (1527–91) and Antoine Favre (1557–1624) stand out with systematic treatises of Modern Roman Law. Jean Domat (1625–96) treats "Civil Law" in its natural order. Robert Joseph Pothier (1699–1772), another outstanding name among jurists of the eighteenth and nineteenth centuries, prepared the groundwork for the *code civil* with his systematic Civil Law treatises; the collection of his works in the Law Library numbers over one hundred titles.

OPPOSITE: *Le grand coustumier de Normandie,* covered in dark green velvet, is a manuscript on parchment that contains seven illuminated miniatures that appear to have been produced ca. 1450 to 1470. Depicted here is folio 227, "A King of France giving a document to an archbishop." This fabulously illustrated compilation of the Norman *coutumes* is an extremely well preserved masterpiece of medieval paleography and one of the treasures of the Library. (*Law Library Rare Book Collection; LCCN 2004572900*)

The subject base of the collections grows broader through the seventeenth and eighteenth centuries. Of interest are the works on Maritime Law, including marine insurance, and Law of the Sea by several authors, among them Jacques Godefroy (1587–1652) and Robert Joseph Pothier, or René-Josué Valin (1695–1765). The work of the lexicographer Pierre Jacques Brillon (1671–1736) is also significant to these years, as is the standard legal dictionary of the renowned French jurist and philologist Barnabé Brisson (1531–91), the *Lexicon Ivris* or *De verborum quae ad jus pertinent significatione*, in several editions in the Law Library. The Law Library also holds the scarce early edition of *Collection de decisions nouvelles et de notions relatives à jurisprudence actuelle* (Paris, 1757) by Jean Baptiste Denisart (1713–65), a major reference work (or digest) arranged as a dictionary of legal issues.

Royal Legislation. The French monarchs used legislation to their advantage like no other power in Medieval Europe. The laws, called *ordonnances*, were only in force in the so-called royal domains (Crown good or *domanium*), originally very small (in the twelfth century only areas around Paris, Sens, Orléans, and Bourges), while local custom and legislation rested with the local authorities in the region or province. By end of the fifteenth century, however, nearly three quarters of France was in the hands of the king. The Law Library holds some chronological or substantive collections, among them the comprehensive well-known *Ordonnances des roys de France* in 21 volumes (Paris, 1723–1849; reprint edition, Farnborough, 1967–), edited by Eusèbe Jacob Laurière (1659–1728), Louis Guillaume de Vilevault (d. 1786), and others.

The Library holds four interesting incunabula, all published in Paris 1499: *Les ordonnances royaulx, nouvellement publiees a Paris*; an interesting manual *Le stille de Perlement, avic instruction et stille des requestes*; *Le stille de Chastellet*; and *La nouuelle ordonnance faicte par le roy . . . touchant la reformation des privileges des vniuersitez de ce royaume*. A collection of royal *ordonnances* deals with the administration of justice and procedure, *Ordonnances royaux svr le faict de la ivstice . . . faites par les rois François* (Roven, 1645). The Law Library also holds a large number of individual *ordonnances* on particular subjects, including commentaries.

Court Decisions. Originally known as the Assembly of Provincial Estates, the *Parlement* gradually metamorphosed during the fourteenth century into superior judicial courts; the legislation, however, remained with the *Conseil*. In the Library's collections, one may study this unique development in France in the interesting treatise *Treize liures des parlemens de France, esqvels est amplement traicté de levr origine et institvtion* (Geneva, 1621) by Bernard de la Roche Flavin (1552–1627). The Law Library holds several editions of Jean Papon's (1505–ca. 1590) work *Recveil 'arrestz notables des covrts sovveraines de France* (Lyon, 1557, second edition). The records, cases, and decisions of these courts, mainly the *Parlement de Paris* and the provincial sovereign courts (also under the name of *Parlement*), constitute another source collection providing insight into pre-revolutionary court process and procedures. Of particular interest are the provincial sovereign courts of Normandie, Toulouse, Grenoble, Bordeaux, Dijon, and Aix-en-Provence.

Examples of some relevant holdings include a collection of treatises by Cardin Le Bret (1558–1655), including the decisions of the *Parlement de Paris* (Paris, 1642); the *Parlement of Grenoble Decisiones Parlamenti Delphinatus* (Lyon, 1562) by Guy de La Pape (ca. 1402–ca. 1487); the *Novveav recveil des arrests de Bourgongne. . . . Decidees par ivgements et arrests de la Cour souueraine du Parlement de Dijone*, by J. Bouvot (Cologny, 1623–28), and the anonymous *Recueil des arrêts, arrêtés, remonstrances et autre pieces . . . du Parlement de Bretagne* (France?, 1765). There are, of course, registers or *dictionnaires des arrêts* of the Parlements of France; one of the better known is a six-volume work by Pierre Jacques Brillon (1671–1736).

The Codification. In an effort to harmonize France's varied regional laws and to disseminate the political principles of the French Revolution, the French *Code civil*, or *Code Napoléon* as it became known, was developed at Napoléon's direction and promulgated in 1804. Influenced by Roman Law, this seminal work aimed at a rational Common Law uniformly applied throughout the indivisible nation, granting equality before the law. At the same time, it brought about a formal break with the earlier "feudal" particularism or regionalism, so dominant during the *ancien régime*. In substance, the *Code civil des français* presented a logical organization of legal concepts and principles of law and, as such, was a major influence on the development of Modern Civil Law, leaving the legacy of French rules in many parts of the world. The term "civil" was to indicate that it was the code of the "Third Estate," i.e., the bourgeoisie, regulating the family as the most important "cell" of the state, including matters of property, inheritance, contracts, and obligations in the daily affairs and relations of "men of means."

The *Code civil*, the first of the *Cinq codes de l'Empire française* to become known the world over, became a model for other European codes and was a major influence on Québec (*Nouvelle-France*) law and on the law of the U.S. State of Louisiana, whose original code was also drafted in the French language.

Following the *Code Napoléon* other codes appeared in rapid sequence, i.e., the *Code de procédure civile* (1806), *Code de commerce* (1807), *Code d'instruction criminel* (1809), and

Code pénal (1810), forming the core of the new French Law. Of course, as in other Civil Law jurisdictions, most areas of the law were codified over time; two other early codes included the *Code des douanes* (1806) and the *Code rural, forestier et féodal* (1808).

The Law Library's collection of the French codes is extensive, including the original and official editions, comparative works on the law of the *ancien régime* and the new codifications, as well as comparative works on the French codes and other early European codifications—e.g., *Concordance entre les codes de commerce étrangers et le Code de commerce français* (Paris, 1851) by Fortune Anthoine de Saint-Joseph (1794–1853), *a comparison of the French commercial code with different countries' legislation, including that of South America*; or his *Concordance entre les code civils étrangers et le code Napoléon* (Paris, 1840), covering the codes of such countries as Sweden, the Kingdom of Württemberg (Germany), and the Two Sicilies. In addition, there are collections of decrees and manifests issued during the Consulate and Empire (1799–1815), such as the *Recueil* and *Supplément au Recueil des décrets, manifestes, discours, etc. de Napoléon Bonaparte et des membres de son gouvernement* (London, 1816).

The Constitutional Law and history of France is an equally if not more interesting collection. The Constitution of 1791 (*Constitution françoise.* Paris, 1791) was issued by the *Assemblée nationale constituante* (1789–91); the draft was introduced in the session of the *Assemblée nationale* in August 1791 (*Chartre constitutionelle des François.* Paris and Liege, 1791). *An authentic copy of the French Constitution* (London, 1791) is in the collections of the Library, followed by the *Constitutions de l'Empire*, 1852, of Napoléon III. Following suit are the constitutions of the various republics up to the most recent. The Law Library also holds collections on French overseas departments (*Départements d'Outre-mer*), such as French Guiana, Martinique, Guadeloupe, and Réunion, and the French overseas territories (*Territoires d'outre mer*), among them French Polynesia, Mayotte, and the contested Southern and Antarctic Territories (*Terres australes et antarctiques françaises*); law collections of New France (*Nouvelle-France*), now the Canadian Province of Québec; and collections of laws for the French colonies.

In times of war, when various kinds of financial legislation must be passed to support the war effort, governments normally engage in various public campaigns. To carry out its fund-raising aims during the First World War, France created a series of evocative posters, which form part of the French Poster Collection accessed through the Prints and Photographs Division. The one shown here fostered the implementation of wartime legislation and economic regulation.

On the other hand, researchers in the Law Library can find historic legislation from France and other nations to control windfall profits that were generated by the war effort.

OPPOSITE: "We'll get them!" A French soldier's cry to his compatriots doubles here as an urging for the French public to contribute to the war effort through bonds. Published in 1916, this image became the most popular French poster of World War I. (*Prints and Photographs Division; LC-USZC2-3864*)

OTHER EUROPEAN LAW

Among other Civil Law jurisdictions, Spain is represented by numerous rare law-related materials in the Library's Manuscript Division and Rare Book and Special Collections Division, but the Law Library has a particularly rich trove of rare Spanish holdings numbering over twelve hundred volumes. Early editions of ancient and Medieval Spanish codes, manuscripts (some of which are signed or autographed), legal documents relating to the Spanish colonies in the Americas, and other materials of significance to the history of the legal development of Spain, Portugal, and other Hispanic-derived jurisdictions are housed in the Law Library's Rare Book Collection.

The history of Spanish Law assumes far more than local importance. The early Spanish codes represent some of the most lasting institutions of Roman Law, and they were the medium through which Spain carried her law into the world. The earliest extant Spanish code is the *Breviary* of Alaric, A.D. 506, also known as the *Lex Romana Visigothorum*. The *Breviary* contains no Visigothic elements but is rather post-classical, pre-Justinian Roman Law. The text is in Latin, and it has come down to us in its entirety. Until the revival of Justinian's *Corpus Iuris Civilis* in thirteenth-century Bologna, the *Breviary* constituted virtually the only

A beautiful edition of the *Summa Hostiensis* of Cardinal Henricus de Segusio (ca. 1200–71). (*Law Library Rare Book Collection*; LCCN 2004572906). The 1579 Turin edition of the *Summa Hostiensis* contains the *Arbor Bigamiae* diagram.

Roman Law known in Europe. The earliest edition of this work found in the Law Library collection was printed in Paris in 1550 by Carolam Buillard by order of the president of the Parlement of Paris, Cardinal Jean Bertrand. This is believed to be the first printed edition of the *Breviary*. The Law Library also possesses Max Conrat's German translation (Leipzig, 1903) and Gustav Haenel's Latin edition (Leipzig, 1849).

The *Breviary* of Alaric was superseded by the late seventh-century *Lex Visigothorum* (*Forum judicum*) in the thirteenth century, translated from the original Latin text into vernacular Spanish as *Fuero juzgo*. The *Fuero juzgo* is considered the first comprehensive Spanish code of laws. Through its amalgamation of Roman elements with the enactments of Visigothic kings, a uniform legal system equally applicable to the Germanic and Roman populations of ancient Spain was formed. The *Fuero juzgo* was incorporated into *Las siete partidas* and influenced the nineteenth-century Spanish Civil Code. The earliest Law Library copy of the *Fuero juzgo* is a thirteenth-century Spanish manuscript on vellum. It is also the earliest Spanish legal manuscript in the Library of Congress. In addition to the manuscript copy, the Law Library contains other important editions of the *Fuero juzgo*, including that in Karl Zeumer's *Monumenta Germaniae historia* and the edition prepared in Madrid in 1815 by the Royal Academy of Spain. Another important code of laws was the *Fuero Real* (*Fuero Castellano*; 1252/55, edited in Catalan), which in some regions replaced the *Fuero juzgo*. The Library holds a 1491 edition of this code with the Latin gloss by Alonso Díaz de Montalvo (1405–99) and several sixteenth-century editions of the same work, as well as the *Ordenanzas reales* (Castile), in several 1485 editions, compiled by Alonso Díaz de Montalvo as well.

The most important Medieval Spanish Code and one of the most important of the old European codes is the *Libro del fuero* (1256/58). Regarded by many as a cultural as well as a legal monument in the history of Spain, it was initiated on June 23, 1256, by King Alfonso X (Alfonso the Wise), King of Castile and Leon, and the work was completed on August 28, 1265. The original compilation underwent four revisions, each time slightly changing the name (*Libro del fuero de las leyes; Libro de las leyes; Espéculo;* and finally *Siete partidas* or the Book of Seven Divisions). The character of the work changed at the same time, from a compilation of the law to a scholarly presentation in seven distinct parts of the then known substantive law. To establish the authority of the *Siete partidas* over the local *Fueros* and the *Fuero Real,* the *Ordenamiento de Alcalá* was issued by King Alfonso XI (1348). The Law Library holds a rare manuscript of the *Ordenamiento,* written towards the end of the fourteenth century.

Siete partidas shows an immense range of Roman, Canon, and Feudal Law in the formulation of its constitutional, civil, and criminal statutes. Renowned equally for its style as for its authority, it remained for centuries the principal instrument in the training of Spanish judges and became the foundation for the legislation of the Spanish colonies in America. Some of its provisions have been invoked in modern times by the courts of Texas, Louisiana, California, the Philippines, and Puerto Rico.

Siete partidas was printed for the first time in 1491, edited by Alonso Díaz de Montalvo. There are two printed "first editions": one dated October 25, 1491, and the other December 24, 1491, both done in Seville. The Law Library copy is the real first edition, dated October 25, 1491, and printed by Mainardus Ungut and Stanislaus Polonus. Other editions of the *Partidas* represented in the Law Library begin with the 1555 Salamanca edition printed by Andrea de Portonaris in four folio volumes, which contains the first gloss of Gregorio López de Tovar. The collection includes several other sixteenth- and seventeenth-century editions and the scholarly editions undertaken by the Royal Academy of Spain beginning in 1807.

An eminent legal source, the *Consolat de mar* (Consulat of the sea), which would become one of the most influential sources in the development of modern maritime law, was compiled in fifteenth-century Barcelona. The Library holds

OPPOSITE: The *Fuero Real,* the *Ordenamiento de Alcalá,* was issued by King Alfonso XI (1348). In addition to the *Ordenamiento de Alcalá,* this manuscript contains laws of Enrique II, *Leyes de la Margarita,* dating from the end of the fourteenth century (139?), written by at least two scribes in the *alcalá* script, with some later additions in *courtesan.* (*Law Library Rare Book Collection;* LCCN 83461371)

Libro del ordenamiento Real q[ue] el
muy alto Rey. Don alfon[so] por la g[racia]
de dios Rey de castilla fiso en al
cala de henares con acuerdo e con
sejo delos plados. E [con] m[ucho]s om[ne]s
om[ne]s e cavalleros e om[ne]s buenos
q[ue] con el fueron ayuntados en el di
cho consejo p[ar]a faser este dicho
ordenamiento

E nel nombre de dios
e de santa maria
dios padre e fijo e
sp[irit]u santo q[ue] son tres p[er]sonas e vn dios
verdadero por q[ue] la justiça es muy alta
virtud e la mas co[m]pli da ya el gove[r]
namento delos pueblos E por q[ue]
por ella se matienen todas las cosas
en el estado q[ue] deve[n] la qual senala
da mente son tenudos los Reys de
g[uar]dar e de mantener Por ende
an de tirar todo aq[ue]llo q[ue] seria arrep
delo alongar o enbargar E por q[ue]
las solepnidades e las sotilesas
delos derechos q[ue] se vsaro[n] de f[as]ta a

en la ordenaço delos juysios e
en los enplasamjentos como en las
mandas e en las co[n]testaçiones delos
pleytos e en las defensiones delas p[ar]
tes e en los plasos e en las co[n]tra
diçones delos testigos e delas se
rengas e en las alegadas e en las su
plicaçiones e en las otras cosas q[ue]
tenesçen alos juysios e por algu[n]as
escribtu[r]as q[ue] son co[n]tra derecho E
otrosi por los dones q[ue] son dados o pm
etidos alos jueses o por temor q[ue] an
alas veses algu[n]as delas p[ar]tes
se alueng[an] los pleytos E por esto
la justiça no se puede faser como
deve E los q[ue] ellos no pueden av[er]
co[m]plemjento de derecho Por ende
Nos don alfon[so] por la g[ra]çia de dios
Rey de castilla de toledo de leo[n] de
galli[z]ia de sevilla de cordova de m[u]r
çia de jahen del algarbe e de alge[z]i
ra E Señor de molina Con co[n]sejo
delos plados e ricos om[ne]s e cavallos e
om[ne]s buenos q[ue] son conusco en estas

PHILIPPVS HISPANIA
RVM ET INDIARVM
REX.

Prouisiões cedulas
Instruciones desu Magestad: orde
nãças ó visitos y audiêcia, pa la bue
na expediciõ delos negocios, y admi
nistraciõ ǫ justicia: y gouernaciõ ésta
nueua España: y pa el buẽ tratamiẽ
to y oseruaciõ ólos yndios, vende el
año 1525. hasta este presente ōe. 63.

EN MEXICO EN CASA
De Pedro Ocharte. M.D.LXIII.

Cédulario de Puga, published in Mexico City in 1563, is the second law book printed in North America. (*Law Library Rare Book Collection*; LCCN 04008197; LC-USZ62-61147)

about twenty editions of the work, including the *Libre de Consolat dels fets maritims* (Barcelona, 1592) and reprints of the original 1408 Barcelona version of the *Llibre del Consolat de mar*. On its early course as the principal Maritime Commercial Law and Mediterranean Law of the Sea, it was printed in other places in the region. In addition to these Spanish works, the Library holds six Italian editions.

The early legal development of Portugal was linked to that of Spain, and the Roman and Visigothic legislation discussed above applied throughout the Iberian Peninsula. The first systematic collection of strictly Portuguese Law was the *Ordenacoes Manuelinas*, 1521, and the *Ordenacoes Filipinas*, 1603. These were the chief sources of Portuguese Law before the establishment of the present codes, and they remained in effect until modern times not only in Portugal itself, but also in its colonies, including Brazil. The Law Library has editions of each of these three Portuguese legislative collections. The legislation issued by Alfonso V is contained in a later edition published by the Real Imprensa da Universidade in Coimbra in 1792. From a bibliographical point of view, the volume containing the legislation of King Manuel I is perhaps the most noteworthy. The work contains the second compilation of Manuel's laws, since all copies of the first, which appeared between 1512 and 1514, were destroyed after the prohibition of the work in 1521. The various parts of the second compilation were published in Spain and Portugal between 1521 and 1539, and their production involved three printers, including Juan Cromberger of Seville, who introduced printing into the New World, when in 1539 he organized a press in Mexico. The Law Library is also fortunate in having a first edition of the 1603 Lisbon compilation *Ordenacoes Filipinas*, issued by Philip II.

Among the rarities in the Hispanic Law Collection are a number of works that hold a special place in the development of law in the Spanish and Portuguese possessions in the New World. Among these is the *Cédulario de Puga*, compiled by Vasco de Puga, a judge of the Audiencia—a Spanish colonial court of appeals—pursuant to a commission given by Viceroy Luis de Velasco, who in turn was acting in fulfillment of a royal order (*cédula*) calling for the compilation of all statutes, decrees, and *cédula*s relating to the viceroyalty of New Spain. The compilation, covering the period 1525 to 1563 and published 1563 in Mexico City, was considered the second law book printed on the continent of North America and is often cited as the first compilation of laws of America (LCCN 09001871). It was actually the second, however, since a compilation prepared by Antonio de Mendoza—one not present in the collection—antedated the Puga work by fifteen years. Mendoza's compilation, however, was confined to the ordinances and instructions that could serve as a guide to the officers of the Audiencia and thus was more restrictive in scope than that of Puga. The *Cédulario de Puga* was reflected over the next hundred years in a series of important legal compilations.

The *Cédulario indiano* (Madrid, 1596) is another of these early compilations in the Law Library collection. Compiled in four folio volumes by Diego de Encinas, a clerk of the Royal Council of the Indies, it is considered a monument in Spanish legislation. The council itself had the work published in response to demands from officials, lawyers, and the public. It contains the *cédulas, capitulos de ordenanzas, instrucciones,* and *cartas* issued at different times by the monarchs Fernando and Isabella, the Emperor Carlos, his mother Juana, and the Catholic King Felipe. The *Cédulario indiano* covers the years from Columbus's voyages to America to 1596.

The *Recopilacion de leyes de loys reynos de las Indias*, 1680, usually referred to as *Recopilacion de Indias*, was regarded as the basic collection of the laws and regulations issued by the Spanish Crown for the colonies throughout their entire colonial period. The *Recopilacion* was ordered printed by a decree of November 1, 1680, and the four-volume work was completed in Madrid in 1681. As the laws were modified, new editions were issued in 1756 in four volumes, in 1774 in four volumes, in 1791 in three volumes, and in 1841 in four volumes. Volume 2 of the 1841 edition, compiled by Jose Maria Alvarez (1777–1820), was furnished with materials concerning laws issued for the Indies after 1680, including a chronological index. All five editions of the *Recopilacion de Indias* are represented in the Hispanic Law Collection.

The items cited here are merely representative of the hundreds of rare volumes in the collection relating to the development of law in Spain, Portugal, and their colonies and possessions. Spain ceded its two provinces of the Floridas to the United States by a treaty concluded in 1819 which was formally ratified two years later. On March 10, 1821, President Monroe appointed Andrew Jackson as Governor of the Floridas and as commissioner to take over the provinces from Spain. In the interim, before the establishment of a regular territorial government and legislature, Jackson ordered that all previous laws and municipal regulations remain in effect as under the Spanish regime. During that interim period, Jackson had certain necessary regulations published in a pamphlet entitled *Ordinances by Major-General Andrew Jackson, then governor of the provinces of the Floridas, exercising the powers of the captain-general, and of the intendant of the island of Cuba, over the said provinces, and of the governors of the said provinces, respectively* (St. Augustine, printed by R.W. Edes, 1821). This twenty-eight-page brochure in the Law Library's collection is the only existing copy.

Capituli et ordinatione di mare [et] di mercantie (Consolat de mar) (Rome, 1519). (*Law Library Rare Book Collection; LCCN 92139744*)

OPPOSITE: An illumination from *Statuta et leges Venetorum* (*Statuta Venetorum: 1242–1346*), a manuscript written on fourteenth-century vellum. The illustration shows one of the eight miniatures that are placed within initials. (*Law Library Rare Book Collection; LCCN 99478565*)

In Medieval Italy, alongside Roman, Canon, and Germanic Law, emerged the Local Law of the independent city states. Beginning in the twelfth century, these cities started to collect their Customary Laws in written form. These collections were succeeded by comprehensive codes or *statuta*, enactments of local legislative bodies, which prevailed until the codification of the eighteenth century. These laws of the city states on maritime commerce eventually began to have international application. Of the five hundred volumes of *statuta* maintained by the Law Library, the most outstanding item is the manuscript of the *Statuta et leges Venetorum*.

Among the early printed *statuta* in the collection are those of Genoa (Bologna, 1498), bound with a 1538 edition of the *Leges Rotae Genuensis*; the *Liber statutorum inclite ciuitatis Mediolani* (Milan, 1480); and the *Constitutiones dominii mediolanensis* (Milan, 1541). The collection also contains contemporaneous regulations on particular subjects from the major municipalities or city states of Medieval and Renaissance Italy, as well as numerous *statuta* from the sixteenth through the eighteenth centuries. Such collections include interesting civil and criminal statutes of Bologna, among them *Statvta criminalis commvnis Bononiae* (Bologna, 1525) and *Statuta civilia, et criminalia civitatis Noniae* (Bologna, 1735–37); the *Statvta magnificae civitatis Veronae* (Venice, 1611); and the *Novissimum statutorum ac venetarum legum volumen* (Venice, 1729).

Throughout the Middle Ages and the Renaissance, Venice was a major power in maritime trade. Together with other Italian city states, it contributed considerably to the formation of the Mediterranean Law of the Sea. Early editions of several documents and works that were instrumental in the development of Maritime Law may be found in the Law Library's collections, among those two fourteenth-century manuscripts on Venetian Maritime Law. The first, *Statuta et ordinamenta super navibus*, contains a maritime statute enacted in Venice by the Doge Rinerio Zeno in 1255. Penned in a good gothic hand, on twenty-five vellum leaves, are one hundred eighty-six chapters of regulations on all aspects of shipbuilding and on relations between ship owners and crews, etc. The second, a fourteenth-century manuscript, *Capitulare officialium cataveris Venetiarum*, contains laws and regulations on Venetian trade and contraband. The Spanish *Consolat de mar* (Consulat of the sea) was an important model for the development of Maritime Commercial Law. The Library holds—besides the Spanish editions discussed earlier—six Italian editions, the earliest a Rome edition of 1519, *Capituli et ordinatione di mare [et] di marcantie*; four Venetian editions, *Libro di Consolato novamente stampato et ricorretto* (1539) and *Il Consolato del mare* (1584, 1612, and 1713); and one Luca edition of 1720.

Many treatises and commentaries have attained the status of classical works in Maritime and Commercial Law. Among these is Benvenuto Stracca (1509–78)

I xpi noumine Amen. Incipit prologus libri statu
torum et legum Venetorum illustris domini Ja
cobi teuupoli incliti duus Venetiarum.

EO auctore ducarum nrm
leuat marti suffragius gub
nante. q nobis pmissione
celestis gratie est collatus.
et bella feliciter pagimus t
pacem muribus decorantes.
statum patrie honorabilu
subite neunimus. Vnde trsq
a deo nostros animos ad au
xilium dei erigimus. ut no
de nostra nostrorumq, situ
lium potentia seu ingenio

confidamus. sed omnem spem ad solum referam
summe prudentiam trinitatis unte et mundi
huius elementa sub quadam nebula presserit
et orbem terrarum eius dispositio est. ponit.
Cum igitur nil tam studiosum reputatur in reb,
quam uenerabiles sanctiones. p quas res diuine
humaneq, ab improbis preguntur. t suis ippl
sionibus omnis iniqtas refrenatur. criminamu
necessarium utile possibile et honestum. ad ip
sarum tramitem pperare. ut eorum metu huma
ni refrenetur audacia tutaq, sit inter ploss inno
centia. q in ipsis impiis refrenetur nocendi fa
cultas supplicio formidato. p quas etiam ius su
um unicuique tribuitur. Reperimus namque
omnia statuta a nobis et predecessoribus nris
edita tanta confusione submissa iuxta eorum in
debitam compositionem de quorundam obsruat
one quibusdam omnibus ptermissis frequenter no

Løgbok Jslendín
ga huoria saman hefur sett
Magnus Noregs Konngur
lofingra Miuinga so
sem / hur bref og
formale von

Hvor ad til heirer
Ernuerdugu og dygdu vor
du Heidurs mañe Stein
dore mynu presije
Eu skrifut / ey so nofuest ma
af Gudmunde Jonssyne
ANNO CHRI 1637

Tractatus de mercaturia seu mercatore (Venice, 1553) in the collection with 1556, 1558, 1575, 1595, and many later editions of the same work. His *Tractatus* is considered one of the first attempts to construe Commercial Law as a coherent system distinct from Civil Law.

The Library's vast law or law-related collections on European Continental jurisdictions include many items unique for their rarity or other historic attributes, and the works are far too great in number and scope to summarize adequately. The illustrations on these pages are thus but a few more examples of the riches of the Library's law holdings.

A study of the legal collections of the Nordic countries of Denmark, Finland, Iceland, Norway, and Sweden reveals readily both the unique aspects of each particular jurisdiction and their influences from the major Western Civil and Common Law traditions. Although borders and political power have shifted back and forth from earliest time on until as late as the twentieth century, the legal systems of these small nations were remarkably distinct from each other. Once the rivalries had been settled and the identity and border of each nation had been permanently defined, the desire for contact, inspiration, and outside ideas developed into intense formal and informal cross-border cooperation, under the auspices of the Nordic Council and the European Union. Many of the present-day statutes of these five neighboring countries, therefore, often have quite similar or identical language.

One of the Library's Scandinavian treasures is the Icelandic manuscript titled the *Jónsbók*. It contains the code of law that was issued in the thirteenth century by the Norwegian King Magnus VII to the people of Iceland, many of whom descended from Norwegian settlers. In the sixteenth and seventeenth centuries, manuscripts as well as printed copies of the *Jónsbók* were in great demand because of the requirement that all Icelandic boys learn it by heart. The *Jónsbók* was an item brought to every courthouse meeting. The Library's copy is a manuscript from the seventeenth century, noteworthy for its unusual gothic script and decoration.

Among the various early European codes held by the Law Library are several Swedish ones that demonstrate Sweden's continental legal heritage, specifically its German-Roman roots. The first comprehensive legal codification, the *Sveriges Rikes Lag*, enacted in 1734 and still in force today, is in an original copy in the Law Library's collections. The systematic arrangement into nine *balks* (literally "beams," i.e., books), covering such areas as Family and Inheritance Law, Land Law, commerce, judicial procedure, and criminal justice, reveal the strong

OPPOSITE: *Jónsbók. Lavgbok islendinga huoria samañ hefur sett Magnus Noregs kongur* (1637). This is actually a facsimile, which was produced in 1637, of the lawbook manuscript of King Magnus VII of Norway. It is executed in a Gothic script with Romanesque initialing throughout. (*Law Library Rare Book Collection; Law Ms J6 LLRBR*)

Portrait of Frederick III of Denmark from the 1709 edition of *Lex regia.*

influences of the Continental tradition on the Swedish legal system. It has remained the foundation for modern Swedish Law and the primary tool for every Swedish lawyer. The Code has been published annually since 1942, reflecting the constant changes and amendments to the law.

The voluminous collections on the law of the Netherlands include the works of a wide range of celebrated humanist legal scholars, such as Johannes Arnoldus Corvinus (ca. 1582–1650); Cornelis van Bijnkershoek (1673–1743); Ulrich Huber (d. 1694); Joannes Voet (1647–1713); and the immense scholarly production of Hugo Grotius (1583–1645). The work of this polyhistorian was devoted not only to the Roman-Dutch Law. A Christian Hebraist like John Selden, Grotius wrote tractates on Natural Law, theology and religion in general, and on the Old Testament in particular, e.g., *Annotationes in Vetus Testamentum* (Halle, 1775–76); *Annotationes in Libros Evangeliorum* (Amsterdam, 1641); and *De veritate religionis Christian* (Lyons, 1640); all covered at the Library in several editions. He wrote also on Roman law, *Florum sparsio ad ius Iustinianeum* (Paris, 1642), and poetry. The Library holds copies of his poetic work, *Poemata* (Lyons, 1617 and 1639), edited by Willem de Groot (1597–1662); a 1664 Leiden edition and a Dutch/Latin translation, *De dichtwerken van Hugo Grotius* (Assen, 1970); and a five-volume Greek anthology (*Anthologia Graeca, cum versione Latina Hugonis Grotii.* Utrecht, 1795–1822). An interesting work on the origins of the American Indians (*De origine gentium americanarum dissertatio.* N.p., 1642, reprinted in Amsterdam and Paris in the same year) may have been inspired by the excitement of that time over the reports on the explorations by the *Nederlandsche West-Indische Compagnie* (1621–75) and the Dutch colonization of what was to become New Netherlands (later New York). An Amsterdam and Paris edition of the same year, as well as a comment on it, *Notae ad dissertationum Hugonis Grotii De origine Gentium americanarum* (Amsterdam, 1643) by Johannes de Laet (1593–1649), and a translation *On the origin of the native races of America* by Edmund Goldsmid (Edinburgh, 1884) are in the collections of the Library.

A notable title of the Czech treasures in the Law Library Rare Book Collection is the most important early systematic treatise on Czech Law, *O práwiech Zemie Czeskee Wiktorina Ze Wssehrd poczinagij knihy prwnije [-dewaatee]* (Nine Books on the Laws of the Czech Kingdom; LCCN 2003558112). Referred to as the "Všehrd" and written by Viktorin Kornel ze Všehrd (1460–1520), a lawyer, professor, and Dean of the Faculty of Philosophy of the Charles University in Prague, this manuscript dates to 1504 and demonstrates that the Czech Law of the time eschewed Roman Law influence in favor of Customary Law.

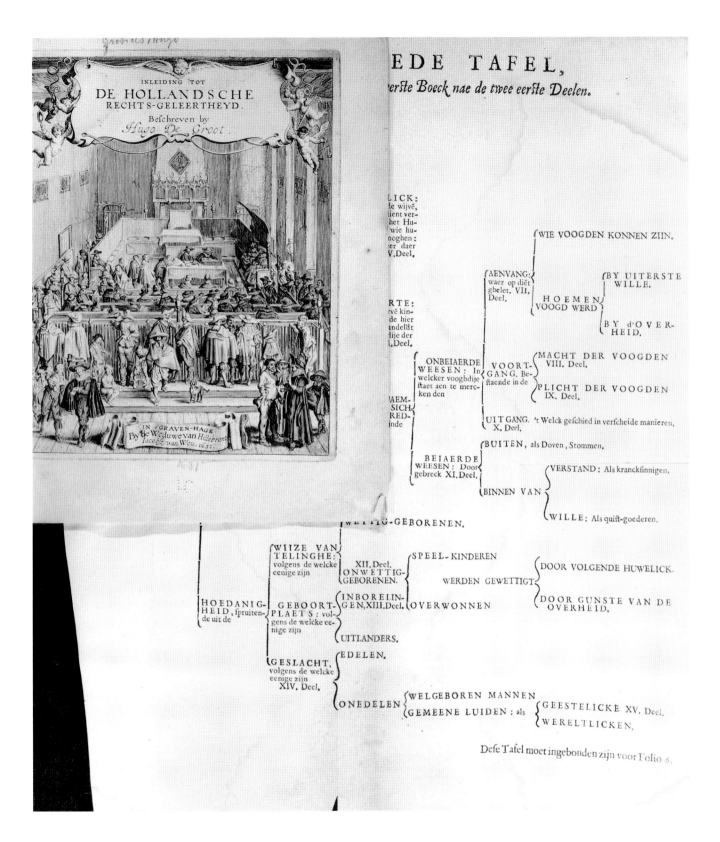

INLEIDING TOT
DE HOLLANDSCHE
RECHTS-GELEERTHEYD.
Beschreven by
Hugo De Groot.

IN 'S GRAVEN-HAGE
By de Weduwe van Hillebrant
Iacobsz. van Wou. 1631.

...EDE TAFEL,
...eerste Boeck nae de twee eerste Deelen.

...LICK:
...de wijvē,
...ient ver-
...het Hu-
...wie hu-
...noghen
...er daer
...V. Deel.

...RTE:
...vē kin-
...de hier
...andelt
...dije der
...I. Deel.

...AEM-
SICH-
RED-
...inde

WIE VOOGDEN KONNEN ZIIN.

AENVANG: waer op diet ghelet. VII. Deel.

BY UITERSTE WILLE.

HOE MEN VOOGD WERD

BY d'OVER-HEID.

ONBEIAERDE WEESEN: In welcker vooghdije staet aen te mercken den

VOORT-GANG. Bestaende in de

MACHT DER VOOGDEN VIII. Deel.

PLICHT DER VOOGDEN IX. Deel.

UIT GANG. 't Welck geschied in verscheide manieren, X. Deel.

BEIAERDE WEESEN: Door gebreck XI. Deel.

BUITEN, als Doven, Stommen.

BINNEN VAN

VERSTAND: Als kranckfinnigen,

WILLE: Als quift-goederen.

HOEDANIG-HEID, spruiten-de uit de

WIIZE VAN TELINGHE: volgens de welcke eenige zijn XII. Deel.

WETTIG-GEBORENEN.

ONWETTIG-GEBORENEN.

SPEEL-KINDEREN

WERDEN GEWETTIGT

DOOR VOLGENDE HUWELICK.

DOOR GUNSTE VAN DE OVERHEID.

GEBOORT-PLAETS: volgens de welcke ee-nige zijn

INBORELIN-GEN, XIII. Deel.

OVERWONNEN

UITLANDERS.

GESLACHT, volgens de welcke eenige zijn XIV. Deel.

EDELEN.

ONEDELEN

WELGEBOREN MANNEN

GEMEENE LUIDEN: als

GEESTELICKE XV. Deel.

WERELTLICKEN.

Dese Tafel moet ingebonden zijn voor Folio 6.

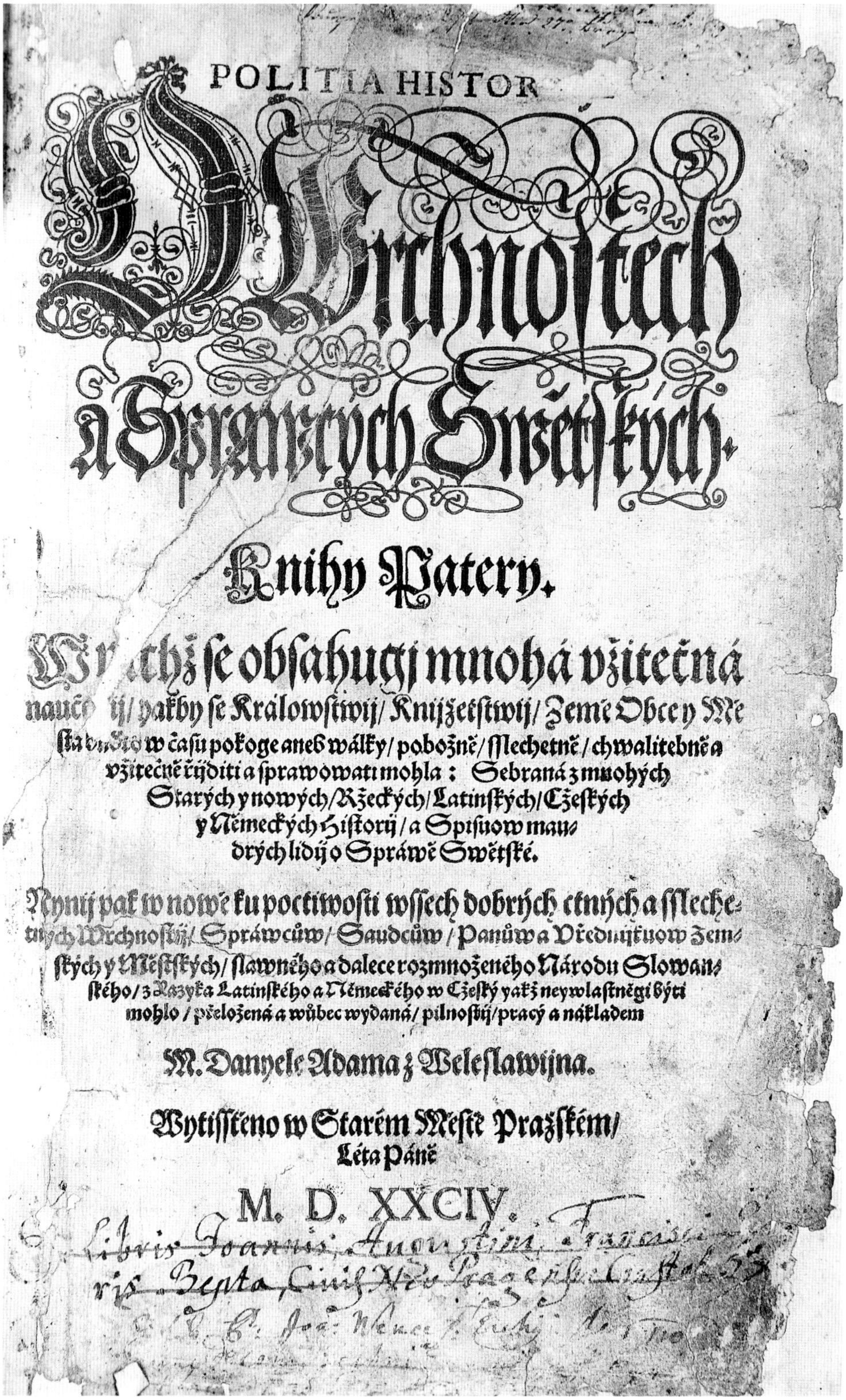

POLITIA HISTOR

O Wrchnostech a Sprawcých Swětských.

Knihy Patery.

W nichž se obsahugj mnohá vžitečná naučenij/ yakby se Králowstwij/ Knijžetstwij/ Země Obce y Města w času pokoge aneb wálky/ pobožně/ sslechetně/ chwalitebně a vžitečně řijditi a sprawowati mohla: Sebraná z mnohých Starých y nowých/ Řeckých/ Latinských/ Cžeských y Německých Historij/ a Spisuow maudrých lidij o Sprawě Swětské.

Nynij pak w nowě ku poctiwosti wssech dobrých/ ctných a sslechetných Wrchnostij/ Sprawcůw/ Saudcůw/ Panůw a Vřednijkuow Zemských y Městských/ slawného a daleče rozmnoženého Národu Slowanského/ z Yazyka Latinského a Německého w Cžeský yakž neywlastněgi býti mohlo/ přeložená a wůbec wydaná/ pilnostij/ pracý a nákladem

M. Danyele Adama z Weleslawijna.

Wytisstěno w Starém Městě Pražském/ Léta Páně

M. D. XXCIV.

Politia historica. O wrchnostech a sprwcých swetských knihy patery by Georg Lauterbeck (Prague, 1584). This early Czech work concerns the rules for kings and rulers. (*Law Library Rare Book Collection; LCCN 56055128*). Another earlier related work by Lauterbeck in the Law Library is his *Regentenbuch* of 1567, which includes the author's translations of various earlier authors on the duties of kings and rulers. This is one of only two recorded copies in the United States. (*Law Library Rare Book Collection; LCCN 85157937*)

As noted in *Poland in the Collections of the Library of Congress: An Overview*, by Kazimierz Grzybowski (Washington: Library of Congress, 1968), the Law Library's Polish Law Collection includes a complete set of the laws and constitutions adopted by the Diets of the Commonwealth since 1550, the original and modern editions of the *Volumina Legum*, the complete collection of Polish legislation beginning with the Statutes of the Diet of Wislica of 1347, early enactments of the provincial diets and synods, as well as an early edition of the Polish Municipal Laws governing legal relations in the cities and towns throughout the Polish-Lithuanian Commonwealth from Silesia to Kyiv. Three consecutive codes of the Grand Duchy of Lithuania from 1529, 1566, and 1588 likewise may be found in the Law Library's Rare Book Collection.

When the Ukrainian provinces of the Grand Duchy were incorporated into Poland proper, their legal system retained the 1566 version of the Statutes. The Law Library has the original and modern editions of the Statutes, both in the official language of the Grand Duchy and in contemporary Polish translations. Legislative materials pertaining to the enactment of the Constitution of May 3, 1791, are also housed in the Law Library.

RUSSIAN LAW

In their study of the Law Library's collections, *The Law Library of the Library of Congress* (Library of Congress, Washington, 1978), Kimberly Dobbs and Kathryn Haun estimated the entire Russian Collection of the Law Library at approximately twenty-seven thousand volumes, with the pre-1917 works numbering about thirteen thousand items and the Soviet materials about fourteen thousand. Today the number of volumes in the collections from the now defunct Soviet Union, Russia, and former Soviet-occupied nations is much higher, reflecting the explosion of publishing from the fifteen jurisdictions that emerged as independent nations after the breakup of the Soviet Union in August 1991. The Law Library's Russian and Soviet holdings include standard Civil Law materials such as constitutions, official law gazettes, and annotated codes, as well as treatises, monographs, collections of decisions, and legal periodicals. Parliamentary debates and works relating to political infrastructure are not in the custody of the Law Library but are found in the General Collections of the Library of Congress.

After the Russian Revolution of 1905 and throughout the war years in the Soviet Union, conditions were such that the Library of Congress was able to purchase a variety of important Russian and Soviet collections. In 1906, Siberian merchant Gennadii Vasil'evich Yudin (IUdin), seeking a safe home for his vast personal library, offered the Library of Congress eighty thousand books at a nominal cost. These were distributed among the custodial divisions of the Library according to subject, and a portion of the law materials, mainly eighteenth-century, reached the Law Library in 1914. Another great influx of important Russian and Soviet works arrived at the Library through book dealer Israel Perlstein, who from 1927 until his death in 1975 purchased large quantities of books from the Soviet authorities that had confiscated them from the Imperial and other libraries and sold them to obtain much needed hard currency. According to one source, these collections were on occasion sold by the linear yard. The rare Russian Law items from the Imperial collections that found their way into the Law Library include material from the Winter Palace Collection, seminal legal sources, and unique items, including illuminated manuscript charters, patents of nobility, manuscript scrolls, and other documentary works.

Printing was introduced in Russia in 1564—a comparatively late date—and the first printed Russian law book did not appear until 1649, when the *Ulozhenie Tsaria Alekseia Mikhailovicha* (The Code of Czar Aleksei Mikhailovich) was promulgated and published in Moscow. The *Ulozhenie* was influential in elevating the contemporary Russian vernacular to an official written language and would remain the basic law of the land until 1833. The Law Library holds a manuscript copy of the *Ulozhenie*, a copy of the first and the second printing of the first edition, as well as copies of the 1720, 1737, 1759, 1779, 1790, and 1796 editions, some of these in multiple copies or variants. The second law book printed in Russia, the *Kormchaia Kniga* or "Pilot Book," is a compendium of ecclesiastical and civil (i.e., Roman) Laws, including church canons, epistles, sermons, selections from Byzantine secular legislation, princely statutes, and commentaries. After Kyivan-Rus' adopted the faith of Byzantium in 988, the *Kormchaia Kniga*, also known by its Greek title *Nomocanon*, circulated in Russia for centuries in manuscript form. Russian Church authorities under Patriarch Joseph first printed the text in Moscow in 1650, but in 1651 the Russian Church Council, reflecting a growing schism in the Church, stopped the book's distribution. Joseph died the next year, and Czar Aleksei Mikhailovich appointed a new patriarch, Nikon, investing him with unprecedented authority. Aleksei hoped that Nikon would help to bring order both to Russia and Russian worship. In 1653, Nikon reissued the 1650 text of the *Kormchaia Kniga* with some omissions and his own added text. The Law Library holds two variant copies of the *Kormchaia Kniga*, the second variant showing what is possibly further editing done by Old Believers who owned the book. Subsequent editions in the Law Library include the 1787 and 1804 printings.

Another Russian religious text in the Law Library's Rare Book Collection is the *Charter of the Iur'ev Monastery in Novgorod,* printed in Moscow in 1830. (*Law Library Rare Book Collection; LCCN unk85058820*)

This book gives a first-hand view of Russian life in the capital city as seen through the eyes of a Polish delegation. It includes a section on the Treaty of Andrusovo, 1667, that ended the thirteen-year war between Poland-Lithuania and Russia and resulted in the partitioning of the territory that today constitutes Ukraine.

A work of great rarity in the collection from an area that today is Ukraine is that of Innokentii Gizel (ca. 1600–83), Archimandrite of the Kyivan Cave Monastery from 1656 to 1683. A professor of philosophy and the rector of the Kyivan College (1645–56), Innokentii was the author of the text *Mir s Bogom chelevieku* (Man's Peace with God, 1669, 1671). Written in Old Church Slavonic, the book summarizes his views of contemporary ethics and religious standards (Law Library Rare Book Collection; LCCN 2004573228).

By the mid-1950s, the Library of Congress had purchased some twenty-six hundred Russian Imperial volumes, almost exclusively from the Winter Palace Collection. Eighteenth-century works constitute a rare and valuable part of the collection. The law component of that collection includes at least one hundred twenty-four titles in one hundred fifty-five volumes published between 1710 and 1801. A bibliographic project conducted in the 1990s resulted in the microfilming of the full text of all of the eighteenth-century Russian Law volumes available at the time; a copy of the microfilm may be purchased through the Library's Photoduplication Service. Manuscript materials from the Russian Imperial Collection, mainly charters and other legal documents, may be found in both the Law Library and the Manuscript Division. Most of the remaining law materials in book form came into the custody of the Law Library.

A rare work noted by Andrei I. Pliguzov and Barbara L. Dash in "Russian Law: 18th Century Russian Books in the Law Library of Congress" (*LC Information Bulletin*, March 2000) is a proof copy of a 1715 Russian translation of the French Code of Naval Law (*Ordonnance de Louis XIV pour les armées navales*, 1689). The Library's copy has manuscript corrections and notes throughout made by the translator and proofreaders. The translation is said to have been published under Peter the Great's close supervision. The Law Library's 1763 and 1764 editions of the *Decrees . . . of Catherine the Great* include her *Manifesto*, which was removed from many copies in 1797 by order of Czar Paul I. Other possibly unique items are eight compilations, 1796 to 1800, of the decrees and edicts of the same Paul I, probably working copies for the Russian Senate.

For the guidance of a legislative commission formed in 1766 to undertake the preparation of a code to supplant the extant Code (*Ulozhenie*) of 1649, Empress Catherine the Great (1762–96) wrote a 526-section Instruction (*Instruktsiia*).

OPPOSITE: *Statute of Empress Catherine II of Russia* (St. Petersburg, 1780). This book contains the text of the statute *Blagochestivieishiia Samoderzhavnieishiia Velikiia Gosudaryni Imperatritsy Ekateriny Vtoryia Uchrezhdeniia dlia upravleniia gubernii Vserossiiskiia Imperii* (Institutions for the Administration of the Provinces of the All-Russian Empire [Approved] by the Most Pious and Most Autocratic Empress Catherine the Second). The statute, dated November 7, 1775, laid the foundations for the organization of provincial administration that survived, with changes, until the fall of the Russian Empire in 1917. The Law Library holds the first edition, printed on November 12, 1775 (LCCN 54054007). Shown here is the flamboyant copy of the 1780 edition that belonged to Catherine II; it is bound in rose velvet and shows the Imperial coat of arms, the double-headed eagle, on the front cover and the embroidered monogram of the Empress on the back. (*Law Library Rare Book Collection*; LCCN 61056023)

Incorporating the most advanced ideas of the Enlightenment, the Instruction was published on July 30, 1767, but its circulation was restricted to higher officials and government agencies, and the Russian legislature never produced Catherine's code. The Law Library has a manuscript English translation of the Instruction that may have been produced for the then British ambassador, Sir George Macartney, whose bookplate it contains, as well as a printed version of the English translation, published in London in 1768. Other important volumes from Catherine's reign include her laws governing municipal corporations and the nobility, as well as her rarely found *Ustav narodnym uchilishcham* (Regulations on Public Education), 1786.

The military and naval regulations of the Russian Empire were codified separately. The military regulations issued from 1716 to 1913 are contained in the *Svod voennykh postanovlenii* (Code of military regulations), of which the Law Library possesses all three editions—1838, 1859, and 1869—as well as supplements containing new regulations and amendments enacted after 1869. The naval regulations, published in 1886 to 1890, were codified in *Svod morskikh postanovlenii* (Code of naval regulations). The Law Library has in its collection volumes 1–18 (except for volumes 11 and 12, which were never published). Some of the topics treated in these volumes are the hierarchy of military and civil ranks, statutes on the military and civil Order of St. George the Victorious (established by Catherine II), compulsory Russian military service, and military education.

Russian books printed during the reign of Peter the Great, 1708 to 1725, are of special interest to historians of printing because Peter replaced the Old Church Slavonic characters, which had been used for all printing previously in Russia, with modern Russian Cyrillic type. The first law book printed with this type, the *Instruktsii i artikuly voennye nadlezhashchie k rossiiskomu flotu* (Moscow, 1710) is in the Law Library's collection.

A unique collection in the Law Library is a group of forty-six handwritten scrolls, the longest of which measures eighty-seven feet. Fashioned of strips of often inferior paper pasted together with starch, such scrolls were used in Russia mostly to record petitions to the tsar, questions of judicial procedure, complaints, briefs, records of testimony, and other matters of a transient nature. The scrolls in the Law Library's possession date from 1628 to the mid-eighteenth century and come from jurisdictions including Galich, Kazan, Novgorod, the Novotorzhok Monastery, Pskov, Romanovo, Shatsk, Tomsk, and Vologda. Addressing a variety of judicial matters—land ownership, Siberian affairs, tax collection, and the construction of new churches—they offer a view of daily interactions between the Russian people and the governing authorities. They also include excerpts from the *Ulozhenie*.

OPPOSITE: These illustrations are from the *Polnoe sobranie zakonov Rossiiskoi Imperii* (volume 36, second series, S.-Peterburg, 1861; Russian Imperial Collection). This serial publication on military regulations includes detailed instructions for artillery and cavalry field operations, such as how to mount one's horse from various starting positions. (*Law Library Rare Book Collection*; LCCN 67043126)

Фиг. 1.

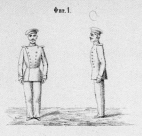

Фиг. 2.

1-й моментъ.

Фиг. 3.

2-й моментъ.

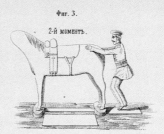

Фиг. 4.

3-й моментъ.

Фиг. 5.

4-й моментъ.

Фиг. 6.

5-й моментъ.

Фиг. 7.

Фиг. 8.

Фиг. 9.

1-й моментъ.

Фиг. 10.

2-й моментъ.

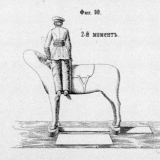

Фиг. 11.

3-й моментъ.

Фиг. 12.

4-й моментъ.

Форма

Для вольнонаемных людей Телеграфнаго Корпуса.

Форма

Для чинов Телеграфнаго Корпуса.

Сигналистъ.   Ревизоръ.   Курьеръ.   Пальто вольнонаемнымъ ревизорамъ, сигналистамъ, курьерамъ и сторожамъ.   Ревизоръ изъ низшихъ чиновъ.

The collection of Imperial decrees of Empress Anna (1730–40), *Ukazy Imperatritsy Anny Ioanovny*, is very rare. This collection of original *ukazy*—Imperial decrees having the force of law—covers the period from March 1732 to December 1737 and was issued to the Chief of the Medical Chancellery. The *ukazy* were often given orally and transcribed by a court official for publication by the Senate or other state printer. Anna's court officials were German, and so a number of reports appear in both Russian and German. The Law Library also holds a collection of more than one hundred individual decrees, acts, and treaties (printed broadsides and fliers) issued by Catherine the Great and at least three decrees (also printed broadsides) issued by Peter the Great (1724).

Reforms of the Russian legal system introduced in the nineteenth century are well represented in the Law Library collection. A successful attempt to supplant the 1649 Code was a two-volume draft criminal code entitled *Proekt ugolovnago ulozheniia Rossiiskoi Imperii*, prepared by the Council of State in 1813 to 1814 by order of Tsar Alexander I. Much of this draft was incorporated into the Russian Criminal Code of 1832. In 1830 Tsar Nicholas I ordered the compilation and codification of Russian law, which resulted in the publication of the *Polnoe sobranie zakonov Rossiiskoi Imperii* (Complete collection of the laws of the Russian Empire). The set began with the Code of 1649 and continued into the reign of Nicholas II up to the year 1913. One of the complete sets of the *Polnoe sobranie zakonov* is said to have been owned by a member of the Romanov family.

An important publication from the reign of Nicholas I is the *Ukazy Ego Imperatorskago Velichestva Samoderzhtsa Vserossiiskago iz Pravitel'stvuiushchago Senata* (The Decrees of H.I.M. Autocrat of All the Russias sent from the ruling Senate), covering, with minor gaps, the period from 1768 to 1866 in ninety-seven volumes. And an important record of the last year of the reign of Nicholas II is the *Zhurnaly Soveta Ministrov* (Minutes of the sessions of the Council of Ministers) of 1914. This set of journals records meetings held by the Russian Cabinet throughout 1914, including those dealing with the outbreak of war.

In 1938, the Law Library acquired about a hundred fifty publications relating to the anti-Soviet governments of the Civil War period, 1918 to 1921. These hard-to-obtain items include the laws and decrees signed by Russian White Army General Anton Denikin as the head of the anti-Soviet government of southern Russia and reports of the governmental departments of the Don Cossack region, presented to the regional legislature that met at the end of the summer of 1918. They include as well the official gazettes published by the government of Admiral Aleksandr Kolchak in Siberia.

OPPOSITE: Also From the *Polnoe sobranie zakonov Rossiiskoi Imperii* of 1861, this plate shows Regulation No. 37611, "Uniforms of members of the Cable Corps," and Regulation No. 37636, "Uniforms of railroad and telegraph personnel." (*Law Library Rare Book Collection;* LCCN 67043126)

Common Law Systems

THE COLLECTIONS ON COMMON LAW, constituting the largest collection in the Law Library of Congress, are those founded on, or conceptually derived from, the English legal system: primarily the laws of England, jurisdictions of the former British Empire (now the Commonwealth), American Colonial, and U.S. Law.

Common Law is best described as a body of law whose historical basis is the Customary Law of England, as developed by the courts. It stands in distinction to the Continental Civil Law systems that rely on codes covering large areas of the law.

A major portion of the Common Law is stated in court judgments that have acquired binding or persuasive authority under the doctrine of precedent. Formerly a distinction was made between the Common Law and principles and rules of equity developed by separate courts of chancery. The two systems were mostly fused under the Judicature Act of 1873. In modern times, legislation forms an increasingly important and even a predominant part in certain subject areas in stating the principles and rules of law.

ENGLAND

The Law Library contains an impressive collection of historic English Acts. Other than that, the Law Library Rare Book Collection is about evenly divided between rare Common Law sources and those of European Continental systems.

One of the treasures of the Law Library's English Law Collection is the first edition of *Tenores nouelli* (Littleton's Tenures) by London printers John Lettou and William de Machlinia (London, ca. 1482), generally regarded as the first law book printed in England. The well-preserved copy in the Law Library's collection is one of only three known in existence. Sir Thomas Littleton (d. 1481) wrote this book in Law French, the legal language of the English court, as a teaching aid for his son who was studying law. Sir Edward Coke (1552–1634) translated the book into the English vernacular in the first volume of his *Institutes*, published in 1628. Volume 1 of Coke's *Institutes* was, in fact, titled *Coke on Littleton*. A subsequent edition of *Coke on Littleton* in the Law Library was found to have a handwritten letter in it drafted by a descendant of Coke to a descendant of Littleton (who owned the volume in question) discussing whether or not the handwritten marginalia in the book was the handwriting of the original Sir Edward Coke. Two incunabula, several sixteenth-century editions, and some fifty other editions of *Littleton's Tenures* are housed in the Law Library's Rare Book Collection.

OPPOSITE: *Magna charta.* This is a fourteenth-century miniature version of the famous English charter of 1215 that gave nobles certain rights which prefigured democratic institutions in England; still bound in its original pigskin wrapper, it is a rare item even among collections in Great Britain. (*Law Library Rare Book Collection; LCCN 2004574702*)

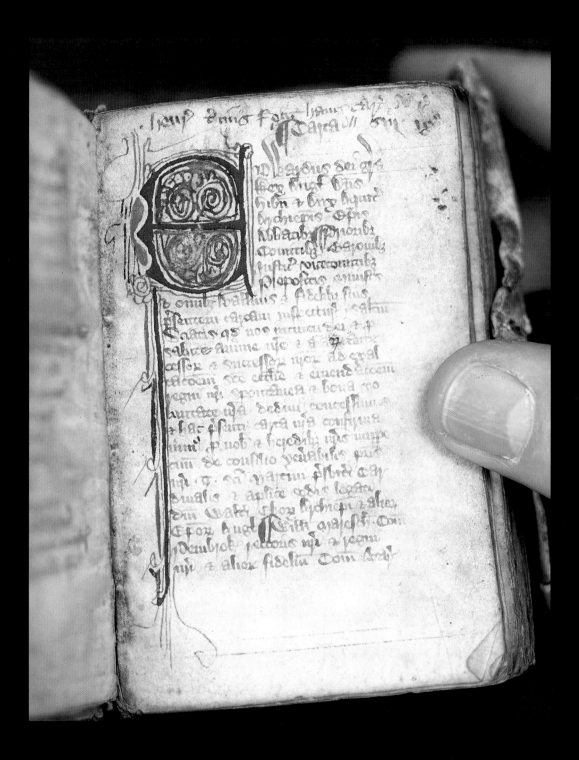

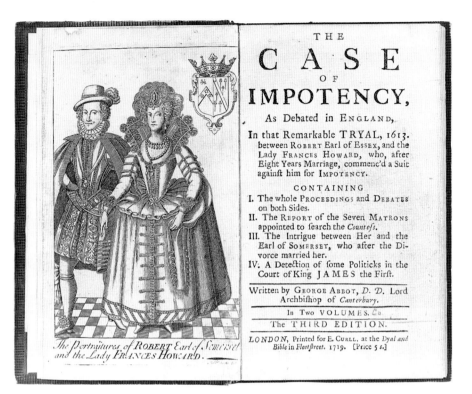

ABOVE, LEFT: This book of English statutes was published by Robert Redman from 1530 to 1540 and again by W. Middleton in the years 1541 to 1547. (*Law Library Rare Book Collection*; LCCN 14003006)

ABOVE, RIGHT: *The case of impotency.* Robert Devereux, the Third Lord Essex, was married at age fourteen to Frances Howard, one year his junior. The marriage, which lasted eight years, may not have been consummated. Frances claimed Devereux was impotent with her but not with other women and sued for divorce in order to marry the man she loved, Robert Carr, a favorite at the English Court. (*The case of impotency, as debated in England, in that remarkable trial. . . .* (London, 1719), by George Abbot (1562–1633). (*Law Library Rare Book Collection*; LCCN 47043247)

Year Book Literature. Among the wealth of sources of early English law in the custody of the Law Library is a superior collection of Year Books, the reports of pleadings in cases decided in English courts from the reign of Edward I (1272–1307) to that of Henry VIII (1509–47). Unlike the contemporary court records, which furnish only a formal recitation of the facts of the case and the decision reached by the court, the Year Books provide an account of the arguments presented by the sergeants at law in court and of the responses of the presiding judges to these arguments. It is thus possible, through close study of the Year Books, to trace the evolution of the Common Law in England through the development of the system of pleadings in use in the courts. However, the Year Books are not just a source for the legal historian but an invaluable source for the study of the development of the English language and of English social history.

The earliest Year Book now known to exist is one of the eighteenth year of Edward I (1289–90)—*18 Edward I*, according to the English system of citation— and the Year Book series stops with that of *27 Henry VIII* in 1535. Year Books for one or more years are available for all intervening reigns although not every year is available, and for those years that were published, not every term was included.

Year Books have been published in three forms: as manuscripts; in multitudinous, so-called black-letter editions published from the advent of printing in England in the late fifteenth century to the late seventeenth century; and, beginning in the late nineteenth century, in bilingual editions edited by scholars. There are as well three famous abridgments of Year Book cases which appeared during the first century of Year Book publishing.

The Law Library's collection, which is strongest in black-letter editions and bilingual editions, does contain the Gell manuscript book (*Liber Antonii Gell*); the book, dating from the mid-sixteenth century, is partly if not wholly in the hand of Anton Gell. Begun in the 1550s, the collection includes Year Book *13 Richard II*, and *18–19* and *26–27 Henry VIII*, with slight variations from the printed reports (Law Library Rare Book Collection; LCCN 2004574703).

Black-Letter Editions. Year Book printing in England began with the issuance by John Lettou and William de Machilina of the Year Books *33–27 Henry VI* during the years 1482 through 1484. Over the subsequent two centuries, Year Books were issued randomly by various printers in overlapping black-letter editions whose diverse composition and abundance have sorely challenged the descriptive powers of modern bibliographers. In 1678 to 1680, a final black-letter edition appeared in eleven parts. In this "standard" or "vulgate" edition, Year Books previously printed in separate editions for the reigns from Edward III to Henry VIII were brought together with the previously unpublished Year Books of *1–19 Edward I*. This edition also includes the *Liber Assisarum*, the accounts of cases heard by the assizes commissioners in the counties during the reign of Edward III (1327–77). With the publication of the standard edition, only the reign of Richard II (1377–99) was left unrepresented in Year Book printing, although, as noted, the materials published for Edward I were memoranda cases heard in the Exchequer and not Year Books proper.

In 1905, the Library of Congress purchased en bloc the outstanding Year Book collection of William V. Kellen, Esq., of Boston, the numerous volumes of which constitute the foundation of the Law Library's Year Book Collection. As described by Charles Carroll Soule (1842–1913) in his pioneer study of Year Book bibliography (14 *Harvard Law Review* no. 8, April 1901: 559), the Kellen collection was "especially rich in editions printed during the latter half of the sixteenth century." Comparisons of the Law Library's holdings against Soule's Year Book bibliography and *A Bibliography of Early English Law Books* by Joseph Henry Beale (1861–1943) reveal that there are very few regnal years for which the Law Library does not have at least one of the available separate black-letter editions. Its holdings include almost two hundred editions printed by Richard Tottell, the preeminent figure in Year Book printing, who between the years 1553 and 1593 printed over two hundred

LADY GROSVENOR & DUKE of CUMBERLAND,

SURPRISED by the SERVANT.

J. Cruikshank fec.t

Pub.d March 1.st 1814 by M. Jones Newgate Str.t

THE

ANNALS OF GALLANTRY;

OR, THE

Conjugal Monitor:

Being a Collection of

CURIOUS AND IMPORTANT

TRIALS FOR DIVORCES,

AND

Actions of Crim. Con.

DURING THE PRESENT REIGN;

Accompanied with

Biographical Memoirs and Anecdotes,

AND

ILLUSTRATED WITH NOTES.

BY A. MOORE, LL.D.

" Is whispering nothing ?
" Is leaning cheek to cheek—kissing with inside lip—
" Stopping the career of laughter with a sigh—
" Skulking in corners—wishing clocks more swift ;
" Hours, minutes ; noon, midnight ; and all eyes
" Blind but their's, their's only, that would, unseen,
" Be wicked—Is this nothing ?
" Why then the world, and all that's in it,
" Is nothing !"   SHAKSPEARE.
                    " Such an act
" That blurs the blush and grace of modesty ;
" Calls virtue, hypocrite ; takes off the rose
" From the fair forehead of an innocent love,
" And sets a blister there ; makes marriage vows
" As false as dicers' oaths."   SHAKSPEARE.

VOL. I.

LONDON:
PRINTED FOR THE PROPRIETORS,
AND SOLD BY M. JONES, NO. 5, NEWGATE STREET.

1814.

fifty editions. There are also a number of editions printed by Richard Pynson, who beginning in 1480 was the first major printer of law books in England. The collection also includes, of course, all eleven parts of the standard edition published in 1678 to 1680.

Later Editions. A major obstacle to full use of the Year Books is the difficulty in reading their texts, both in manuscript form and in the black-letter editions. Not only do they appear in a little-known and now unused language, i.e., the so-called Law French, but they also are replete with arbitrary abbreviations and outright errors made by reporters, copyists, and printers. Putting the Year Books into more readable form has been one of the aims of the three series of modern editions of these early sources of the Common Law. A further aim has been to put together Year Books from available manuscripts that appeared in a black-letter edition. Currently, Year Books have been published in modern editions in three series totaling over fifty volumes, all of which are available in the Law Library collection. The only continuing Year Book series consists of *1–12* and *14 Edward III*, and *49 Henry IV* and *10 Edward VI.* All but one of these volumes is listed in *A Centenary Guide to the Publications of the Selden Society*, published in 1987 by the Society. The Rolls Series, published from 1863 to 1911 under the superintendence of the Master of the Rolls, covers *20–22* and *30–35 Edward I* and is in five volumes, and *11–20 Edward III* is in fifteen volumes. The Ames Foundation published in seven volumes the Year Books for *2* and *6–13 Richard II.* The Law Library has the final three volumes of this series, which cover the years 11 through 13. All of these volumes contain the Anglo-Norman text of the manuscript, along with a modern English translation and editorial enhancements, such as historical commentary and explanations of terms and abbreviations used in the text. The volumes of the Rolls Series edited by L. O. Pike and those of the Selden Society are noted for the fact that they provided additional information about the case at issue beyond the text available in the manuscript.

Abridgments. Also in the Law Library's collections are three of four abridgments of Year Book cases that were published during the hundred-year period following the appearance of the first published Year Book. These abridgments are valued not only because they constitute digests of cases or points presented at greater length in the Year Books themselves, but also because they include abridgments of cases not appearing in the printed Year Books. In each of the three the cases or points which are grouped under various titles generally take their names from the

OPPOSITE: *The annals of gallantry; or, The conjugal monitor: being a collection of curious and important trials for divorces* (London, 1814–15). (*Law Library Rare Book Collection;* LCCN 45022869)

type of writ that initiated the actions giving rise to the abridged reports. The earliest of the three, known as *Abridgment of Cases* by Nicholas Statham (d. 1472), digests over thirty-seven hundred cases or points under two hundred fifty-eight titles; most modern bibliographers place its publication date in the 1490s. *Statham's Abridgment* is included in the Law Library collection both in its rare original edition and in a 1915 translation by Margaret Center Klingelsmith. Possibly the finest of the Year Book abridgments, Sir Anthony Fitzherbert's *La Graunde Abridgement* was first published in 1516. The Law Library has this original edition along with editions printed in 1565 and 1577 and finding tables for these editions. The later abridgment by Robert Brooke, which rivals Fitzherbert's work in repute among scholars, digests some twenty thousand cases under four hundred and four titles. The Law Library has copies of the 1573, 1576, and 1586 editions of this work. The collection also includes multiple sixteenth-century editions of selected cases compiled by Richard Bellewe (fl. 1585) from *Brooke's Abridgement*, which was first published in 1578. In addition to the abridgments of the Year Books, the Law Library also has a collection of the *Abridgement of the Booke of Assises*. Although technically not considered to be a part of the Year Books, the *Boke of the Assises* or *Liber Assisarum*, provides accounts of cases from the Assize courts of Edward III. The Law Library has a 1555 edition of the abridgment printed by Tottell. The Law Library also holds several editions of the *Abridgments of the law* and *Abridgments of cases in equity* of Matthew Bacon (fl. 1730).

A folio volume by Francis Sandford presents to the modern reader an interesting depiction of judges, court officials, and leading lawyers that is an exquisitely detailed source for seventeenth-century English costume as well. Among the legal luminaries of court shown here, the officials of the Court of Chancery were at one time allegedly honest and upright, but were later implicated in various abuses. Courts of chancery still exist in some U.S. states today.

A pillar of the development of the Common Law, the numerous works of Sir William Blackstone (1723–80) in the Law Library include multiple editions of this English jurist's *Commentaries on the Laws of England* from British, Irish, and American sources. The Law Library has close to forty English and Irish editions of the *Commentaries*, including the Oxford first edition of 1765–69, and approximately fifty American editions, including the first American edition, published in 1771–72. Other Blackstone materials include abridgments and extracts of the *Commentaries*, as well as many editions of *An Analysis of the Laws of England*, the *Reports of Cases Determined in the Several Courts of Westminster-Hall, from 1746 to 1779*, and various other legal tractates, essays, and treatises.

OPPOSITE: This magnificent specimen of the *Magna Carta* on cream-colored vellum is the first book to have been printed in England entirely in letters of gold. John Whittaker, a Westminster printer and bookbinder, published this book in 1816 to display his gold typography. (*Law Library Rare Book Collection; LCCN 2004572905*). Some other editions of the *Magna Carta* with subsequent statutes may also be found in the Rosenwald Collection in the Rare Book and Special Collections Division.

Johannes Dei gratia rex Anglie dominus Hyber-
nie dux Normannie et Aquitanie comes An-
degavie archiepiscopis episcopis abbatibus
comitibus baronibus justiciariis forestariis
vicecomitibus prepositis ministris et omnibus
ballivis et fidelibus suis salutem Sciatis nos
intuitu Dei et pro salute anime nostre et
omnium antecessorum et heredum nostrorum ad honorem Dei et
exaltationem sancte ecclesie et emendationem regni nostri per consilium venerabilium patrum nostrorum Stephani Cant' archiepiscopi totius Anglie primatis et sancte Romane ecclesie cardi-
nalis Henrici Dublin' archiepiscopi Willielmi London' Petri
Winton' Joscelini Bathon' et Glaston' Hugonis Lincoln' Willelmi
Wygorn' Willielmi Coventr' et Benedicti Roff' episcoporum ma-
gistri Panduli domini pape subdiaconi et familiaris et fratris
Eymerici magistri milicie templi in Anglia et nobilium virorum
Willielmi Mariscalli comitis Penbrok' Willielmi comitis Sar'
Willielmi comitis Warenn' Willielmi comitis Arundell' Alani de
Galweya constabularii Scottie Warini filii Geroldi Huberti de
Burgo senescalli Pictavie Petri filii Hereberti Hugonis de Nevill'
Mathei filii Hereberti Thome Basset Alani Basset Philippi de
Albin' Roberti de Roppel' Johannis Mariscalli Johannis filii
Hugonis et aliorum fidelium nostrorum In primis concessisse
Deo et hac presenti carta nostra confirmasse pro nobis et heredibus
nostris in perpetuum quod Anglicana ecclesia libera sit et habeat
jura sua integra et libertates suas illesas et ita volumus obser-
vari quod apparet ex eo quod libertatem electionum que maxima et
magis necessaria reputatur ecclesie Anglicane mera et spontanea
voluntate ante discordiam inter nos et barones nostros motam
concessimus et carta nostra confirmavimus et eam optinuimus a
domino papa Innocentio tertio confirmari quam et nos observabi-
mus et ab heredibus nostris in perpetuum bona fide volumus obser-
vari Concessimus etiam omnibus liberis hominibus regni
nostri pro nobis et heredibus nostris in perpetuum omnes libertates
subscriptas habendas et tenendas eis et heredibus suis de nobis et

Masters in Chancery, in number 10.   *The Kings Sergeants at Law, in number 5.*   *The Kings Attorney*   *The So...*

...ry Seven   *Judges, in number 9.*   *The Lᵈ Chief Justice of the Kings Bench.*   *The Lᵈ Chief Baron of the Exchequer.*

(5)

Francis Sandford (1630–94), *The history of the coronation of the most high, most mighty, and most excellent monarch, James II . . . in the City of Westminster, on Thursday the 23 of April . . . 1685* (London, 1687). This folio volume is an excellent depiction of judges, court officials, and leading lawyers, in addition to being an exquisitely detailed source for seventeenth-century English costumes. (*Law Library Rare Book Collection;* LCCN 04003138)

Lincoln's Inn Hall

William John Loftie (1839–1911), *The Inns of court and chancery* (London, 1893). Herbert Railton's picturesque, well-known illustrations grace this historical account of the Inns of Court, England's ancient "rookeries of lawyers"—Lincoln's Inn, Inner Temple, Middle Temple, and Gray's Inn. Lincoln's Inn, whose Hall and Library are depicted here, has been occupied by law students and lawyers since 1311. The Honorable Society of Lincoln's Inn has called to the bar many who rose to fame in the law and other fields, including Sir Thomas More, the poet John Donne, William Penn, Horace Walpole, Lord Denning, and from the United States, President Dwight D. Eisenhower and Dean Acheson. (*Law Library Rare Book Collection;* LCCN 03012115)

Topolski's Legal London, with text by Francis Cowper (published for "The Lawyer," by Stevens and Sons, Ltd., 1961), contains wonderfully gestural drawings of British justices by Feliks Topolski, a famous "master alike of giant murals and small 'scribbles,' as he calls them." Among the interesting facts this delightful book teaches is the answer to why British lawyers wear wigs. The practice dates to the early seventeenth century when the French King Louis XIII, balded at thirty, began the fashion of long-haired wigs. The exiled British Royalists who returned home to England after the Cromwell period brought the habit with them, and though styles of men's clothing changed over time, the habit of wigs continues. (*Law Library Rare Book Collection;* LCCN 62001810)

The Law Library of Congress possesses today the world's largest and most comprehensive collection of Anglo-American Law, although larger collections in specialized subject areas may be found in other research libraries. As the first priority for the Law Library was always to serve Congress, it aimed at a record as complete as possible of American Federal and State Law. Thus, the American materials include original editions of Colonial, State, and Territorial Session Laws, Codes and other compilations of statutes and administrative regulations, and most of all, court reports. The holdings of congressional documents are surpassed only by those of the House of Representatives and the Senate themselves. They begin with the September 5, 1774, issue of the *Journals of the Continental Congress*. Law Library policy is to keep two copies of almost all commercial legal publications at the federal and state level. Until the late nineteenth century, monographic literature on specific topics, though, was almost unknown. Earlier studies often consisted of sporadically published comparative treatises on English and contemporary American jurisprudence and law, in particular on criminal law, process, and execution—cf. John Milton Goodenow (1782–1838), *Historical sketches of the principles and maxims of American jurisprudence, in contrast with the doctrines of English Common Law on the subject of crimes and punishment* (Steubenville, Ohio, 1819); or works such as those of the Continental jurisprudent Carl J. A. Mittermaier (1787– 1867) on comparative criminal procedure of Great Britain seen against the moral, political, and social background of contemporary American legal practice: *Das englische, schottische und nordamerikanische Strafverfahren im Zusammenhange mit den politischen, sittlichen und sozialen Zustaenden. . . .* (Erlangen, 1851). But today, judging by the depth and breadth of the monographic American collections, no other research library will easily measure up to the holdings of the Law Library.

Court Reports and Statutes. American Law—during its early formation—traced itself back to a number of European legal systems that were brought to shore with the settlers of the New World. Common Law of the English strain was one of the major systems breaking ground. But already during the colonial period and the initial years of the Republic, the notion was adopted that English Law, although recognized as a richly developed system with constructs of concepts, seemed not to fit the situation or needs of the young society. Above all, it seemed desirable to have an uncomplicated administration of justice and a process of speedy adjudication. Over time it became apparent that without a record of decisions and the legal reasoning upon which the decisions were based, legal uncertainty was inevitable. The main lasting contribution that the English Common Law system made to American Law was its established reporting system.

Among the Law Library acquisitions in the late 1930s is a rare collection of approximately one hundred cases on appeal to the Privy Council in England from the colonies of Antigua, Barbados, Jamaica, and St. Christopher, as well as Massachusetts, New Hampshire, Rhode Island, and Virginia. These colonial appeals of the second half of the eighteenth century, including all types of litigation, are the only accounts, aside from some fragmentary ones, of early colonial cases because of absence of a regular law reporting system at that time.

American court reports, initially a private endeavor, did not appear before 1789. The first court reports were published in Connecticut (one year earlier than the first U.S. Supreme Court report), "because of uncertainty and contradiction attending the judicial decisions in this state"—*Kirby's Reports of Cases Adjudicated in the Superior Court [of Connecticut] from the year 1785, to May 1788*; cf. Morris L. Cohen, *A Guide to the Early Reports of the Supreme Court of the United States* (Littleton, Colorado, 1995). It was also maintained that the "reporting of decisions of important cases, their histories, grounds and principles of the decisions would in time produce a permanent system of common law."

The *U.S. Supreme Court Reports* were published beginning in 1790 by the seven first reporters: Alexander J. Dallas (1759–1817, 4 volumes); William Cranch (1769–1855, 9 volumes); Henry Wheaton (1785–1848, 12 volumes); Richard Peters (1779–1848, 17 volumes); Benjamin C. Howard (1791–1872, 24 volumes); Jeremiah S. Black (1810–1883, 2 volumes), and John W. Wallace (1815–1884, 23 volumes). For more on the evolving reporting process, biographical sketches, and a bibliography of the early reports, see Cohen's *Guide to the Early Reports.* The important and up-to-date collection of *Supreme Court Reports* in the Law Library, including the early reports, counts five hundred and forty volumes. The Law Library has one of the most complete sets of both the records (going back to 1832) and briefs (going back to 1854) of the U.S. Supreme Court. The Law Library also holds a partial collection of the records and briefs of the Thirteen Circuit Courts.

The largest collections, of course, consist of the complete sets of all *Federal Reports* (ca. 10,000 volumes), the State and regional court reports, and reporter systems, with related digests, indexes, and other bibliographic aids.

An interesting early collection relating to the judicial branch in the Library is the record of the trial of U.S. Supreme Court Justice Samuel Chase, as well as his personal law library of two hundred forty-seven volumes. The Law Library Annual Report of 1931 notes that Chase, born in Somerset County, Maryland, in 1741, "distinguished himself early in life as one of the boldest opponents of the royal governor and later as the most active adversary of the British Government in his State." He was appointed by George Washington in 1796 to the U.S. Supreme Court. His impeachment trial before the Senate was noteworthy for many reasons, "but chiefly," as Law Librarian John Vance wrote, "for the ability with which he defended himself and the nature of his acquittal."

An engaging sixty-page manuscript journal of another gifted judicial mind—that of Justice James Iredell (1751–99)—is found in the Law Library Rare Book Collection. Supreme Court Justice Felix Frankfurter described Iredell as "one of the brilliant minds of his time, and, in fact, of the nation's entire history." The journal (LCCN 93236494) covers a section of Iredell's cases heard on circuit in the spring of 1793. Generally speaking, the papers of most other justices, both early and modern, may be found most often in the Manuscript Division.

Easy access to the early American statutory law is provided in the Microform Reading Room, located within the General Reading Room of the Law Library. It is a microfiche collection arranged by colony, territory and/or state, and session. This collection also includes early U.S. Session Laws, the Session Laws of the Confederate States of America, and the constitutions and laws of various American Indian nations.

The New Plymouth Colony, founded by the Pilgrims who arrived on the *Mayflower* in December 1620, made several contributions to the field of law, including the first code of laws in North America. In all, the Colony's subsequent codes, published in 1658, 1672, and 1684, expressed the fundamental values of the rule of law rather than the personal authority of leaders and of the need for the laws to be known to all members of the community. The punishment for adultery, which was set out in the 1658 Code and the 1694 laws of the Massachusetts Bay Colony, provided the title and background for Nathaniel Hawthorne's novel *The Scarlet Letter.*

Probably the largest individual collections are the Session Laws (statutes at large), the compilations of federal statutes, U.S. Code (containing all general and permanent laws of the United States in force), and the Code of Federal (administrative) Regulations. Important finding aids are the digests, indexes, and citators. The broad-based *Bibliography of Early American Law* by Morris L. Cohen (Buffalo, 1998) is an excellent reference work, organized in six volumes by type of legal materials.

In Congress July 4: 1776

Resolved, That an Application be made to the Committee of Safety of Pennsylvania for a supply of Flints for the Troops at New York.

That the President write to the Colony of Maryland and Delaware, & Request them to Imbody their Militia for the Flying Camp with all Expedition, and to March them without Delay to the City of Philadelphia

That Copies of the Declaration be sent to the several Assemblies, Conventions & Councils of Safety, & to the several Commanding Officers of the Continental Troops, that it be proclaim'd in each of the United States, and at the head of the Army

That the Secret Committee be instructed to order the Flints at Rhode Island which belong to the Continent to be sent to the General at New York,

That Doct. Franklin, Mr John Adams & Mr Jefferson bring in a device for a Seal for the United States of America

July 5:

Resolved, That a Letter be written by the Presidt. to Govr. Cook, Requesting him to order Fifty Ship Carpenters to be Engaged and Sent to General Schuyler at Albany as soon as possible, in order to Build Vessells for the defence of the Lakes, to be Engag'd on the best terms, at the Expence of the Continent,

Resolved, That an order issue to Coll Haslett of the Battalion in Delaware Government to Station one Company at Lewis Town, and to March the Remaining seven Companies of his Battalion to Wilmington & there Remain until the further order of this Congress

That General Washington be empower'd, if he

Known as *Dunlap's Declaration of Independence* (Philadelphia, John Dunlap, [1776]), this copy of the *Declaration* was the copy circulated by George Washington on July 4, 1776. (*Rare Book and Special Collections Division; LCCN 2003576546*)

Fast-Day Proclamation. For students of the relationship between religion and state in the formative years of the American experiment, the collection of presidential and congressional proclamations offers a rich resource. This proclamation, printed in Philadelphia in 1779 by the Continental Congress, for instance, is one of the many so-called fast-day proclamations by the Founding Fathers appealing for such days of prayer and "humiliation" in penance to a Supreme Being. (*Rare Book and Special Collections Division; LCCN 90898103*)

PROCLAMATION.

WHEREAS, in juſt Puniſhment of our manifold Tranſgreſſions, it hath pleaſed the Supreme Diſpoſer of all Events to viſit theſe United States with a calamitous War, through which his Divine Providence hath hitherto in a wonderful Manner conducted us, ſo that we might acknowledge that the Race is not to the Swift, nor the Battle to the Strong: AND WHEREAS, notwithſtanding the Chaſtiſements received and Benefits beſtowed, too few have been ſufficiently awakened to a Senſe of their Guilt, or warmed with Gratitude, or taught to amend their Lives and turn from their Sins, that ſo he might turn from his Wrath: AND WHEREAS, from a Conſciouſneſs of what we have merited at his Hands, and an Apprehenſion that the Malevolence of our diſappointed Enemies, like the Incredulity of Pharaoh, may be uſed as the Scourge of Omnipotence to vindicate his ſlighted Majeſty, there is Reaſon to fear that he may permit much of our Land to become the Prey of the Spoiler, our Borders to be ravaged, and our Habitations deſtroyed:

RESOLVED,

THAT it be recommended to the ſeveral States to appoint the Firſt *Thurſday* in *May* next to be a Day of Faſting, Humiliation, and Prayer to Almighty God, that he will be pleaſed to avert thoſe impending Calamities which we have but too well deſerved: That he will grant us his Grace to repent of our Sins, and amend our Lives according to his Holy Word: That he will continue that wonderful Protection which hath led us through the Paths of Danger and Diſtreſs: That he will be a Huſband to the Widow, and a Father to the fatherleſs Children, who weep over the Barbarities of a Savage Enemy: That he will grant us Patience in Suffering, and Fortitude in Adverſity: That he will inſpire us with Humility, Moderation, and Gratitude in proſperous Circumſtances: That he will give Wiſdom to our Councils, Firmneſs to our Reſolutions, and Victory to our Arms: That he will bleſs the Labours of the Huſbandman, and pour forth Abundance, ſo that we may enjoy the Fruits of the Earth in due Seaſon: That he will cauſe Union, Harmony, and mutual Confidence to prevail throughout theſe States: That he will beſtow on our great Ally all thoſe Bleſſings which may enable him to be gloriouſly inſtrumental in protecting the Rights of Mankind, and promoting the Happineſs of his Subjects: That he will bountifully continue his paternal Care to the Commander in Chief, and the Officers and Soldiers of the United States: That he will grant the Bleſſings of Peace to all contending Nations, Freedom to thoſe who are in Bondage, and Comfort to the Afflicted: That he will diffuſe Uſeful Knowledge, extend the Influence of True Religion, and give us that Peace of Mind which the World cannot give: That he will be our Shield in the Day of Battle, our Comforter in the Hour of Death, and our kind Parent and merciful Judge through Time and through Eternity.

Done in CONGRESS, *this Twentieth Day of March, in the Year of Our Lord One Thouſand Seven Hundred and Seventy-Nine, and in the Third Year of our Independence.*

JOHN JAY, Preſident.

Atteſt. CHARLES THOMSON, Secretary.

PHILADELPHIA: PRINTED BY HALL AND SELLERS.

Constitutional Law. One of the greatest treasures in the Library of Congress is Thomas Jefferson's *Rough Draft of the Declaration of Independence.* The draft, written on four separate pages in Jefferson's small, precise handwriting, is the form in which Jefferson submitted the *Declaration,* together with all corrections, additions, and deletions made by John Adams, Benjamin Franklin, the Committee of Five, and the Congress. In the text, Jefferson enclosed in brackets those parts stricken out by Congress sitting as the committee of the whole. Some time later, perhaps after 1800, Jefferson indicated in the margins some, but not all, of the corrections suggested by Adams and Franklin.

Documents from the years of the Continental Congress (1774–89) may be found in the Library's Continental Congress Broadside Collection, http://memory.loc.gov/ammem/bdsds/contcong.html (253 titles), and the Constitutional Convention Broadside Collection, http://memory.loc.gov/ammem/bdsds/consconv.html (21 titles); these two hundred seventy-four documents cover the work of Congress and the drafting and ratification of the *Constitution.* Items include extracts of the journals of Congress, resolutions, proclamations, committee reports, treaties, and early printed versions of the *U. S. Constitution* (http://hdl.loc.gov/loc.rbc/bdsdcc.c0801), and the *Declaration of Independence* (http://hdl.loc.gov/loc.rbc/bdsdcc.02101). Most Broadsides (http://memory.loc.gov/ammem/bdsds/broadsd.html) are one page in length; others range from one to twenty-eight pages. A number of these items contain manuscript annotations not recorded elsewhere that offer insight into the delicate process of creating consensus. In many cases, multiple copies bearing manuscript annotations are available for comparison and contrast.

The major objection to the new *Constitution* had been the absence of a Bill of Rights, and only after both houses of Congress approved the Bill of Rights on September 25 did the last two holdout states, North Carolina and Rhode Island, join the Union. This collection includes the texts of laws, appropriations, and the proposed amendments to the *Constitution* that formed the Bill of Rights.

A very interesting work by the noted German publicist Johann Jacob Moser (1701–85) may also be found in the collections. It offers students of American history a contemporary glimpse of the New World: *Nord-America nach den Friedensschlüssen vom Jahr 1783. Nebst 1. einem Vorbericht von America überhaupt, 2. einigen Charten, und 3. einem hinlänglichen Register,* Leipzig, 1784–85 (North-America after the peace treaties of 1783, including an introduction to America, accompanied by several maps and a register).

State Law. The collection of pre–Civil War Session Laws of the American states and territories contains approximately sixteen thousand volumes, which in some cases date back to the earliest available issuances of the Session Laws in the initial colonial or territorial period. Among the rare items in the collection are E. Stout's 1804 printing of the *Laws for the Government of the District of Louisiana, Passed by the Governor and Judges of the Indiana Territory, at Their First Session, Uegun* [sic] *and Held at Vincennes, on Monday the First Day of October, 1804* (LCCN 77352030). This is the earliest holding in the Library of an Indiana imprint from the present boundaries of that state.

Many of the Law Library's extensive holdings of state codes and compilations appear in a standard reference work, Grace E. Macdonald's *Check-list of Statutes of States of the United States of America.* Included is a rare edition of the *Code noir; ou, Loi municipale . . . & le commerce des esclaves négres, dans la province de la Louisiana* (New Orléans, 1778; LCCN 34037508), a Louisiana code based on the first *Code noir,* decreed by Louis XIV in 1685 "for the government . . . of the French islands of America, and for the discipline and commerce in negroes and slaves in the said countries."

All but one edition of the Session Laws of both the Provisional government and the Confederate government of the Confederate States of America listed in Grace E. Macdonald's *Check-list of Session Laws* are maintained in the Law Library collection. The collection also includes the sole edition of *The Statutes at Large of the Provisional Government of the Confederate States of America. . . .* (Richmond, R. M. Smith, 1864), listed in Macdonald's *Check-list of Statutes of States of the United States of America.*

The Law Library's separate editions of State Laws include an especially rare eleven-page pamphlet, *A Catalogue of Fees Established by the Governour and Council at the Humble Request of the Assembly,* printed in New York by William Bradford in 1693. It is the Library of Congress's earliest imprint that names New York as the place of publication. It is bound in the back of Bradford's printing of *The Laws & Acts of the General Assembly. . . .* (New-York, 1694), which is the next earliest imprint and the first compilation of the laws printed in the state.

Many other items in the collection of early state materials are also of great bibliographic interest. Printed by Lewis Timothy in 1736, *The Laws of the Province of South-Carolina* is one of the finest examples of early American printing, with its title page printed in red and black and signed by William Bull, Jr., acting governor of South Carolina, 1760 to 1775 (LCCN 32007970). Other items of special note are *A Collection of Charters and Other Publick Acts Relating to the Province of Pennsylvania,* printed and sold by Benjamin Franklin in 1740 (LCCN 66038823), and a *Complete Body of the Laws of Maryland,* the oldest Maryland imprint in the Library of Congress, printed in Annapolis by Thomas Reading in 1700.

Lincoln biographer and investigative jour-
nalist Ida Minerva Tarbell's (1857–1944)
exposé of John D. Rockefeller's illegal activities in the early days of the oil industry inspired this cartoon, entitled "Next!"
by Udo Keppler in 1904, showing a Standard Oil tank as an octopus with tenta-
cles grasping the steel, copper, and shipping industries, as well as a state house
and the U.S. Capitol, and reaching for
the White House. (*Prints and Photographs
Division; LC-USZ4-435*)

The *Laws of the territory of Illinois*, published in 1815, is another first state
compilation and is of especial interest in that it includes a topical-alphabetical
arrangement and contains the laws of 1812 to 1814, which were not published in
any other source until 1920. This is also the earliest Illinois imprint in the
Library of Congress.

Lincolniana. The Library of Congress has a wealth of Lincolniana, including two
manuscript copies of the Gettysburg Address, Lincoln's letters, presidential
papers and other papers, as well as the contents of his pockets the night he was
assassinated in Ford's Theater. Lincoln scholarship has been given an added
impetus by the founding in 1997 of the Abraham Lincoln Institute, which holds
symposia and various research presentations at the Library of Congress. A vast
amount of Lincoln-related material has been uncovered in recent years, much of
it having to do with his law practice.

Political Cartoons. Topical drawings have had a powerful contributing effect on developments in the field of law. The Library has voluminous historic and contemporary cartoon collections, found especially in the Prints and Photographs Division, Manuscript Division, and the Rare Book and Special Collections Division.

Civil Rights. Slavery in the United States was governed by an extensive body of law developed between the 1660s and the 1860s. Every slave state had its slave code and body of court decisions. Slavery was defined as a permanent condition, inherited through the mother, and slaves were defined as property, usually in terms similar to real estate. Slaves could not own property or enter into contracts; thus no slave marriage had any legal standing. Under the slave codes, free blacks were also regulated, often with controls on their movements and employment and a requirement to leave the state after emancipation.

When the District of Columbia was established in 1800, the laws of Maryland, including its Slave Laws, remained in force. Additional laws were then made by the cities of Washington and Georgetown and the unincorporated rural section of the District. By southern standards, the District's slave codes were moderate. Slaves were permitted to hire out their services and to live apart from their masters. Free blacks were permitted to live in the city and to operate private schools. On the other hand, Chapter 94 in the printed edition of the *Black Code of the District of Columbia* (New York, 1848) reads as follows:

Chapter XCIV.

PUNISHMENT OF SLAVES FOR BATHING IN CERTAIN WATERS *If any slave shall, before the hour of nine o'clock, P.M., and after the hour of five o'clock, A.M., bathe in the Potomac or Rock Creek, within the jurisdiction of this Corporation, he shall be publicly whipped, not exceeding twenty stripes.*
Ordinances of the Corporation of Georgetown, 1814, April 2d, Sect. 2.

If any slave bathe in the Canal, within the jurisdiction of this Corporation, he shall be publicly whipped, not exceeding twenty-one stripes.
Ordinances of the Corporation of Georgetown, 1840, May 16th.

Chapter 98 of the same Code lists a provision dating from 1827 that any slave caught flying "any kite or kites" within the same jurisdiction who cannot pay a fine of two dollars (the fine to be split between the informant and the corporation) may be punished by whipping at the mayor's discretion. By 1860 the District of Columbia was home to 11,131 free blacks and 3,185 slaves. Slavery in the District of Columbia ended on April 16, 1862.

- Slaves -

A slave is a human being, who is by
law deprived of his or her liberty for
life, and is the property of another.
A slave has no political rights and generally has no civil rights.

When the fact of slavery is clear, the
nature of the relation of Master and slave
admits of no modification; nor will courts
either of law or equity lend aid to the attempts of individuals to ingraft upon it
new and incongruous features. A slave
cannot become partially free. The law
recognizes only freedom on the one side
and slavery on the other; and there is
no intermediate Status. See Maria vs
Surbaugh, 2 Rand. 228. –

Where a negro girl was given by will,
on the terms that she was to be held
not as a bound slave, but under
the care and tuition of the legatee, with
an allowance of wages; and that her
children if she had any, were to come
under the same regulation after they
paid for their raising – their labor to
be equally divided amongst all the tes-
tator's children if they chose to employ
them, the bequest was adjudged void.

(margin notes:)
Slave defined

The nature of slavery admits of no modification

A bequest of conditional slavery void

The Law Library Rare Book Collection also contains the printed slavery code *The Slavery code of the District of Columbia together with notes and judicial decisions explanatory of the same. By a Member of the Washington Bar* (Washington, L. Towers). The code was published on March 17, 1862, one month before slavery in the District ended, when President Lincoln signed a law that provided for compensation to slave owners. An Emancipation Claims Commission hired a Baltimore slave trader to assess the value of each freed slave and awarded compensation for 2,989 slaves.

Some informative research sources in the Library's collection on the subject of slavery include J. Clay Smith, Jr., *Emancipation: The Making of the Black Lawyer 1844–1944* (Philadelphia: University of Pennsylvania Press, 1993, LCCN KF299.A35 S65 1993); Helen Tunnicliff Catterall, editor, *Judicial Cases Concerning American Slavery and the Negro* (Washington, D.C.: Carnegie Institution of Washington, 1926–1937, LCCN KF4545.S5 C3 1926); and Paul Finkelman, *Slavery in the Courtroom: An Annotated Bibliography of American Cases* (Washington, D.C.: Library of Congress, 1985, LCCN KF4545.S5 A123 1985).

Legislation that is passed during wartime can be an especially absorbing study when it concerns the treatment of human and civil rights. The United States sent Japanese-American citizens born in the United States as well as Japanese aliens residing in the United States to such isolated locations as the Manzanar War Relocation Camp in California. Despite having his parents in a U.S. relocation center, one U.S. citizen of Japanese ancestry, Private Mitchie M. Miyamoto of the U.S. Army's Ninth Armored Division, was assigned to special duty as a cartoonist in the public relations section of his division. The numerous World War II–era cartoons drawn by this young San Francisco-born soldier may be viewed in the collection of the Prints and Photographs Division.

Accounts of trials provide interesting reading. The Law Library has an extensive collection of trials from various countries, although the majority are American and British, dating from the 1500s to the present. Many tabloid-like accounts, while in some instances exaggerated and sensational, nevertheless provide important source material for social historians. Although official and quasi-official transcripts are included, the major portion of the volumes on trials are in the form of monographic publications, pamphlets, and serialized accounts of trials. Graphic materials from famous trials also exist in the Prints and Photographs Collection.

The civil rights movement in the United States has been fought on many fronts and for many different individuals and groups, for American Indians, for African Americans, for women, for non-citizens of various nationalities, and for others. The Library's historic photographic and poster collections as well as

OPPOSITE: *Slavery code of the District of Columbia*, Manuscript, 1860. This manuscript, almost certainly a "practice book" produced by a law firm for its attorneys for drafting contracts and legal briefs, indicates something of the volume and routine character of legal work surrounding transactions in human property. (*Law Library Rare Book Collection*; LCCN ltf 96001559)

book collections on a wide range of human and civil rights issues provide haunting documentation of these many struggles. Victories, however, have almost always been won in the form of a case before one or more courts of law.

One of the most famous U.S. court cases is *Brown v. Board of Education of Topeka, Kansas, 347 U.S. 483* (1954), which resulted when the parents of Linda Carol Brown, African Americans, filed a suit in 1950 in a Topeka, Kansas, court so that their daughter could attend a local elementary school. When the case eventually reached the Supreme Court, Thurgood Marshall, Director of the Legal Defense and Education Fund, Inc., of the National Association for the Advancement of Colored People, gave the oral argument. In the Library's juvenile literature collection, an informative source for children learning about this landmark case is *Brown v. Board of Education: Equal Schooling for All* (Hillside, New Jersey: Enslow, 1994; LCCN KF228.B76 F57 1994).

Women's Issues. Resources concerning the efforts of women in the United States to achieve legal parity with men may be found scattered throughout the Library. An excellent introduction to legal research on women and law in the United States may be found in *American Women: A Library of Congress Guide for the Study of Women's History and Culture in the United States* (Library of Congress, 2001). Researchers interested in gender studies may also find additional relevant material on the history of the status of women among Native Americans, the slave population, African Americans, and other minorities in colonial times and in U.S. history.

The Federal Law, State Law, and Rare Law Book Collections in the Law Library all contain significant material for legal research concerning women, although as the *American Women Library of Congress Guide* points out, index terms related specifically to women often do not exist in earlier sources and call for an imaginative approach. Property, Succession, and Marriage Laws are often the exception. In addition to being generally subject to their spouses and unable to vote, women at various times in American history could not be witnesses in trials, could not enter into certain professions or trades, could not go to law school or become lawyers or judges, could not run for public office, could not enter into contracts, and did not receive equal pay for equal work.

On the other hand, the history of matriarchal regimes may be studied in the sources of the Law Library's Rare Book Collection in such works as those from the Hawaiian Islands before 1896 during the reign of Queen Liliuokalani or from certain Native American tribes living in matrilineal societies. The Law Library possesses a copy of the Wyoming Territory's act in its original format

OPPOSITE: Thurgood Marshall (1908–93) attended Howard University Law School after having been denied admission to the University of Maryland Law School in 1930. Marshall went on to win twenty-nine cases before the U.S. Supreme Court and eventually become the first African American to become a Justice on the Court (1967–91). In this photograph, the twenty-seven-year-old lawyer Marshall and another lawyer, probably Charles Houston, are shown during the court proceedings with law client Donald Gaines Murray, who had also been denied entry into the University of Maryland Law School. (*Prints and Photographs Division; LC-USZC4-4633*)

The American women's suffrage movement used dramatic means to call attention to the quest for voting rights. Lawyer Inez Boissevain, clad in white and seated on a white horse, took part in the National American Woman Suffrage Association parade on March 3, 1913, Washington, D.C. (*Prints and Photographs Division; LC-USZ62-77359*)

OPPOSITE: The Law Library's copy of the first volume of the *Chicago Law Journal* (ed. Myra Bradwell; October 1868), contains an inscription by political activist Susan B. Anthony that reads: *The first legal paper* [i.e., journal] *edited by a woman—Myra Bradwell—This file is from 1868–1869—It was Mrs. Bradwell whose right to be admitted to the Bar of Illinois was carried up to the United States Supreme Court—Senator Matthew Carpenter made the argument for her—Congressional Library Washington—D.C.—Susan B. Anthony Rochester 2.8—Jan. 1. 1903.* (*Law Library Rare Book Collection; LCCN 98178271*)

granting female suffrage in 1869, the first of all the territories and states to do so, well before the passage of the Nineteenth Amendment to the Constitution in 1920 that finally granted women the right to vote.

Myra Bradwell, the first woman lawyer in the United States, passed the Illinois Bar Exam with honors, but her application for admission to the Illinois Bar was rejected because she was a woman. The U.S. Supreme Court upheld the state's rejection of her application in *Bradwell vs. Illinois*, but Mrs. Bradwell was finally admitted in 1890 when Illinois changed its rules; she received a license to practice before the U.S. Supreme Court in 1892, two years before her death.

Another famous and engaging legal personality who championed women's rights was Belva Lockwood. Educator, lawyer, reformer, and political activist, Lockwood is remembered for many firsts, including being the first woman to run for president of the United States, the first woman to be admitted to the bar in Washington, D.C. (1873), the first woman lawyer to be admitted to practice before the Supreme Court, and the first woman to ride a tricycle through the streets of Washington, D.C., for the purpose of practical transportation. Her most outstanding legal case was to win an award totaling five million dollars in damages for the Cherokee Nation arising from encroachment on their territory.

The legal status of women throughout history and around the world, in some instances superior or much worse than that of U.S. women, may also be traced in the collections of the Law Library. Works by and about women leaders, both modern and historic, may of course be found in the General Collections, such as in *Women Who Led Nations* by Joan Axelrod-Contrada (Minneapolis, 1999).

The first legal paper edited by a
woman — Myra Bradwell — This file is from 1868 & 1869 —
It was Mrs Bradwell whose right to be admitted to the
Bar of Illinois was carried up to the United States Supreme Court
Snator Matthew Carpenter made the argument for her —

Congressional Library
Washington D.C. —

Susan B. Anthony
Rochester — N.Y. —

Jan. 1. 1903

Asian and African Law

The largest single Asian collection is Japanese. Although a comprehensive collection on all aspects of Modern Law, it offers a rich core of historic interest. The very extensive collection of legal periodicals, including gazettes, is a special strength of the Japanese holdings.

Historic Japanese society is characterized by its strict organization in "estates" or "classes" (warriors, peasants, artisans, and merchants); early administration of the country shows the influence of China (to about the mid-seventeenth century), and legal norms appear to reflect the Chinese model. Special collections include works on all historic periods of Japanese Constitutional and Feudal Law, in which the shoganate (ca. 1185–1868) occupies a special place.

Among the important historic Japanese laws are several editions of the *Goseibai shikimoku*, the Formulary for Adjudications, a compendium of precedents of mostly civil cases that was employed for the samurai of the Kamakura shogunate (1185–1333) to give them an overview of substantive and procedural rules of the period. The Asian Division's collections hold several important Japanese law sources, including a manuscript produced in the second half of the eighteenth century regarding Criminal Law, the *Kujikata osadamegaki*, and two manuscripts concerning the history of Feudal Law in Japan—one written about 1790 and entitled *Buden sōsho*, and the other written about 1801, entitled *Buke gohatto oyobi jiin ofuregaki*.

When U.S. President Fillmore's administration negotiated Japan's opening up to the West beginning in 1853, the island nation gradually began accepting certain Western ideas and influences. Especially since the 1868 Meiji Restoration, social organization and institutions were dramatically changed. Legislation and codifications follow in the footsteps of the Continental European codification movement of the mid-nineteenth century. Japan leaned initially strongly towards the French codes; a translation of the Civil Code was undertaken between 1869 and 1874. Supported by French, German, and English jurists, the first Japanese codes were drafted. A Criminal Code and Criminal Procedure Code of 1882 followed the French model; the court organization and Civil Procedure Code of 1890 were based on the German codes.

The draft of Japanese Civil Codes of 1891, initially a mirror of French Law, was never promulgated. The new draft code in its final version, promulgated in 1898, is based on the German Civil Code, although it incorporated patterns of other European civil systems. The researcher will find the various drafts of all codes, also translated in various European languages, and many editions of the six

OPPOSITE: This 1861 Japanese color woodcut shows a Dutch man and a German writing up a contract in a Yokohama mercantile house. It is demonstrative of the opening up of Japan to foreign trade. (*Prints and Photographs Division; LC-USZC4-9986*)

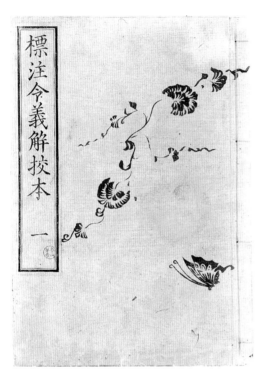

main codes with supplementary legislation and commentaries in the collections. The numerous treatises on legal philosophical axioms and jurisprudence are basically evaluations of Western concepts and rarely present comparative aspects.

A unique Japanese item from the modern period is a largely handwritten compilation of notes on lectures on Constitutional Law, taken in 1935 by special agents from the Ministry of Education's Thought Bureau, *Kaku Daigaku ni Okeru Kenpo Gakusetsu Chosa ni Kansuru Bunsho.* In a straightforward exercise in thought control, the lectures of professors of Constitutional Law at Japan's major universities were monitored by special agents.

For the reader interested in modern trends of law and society, collections on the post–World War II period provide an insight in shifting patterns of law and fluctuating societal patterns in the tension between modern capitalist-corporate standards and historically predestined social norms. The study of Japan's constitutional developments during the period of Allied Occupation (1945–52) invites the comparative evaluation of the state-religion complex under the new order, disestablishment of the State Shinto, and renunciation of the divinity of the Tennō, all documented in the collection. A Law Library volume bearing prominent "Secret" and "Top Secret" stamps was probably seized from the Ministry of Education Archives during the American Occupation of Japan (1945–52) and eventually made its way to the Library of Congress.

CHINESE LAW

The Chinese collection of the Law Library includes some four hundred titles of traditional legal material, many of which are multi-volume compilations. Most of these date from the eighteenth and nineteenth centuries. The various editions of the Code of the Qing Dynasty (1644–1911) (*Da Qing hui dian*), which each consist of sets of up to eighty volumes of Chinese woodblock editions, are complemented by collections of cases and precedents. The collection also contains numerous regulations of the ministries of the Imperial government and of the provinces. There are many volumes of the administrative regulations and activities of the provincial branches of the Imperial Salt Monopoly.

The codes of various Chinese dynasties from the Tang (618–907) through the Qing (1644–1911) were transmitted to and used as models for Korea, Japan, and Vietnam. Although the social and political structures of these countries differed considerably from those of Imperial China, Chinese law provided the basic framework and categories for indigenous systems. The Chinese codes and legal

Hyōchu ryō no gige kōhon, or Code of Ethics for Japanese Nobles, is a seventeenth-century edition of the original, initially prepared by Sanuki chief Kiyohara no Natsuno (782–837) and others. The volume includes writing in *kanbun* with reading marks and *okurigana*. (*Law Library Rare Book Collection;* LCCN 93214491)

system can be seen as a matching counterpart to the Roman Law that dominated the western end of the Eurasian continent.

The Law Library holds several editions of the *Great Qing Code* promulgated by the Qianlong Emperor in 1740 that remained substantially unchanged until the end of the dynasty in 1911. It incorporated much material from the *Code of the Ming Dynasty* (1368 to 1644), and there is clear continuity back to at least the Tang Dynasty. Probably the first translation into a European language was the Russian version, published at St. Petersburg in 1778. Its title page identifies it as a translation from "Manchurian" into Russian, which may indicate that the original was the Manchu rather than the Chinese version of the *Code*.

The English translation of the *Da Qing lü li* was originally published in 1810. This was produced by Sir George Staunton (*Ta-Tsing-Leu-Lee; Being the Fundamental Laws . . . of the Penal Code of China*), who served as an interpreter and later head of the East India Company's office at Canton between 1798 and 1817. A French translation of Staunton was published in Paris in 1812. The Law Library has a copy of Staunton's book translated into Italian and published in Milan in 1812. In 1862, a Spanish translation of Staunton appeared in Havana. This slightly antedates the abolition of slavery in Cuba (1865) and may be related to the large-scale recruitment of Chinese labor for the Cuban sugar plantations. The 1812 French translation was in turn translated into Spanish and published in Madrid in 1884.

By the time the Chinese text had been translated first into English, then into French, and then into Spanish, the questionable accuracy of these successive translations was further diminished. To compound the problems of understanding what was to Europeans a very alien legal tradition, Staunton's translation has been dismissed by William T. Jones, author of *The Great Qing Code*, who, in the most recent translation of the *Code* (Oxford, 1994, p.v.), describes Staunton's work as "essentially useless since it was so free as to be inaccurate." According to Professor Jones, the best previous translation into a European language was P.L.F. Philastre's translation of the *Annamite Code* into French, which was published in Paris in 1876. Annam was in central Vietnam, where a French-dominated Emperor held court at Hue. What the French called the *Yih king* was the 1815 *Gia Long Code*, in which the Vietnamese Emperor Gia Long took the entire *Qing Code*, in Chinese, as the basic code for his state. One problem with the French translation, however, was Philastre's decision to employ French legal and administrative terminology, which made China and Vietnam appear much more like nineteenth-century France than was ever the case. Jones notes that a Confucian district magistrate becomes "in effect, a *juge d'instruction* who was instructing himself on the case."

The *Qing Code* Collection includes a large number of handbooks for magistrates or their specialized legal or taxation secretaries, which provide brief summaries of the code, arranged by topic. Examples include the *Bo An Xiu Bian* (How to Decide a Case) (nineteenth century?) by Quan Shizhao, and 1835 and 1882 editions of Xu Lian's *Zhe yu qui jian* (How to Decide a Criminal Case). A specialty of traditional Chinese murder cases was detailed forensic examinations of corpses, and the Law Library holds many editions of the classic text on the subject, *Xi Yuan ji lu*, first published in 1247. Later editions include cases and supplementary notes. Books that reduce the Criminal Code to easily grasped charts were also popular in the nineteenth century. In one format, illustrated by the 1836 *Du Fa Cun* (Learning Law Through Charts), each article of the code is represented by a one-page chart or diagram with brief text in as many as forty-five subordinate boxes or "windows," bearing such information as "Principle," "Accessories," "Penalty," or "Penalties for Those Under the Age of 12."

These "how-to-be-a-mandarin" books are of great interest to historians, as they provide evidence for the way the Imperial government actually operated. The complete editions of the codes and the relatively brief handbooks and treatises on such topics as instructions to coroners mean that it would be possible to replicate the contents of the bookshelves of a representative late Imperial magistrate. The depth of the collection means that it frequently has multiple editions of the same titles, sometimes produced over the course of more than a century. These, too, can be used by historians to trace changes in all the matters that have been regulated or touched by law—commerce, population growth and migration, variation in harvests, irrigation disputes, and so on. They also illustrate a general principle. Although the Chinese and the Western legal traditions differ in many ways, both illustrate the tendency for statutes, regulations, interpretations, and precedents to grow over time, with each successive edition of the general code or the regulations of such specialized bodies as the Imperial Salt Monopoly being longer than its predecessor. The tendency to expansion and elaboration has elicited a need for digests, epitomes, outlines, and how-to books, in this instance, for the practical Mandarin.

The greatest strength of the Modern Chinese collection is probably the extensive set of official gazettes. The several thousand bound volumes range from the very last years of the Qing Dynasty to the present, and include material from both the Nationalist Government (1927–), which moved to Taiwan in 1949, and the People's Republic of China (1949–). Besides the central government, the holdings include less complete sets of gazettes from some provincial

現擬屍圖　合面

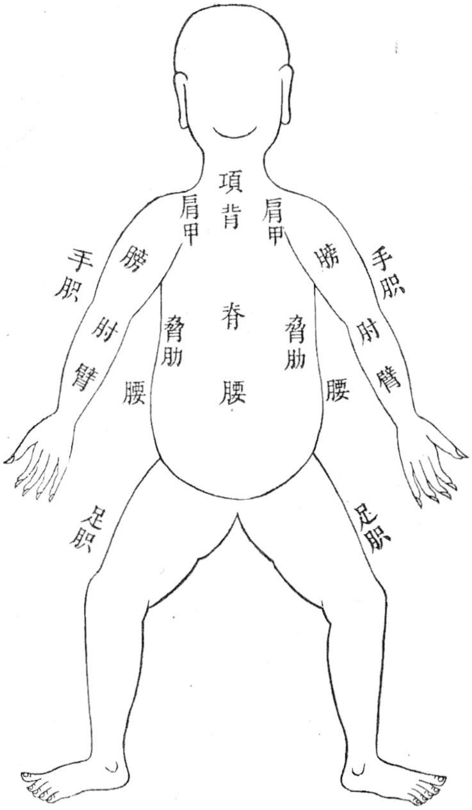

項背　脊腰
肩甲　肩甲
晒脉　手脉
脅肋　脅肋
膀胱腰　腰
肘臂　肘臂
手脉　手脉
足脉　足脉
腰

詳義

右圖所列各條其說解摘敘簡要數語逐條開
載於後俾司牧者臨場易於檢查其與原圖不相符
合之處可一覽即知矣

顖門在頂心前三寸原圖距頂心太近應改

額顱在髮際下左右兩角與額顱應改

額角在髮際之上與額顱高下懸殊應改

髮際之上與額顱相平原圖列在

大陽穴在眉際之末斜上少許原圖列在額角部
位應改

眉叢係左右兩眉叢聚處並非正中額應改

腮在顴骨之下頰車之上處無骨處頰即下把
改殼之兩旁原圖合腮頰為一列在頰車之尾應

頦為下唇至末即下把殼之正中額為結喉之上

額兩旁虛輭無骨處原圖合頦頦為一列在頰車
部位應改

頸項前也即自頷下至喉上統名為頸項頭後也即

頸項受枕之處然則頸為仰面項為合面原圖誤合

為一屍圖

and major municipal governments, as well as from such major ministries as those of Transportation, Taxation, the Railroads, the Trademark Bureau, and so on. The post-1950 holdings from the Republic of China on Taiwan are especially extensive and include the proceedings of the National Legislature (*Li Fa Yüan*). These are primary sources for the study of the country's history and administration.

Apart from the official gazettes and recent compilations of laws and regulations from the People's Republic of China, the Law Library holds some relatively rare materials from the several regional governments established by the Communist Party of China during the 1940s, before its victory in the 1946 to 1949 Civil War and the establishment of the People's Republic of China on October 1, 1949. These include copies of documents held by the Ministry of Justice of the Nationalist Government on Taiwan, as well as such published material as the 1943 *Proceedings of the First Session of the People's Political Convention of the Shanxi-Zhaha-Hebei Border District* (*Jin Cha Ji Bianqu Diyijie Canyihui*). The extensive collection of contemporary provincial-level legal newspapers and such publications as *Renmin Gonganbao* (China Police News) permits a more finely grained understanding of the operation of China's legal and police systems than does the national-level legal newspaper, *Fazhi Ribao* (Legal Daily). The Law Library receives some dozens of

legal periodicals from China, ranging from the scholarly to the popular, as well as English-language periodicals detailing and sometimes translating Chinese Law, with most of these directed at companies doing business in or investing in China.

The policy of the Law Library is to collect primary sources whenever possible, but it is not always feasible to do so, especially from some isolated, belligerent, or no longer extant jurisdictions. In such cases the collections are enriched by copies, facsimiles, or even, as with some rare Chinese Communist legislation, handwritten photocopies. Individual items in the Law collections thus range from sumptuously printed and decorated tomes to mimeograph copies or various types of facsimiles. Certain items have been reproduced in facsimile by the Library in order to allow researchers access to texts without threatening the fragile condition of the originals.

KOREAN LAW

Twenty-nine volumes of legal material from Korea's Yi Dynasty (1392–1910) are considered rare books, the most noteworthy of which is the six-volume title *Kyongguk Taejon,* the first comprehensive set of legal codes of the Dynasty. The codification project was begun in 1460 and completed under King Songjong in 1485. The Library has a copy of the 1630 edition, which includes much supplemental material. Researchers interested in modern, English-language Korean legislation make much use of the twenty loose-leaf volumes of *The Statutes of the Republic of Korea,* a twentieth-century English translation of some eight hundred important Acts and Presidential Decrees. Similar loose-leaf services on modern law exist in the Law Library for most other major jurisdictions, both in Asia and throughout the world.

Although legal material from the Democratic People's Republic of Korea (North Korea) is scarce and very difficult to obtain, the Law Library's collection is one of the most complete outside of Korea or Japan. A bibliography of this material, *Law and Legal Literature of North Korea: A Guide,* was published by the Law Library in 1988 and features an annotated list of 1,015 items published between 1945 and 1987. The collection includes a copy of the very rare 790-page legal dictionary *Pophak Sajon.* Originally published in Pyongyang in 1971, the dictionary in the Library's collection is a photocopy of the original, donated by a visiting South Korean scholar from Beijing.

The Asian collections also include those on Cambodia, Indonesia (previously Dutch East Indies), Thailand (previously Siam), and the Philippines. All these

OPPOSITE: The work pictured, entitled *Supplemented Collection of Categories of Law Cases,* is an eighteenth-century block-printed edition of an earlier manuscript, with some additional material. The manuscript version is a copy of another manuscript work, with the simpler title "Collection of Categories of Law Cases." This first work was hand copied in Korea but based on a Ming Dynasty Chinese text describing the various types of legal proceedings, including what would today be classed as criminal matters, such as assassinations and burglaries, and civil matters, such as issues related to property holdings and sales. It also includes a table of Ming Imperial reigns and their Korean Imperial reigns for the same time periods. The handwritten supplemented version includes a preface, describing the necessity of having a collection of these types of cases and the fact that it was borrowed from China. The supplemental material consists of sub-categories of types of cases based on Korean laws and situations. The block-print version includes the material in the second manuscript version, with an addendum showing the added later Imperial chronology, plus a table on the five kinds of punishments, including beating, beating with sticks, two forms of exile, and the death sentence. (*Law Library Collection;* LCCN 77825292 *and* LCCN 2004597299)

Among the Vietnamese law holdings in the Law Library this "Popular Handbook," titled *Phụ-Nữ Việt-Nam* (Vietnamese Women Before the Law), concerns the law as it was in South Vietnam. The contents lists the following categories: 1) Unmarried, 2) Married, 3) Divorced or Widowed, and 4) Succession of Property. (*Law Library Collection; LCCN 75984777*)

collections have a Customary Law component. The Vietnam collection is developed along its historic divides: before 1945, including Annam, Tonkin, and Cochin-China before 1883/1899, when these entities were absorbed into French Indo-China; the Democratic Republic of Vietnam (North Vietnam, 1945–75); the Republic of Vietnam (South Vietnam, ca. 1956–75); and the collection of the reunified Vietnam (Socialist Republic of Vietnam, since 1975). All collections contain official gazettes and—however limited—law compilations. An interesting overview of Vietnam's dynastic and legal history is *Lê Code. Law in traditional Vietnam: a comparative Sino-Vietnamese legal study with historical-juridical analysis,* by Nguyễn Ngọc Huy and Ṭ Văn Tài (translated into English; Athens/Ohio, 1986).

INDIAN LAW

Indian Law was formed over the course of centuries under many cultural, ethnic, and foreign legal influences. The historic periods of India—the ancient and Medieval to the tenth century, the period of Muslim rule (997–1761), the British/European colonial period (1761–1949), and India of today—translate as the periods of Hindu Law, Islamic Law, and Common Law of England. It is speculated that invading Aryans from Central Asia brought their language and caste, or social class system, to the northern part of the Indian subcontinent between 1500 and 500 B.C. In the course of history, Sanskrit became the language of the educated castes throughout India. Between 500 B.C. and the beginning of the Muslim period, Hinduism, or Hindu civilization, propagated in a number of Hindu kingdoms, has evolved from this contact of indigenous people with Aryan culture, and is one of the oldest religious, legal, and social systems, originating from the *Veda* (compilations of prayers and liturgy) and in the *Mānava-dharma-śāstra,* the code of the First Patriarch Manu, the Lawgiver, who compiled the code sometime during the first and second centuries A.D.

Thus, the legal literature of ancient and Medieval India, referred to as *dharma* literature, is a large body constituted of primary and secondary sources, and includes the *sūtras, smṛtis, śāstras,* and *nibandhas*: the primary sources are Sanskrit texts; the secondary literature in the collection represents itself in many languages such as Hindi, Bengali, Burmese, Indonesian, Malayalam, Arabic, and European languages, often presented parallel with the original Sanskrit text. The texts can be broken down in the three chronological periods: the *sūtra* period (eighth century B.C. to A.D. 0); the *smṛtis* period (A.D. 0 to eighth century); and the commentary period (eighth to eighteenth century), overlapping with the Muslim rule in India and ending with the emergence of British rule. The literature reflects the literary style of the period as well. The *sūtras* are epigrammatical prose compositions which require for their understanding exegesis or commentary. The *smṛtis* (also called *śāstras*) are compositions in metric verse, the usual verse being the *śloka* (comprising thirty-two syllables). The commentary literature is constituted of two types, commentaries on particular works and digests (*nibandhas*). *Sūtras* and *smṛtis/śāstras* form the canonical literature. One should bear in mind that *smṛtis* and *śāstras* are not clearly distinguished, even the Code of Manu is sometimes called *smṛti* and sometimes *śāstra*. The Library has a modest collection of Hindu Law, including digests, treatises, and other types of legal reference books; works in Sanskrit add up to approximately six hundred. The most important works in this group are the over fifty editions of the *Mānava-dharma-śāstra*, the Code of Manu and some on its chapters, mostly published in Sanskrit, with or without translations, independent translations, and commentaries. In the following centuries, legal texts were elaborations on the *Mānava-dharma-śāstra*. The Law Library holds collections, translations, and studies on the *sūtras* and *smṛtis/śāstras*, e.g., *Dharma śāstrasaṅgrahaḥ: Atri, Viṣṇu, Hārīta . . .* etc. (Kalikātā, 1876).

This first edition of the English translation and bilingual edition of the *Gentoo Code* was published in 1776. The term *Gentoo* was an anglicization of *Hindu*. One of the stated purposes of the book was to increase Westerners' understanding of Hindus and thus foster better treatment for them under British rule. (*Law Library Rare Book Collection; LCCN 32018556*)

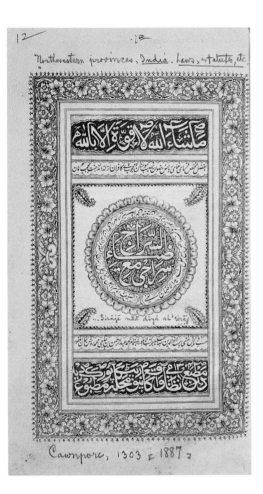

This volume contains Islamic inheritance law. Published in Cawnpore in the Northwestern Provinces of India in 1887, it is evidence of the historic extent of Islamic law in Asia. (*Law Library Rare Book Collection*)

Nibhandas (Digests) are also in the collection, e.g., S.S. Vidya-Bhushan, *Vyavastha-Darpana; A digest of Hindu law, as current in Bengal* (Calcutta, 1883).

The colonial introduction of British legal institutions, including a heavy reliance on precedents and collections of judicial decisions, to South Asia, combined with the post-independence publication of legal materials of all sorts in India and their purchase with US PL 480 funds, has resulted in very substantial holdings from India, Pakistan, and Sri Lanka. Let us pause and look at the historical background of some of the collections. In 1857 and 1858—in response to the British takeover of India (India Act, 1858)—uprisings erupted and led to the "First War of Independence." When the Indian forces surrendered, the Moghul (Muslim) Empire formally came to an end. The rule of the East India Company passed over to Britain. A Viceroy was nominated by Queen Victoria, and British India was subdivided in provinces, each with a governor. But most important, in 1861, a judicial system of independent High Courts was moved in place, subject to the Privy Council in London. The collection of Indian Law reports from the National courts, the Presidencies' courts, Princely States' Law reports, the Privy Council Law reports, and law reports of provinces, territories, and areas before 1947, could be matched only in New Delhi, and perhaps in London, but nowhere else.

Collections on the modern constitutional development of India are just as interesting. Since the end of the nineteenth century, India was pushing for independence from colonial rule. The Library holds the Government of India Acts of 1915, 1919, 1935, the draft Constitution of 1948 signaling independence, and the 1950 Constitution. The Law Library holds *A critical survey and in-depth commentary on constitutional law and history of Government of India, from the grant of the first charter to East India Company in the year 1600 to Government of India Act, 1935 . . . culminating in the present constitution,* by C. L. Anand (sixth edition, Allahabad, 1990).

A rare acquisition by the Law Library in 2002 details an important episode in current Indian history: the assassination on January 30, 1948, of the legendary advocate of nonviolence, Mahatma Gandhi, who led the way to freedom. The eight-volume set of the *Gandhi Murder Trial* had originally belonged to the main assassin, Nathuram Vinayak Godse, before he was executed in November 1949. In the margins this set contains the handwritten notes of the defendant and his counsel during the trial. The police investigation implicated twelve men as having been involved in the plot. The first volume of the Gandhi trial set contains the verbatim testimony of the hundred forty-nine prosecution witnesses; the second volume, the written statements of several of the twelve defendants; and the third,

Title page from the *Constitution of India* (calligraphed by Prem Behari Narain Raizda; illuminated by Nandalal Bose and other artists; Dehra Dun: Photolithographed at the Survey of the India Offices, 1955?; reprinted by National Printers, New Delhi, 1990?). The original of this elaborate edition of the *Constitution of India* took nearly five years to produce. Signed by its framers, most of whom are regarded as the founders of the Republic of India, the original is kept in a special helium-filled case in the Library of the Parliament of India. The illustrations represent styles from the various civilizations of the subcontinent, ranging from the prehistoric Indus valley Mohenjodaro to the present. (*Law Library Rare Book Collection;* LCCN 90902847)

the judgment of the trial court. Volumes 4 through 6 contain a printed record of the trial and all the associated trial documents and exhibits. Volumes 7 and 8 reprint the record used in appeal and the judgment of the High Court in appeal. Other works related to the trial and assassination in the Library's collection include Jeevan Lal Kapur, *Report of Commission of Inquiry into Conspiracy to Murder Mahatma Gandhi* (New Delhi, Ministry of Home Affairs, 1970; LCCN 72905362); V. T. Rajshekar Shetty, *Why Godse Killed Gandhi?: A Philosophical Interpretation of Indian History* (third revised edition, Bangalore, Dalit Sahitya Academy, 1997; LCCN 98901498), and Khalid Latif Gauba, *The Assassination of Mahatma Gandhi* (Bombay, Jaico, 1969; LCCN 709121).

AFRICAN COLLECTIONS

The collection on Africa in the Law Library is a large and multi-faceted collection telling the African story by what it contains and what is missing. Works on early and Customary Law of peoples of Africa are sparse. There are many reasons for this. Much of the continent's early history, including its legal history, went unrecorded or was destroyed in the vagaries of hostile times. The researcher must therefore resort to histories from Roman times, or records and histories from councils of early Christianity and from the early periods of the spread of Islam (between the eighth and tenth centuries) throughout North African regions. For later eras, histories and records of expanding Ottoman rule (in the early 1500s) over much of North Africa may be consulted. General histories of explorations and travelogues as well as records and diaries of missionaries and Christian settlers are other resources that offer some information on the heritages of the peoples on the African continent. Research, thus, has to negotiate sources of disciplines quite different from the field of law, such as archaeology, theocratic studies, legal, social, and cultural anthropology, and folk life studies, all of which are available in the General Collections of the Library. General and political history collections on Africa contain a wealth of works covering historic kingdoms, empires, chiefdoms, and states, as well as individual ethnic peoples of the pre-colonial periods up to the present day. Those general works often include in passing features of legal archaeology and indigenous law. Records of official diplomatic missions, maps, and treatises on foreign relations are another source for the researcher, such as *L'Ethiopie au point de vue du droit international* (Paris, 1928), found in the Library's General Collections. Early treaties of friendship, commerce, and amity between African and other nations in the Library's collection are very important sources for legal research. One such is the *Treaty of peace and amity, concluded September 5, 1795, between Hassan Bashaw, Dey of Algiers, his Divan and subjects, and George Washington, president of the United States of North America, and the citizens of the said United States: with the president's proclamation announcing its ratification, as published in the Philadelphia gazette, March 9, 1796* (Rare Book and Special Collections; LCCN 12034934).

Nineteenth-century African law collections document the full impact of European colonialism: dominance over vast historic empires and peoples, arbitrary imposition of boundaries disrupting societal continuity and shredding the socio-economic fabric of indigenous populations. The *Berlin West Africa Conference* of 1884 to 1885, attended by the major European powers, was a key event in settling contentious questions of colonial expansion between the attending nations. The Library holds editions of the Final Act of the Conference (*Acte général de la Conférence de Berlin.* Berlin, 1885; LCCN 05018407) and related reports, diplomatic documents, correspondence, etc. (LCCN 10016487). Although publishing in some of the colonial regions started earlier, e.g., in South Africa, most of the Law Library's early African collections fall within this period. The holdings, for example, are very strong in official gazettes or journals, law reports, collections of acts and statutes for all the major colonial jurisdictions, such as the (British) East African Protectorate and Kenya Colony (to 1963; today Kenya and Tanzania); British Central Africa Protectorate (today Rhodesia and Malawi); Anglo-Egyptian Sudan (to 1956; today Sudan); French Equatorial Africa (today Central African Republic, Congo/Brazzaville, Chad, and Gabon); French West Africa (today Benin, Burkina Faso, French Guinea, Cote d'Ivoir, Mali, Mauritania, Niger, and Senegal); Italian East Africa (today Ethiopia, Eritrea, and Somalia); Portuguese West Africa (today Angola); and Portuguese East Africa (today Mozambique) to name only a few. The nine-volume work in the Law Library entitled *La tribune des colonies & des protectorats: Journal de Jurisprudence, de Doctrine, et de Legislation Coloniales et Maritimes* (first edition, Paris, 1891–99; LCCN 2200120808) affords a significant insight into the laws applied in the regions affected by the spread of French colonialism. Volume 1, for example, includes judgments, excerpts of French law and applicable Islamic law, and legal writings by various jurists, relating to French Indochina, Algeria, Tunisia, Martinique, and French Guyana, among other places.

The collections of modern legal materials from various jurisdictions on the African continent vary greatly. The acquisition of legal titles from many nations has presented a challenge because of the paucity of legal publishing due to internal or external factors, such as the two World Wars, eruptions of civil

PALM TREE.

NATIVE AND COLONIST.

NEWS FROM AFRICA.

A

COLLECTION OF FACTS,

RELATING TO

THE COLONY IN LIBERIA,

FOR THE INFORMATION OF THE

FREE PEOPLE OF COLOUR

IN MARYLAND.

"Where Freedom is, there is my country."

BALTIMORE:

PUBLISHED BY THE COLONIZATION MANAGERS APPOINTED
BY THE STATE OF MARYLAND,

J. D. TOY, PRINTER.

1832.

unrest, and the drawn out, often violent breakup of the colonial mega-regions. In the collections, among the most important documents of political changes from about 1960 on are the constitutions adopting, country-by-country, Western-style democratic principles and legal institutions. The reader interested in a quick overview may start with *Constitutions of African States* (New York, 1972), a collection of all original constitutions up to the year of publication, together with other works on current law developments, such as *Traditional Authority and Democracy in Southern Africa* (F. M. d'Engelbronner-Kolff, et al., editors, Windhoek/Namibia, 1995); or the periodical publications *Annual Survey of African Law* (London, 1967–); the *African Law Digest* (New York, 1965?–); the *African Law Reports: Commercial Law Series* (New York, 1965–); and for commercial law of Francophone Africa the *Droit des affaires en Afrique* (semi-monthly; Paris, 1997–).

Of interest for constitutional historic research are the increasing references to indigenous rights and institutes in the context of human rights and questions of indigenous ancestry rule couched in terms of "decolonization" and independence of states. In a slow process, in many African countries, modern legislation has set out to preserve residual customs and institutions and to remedy situations where European Continental or British legal acts superceded or restricted the operation of Customary Law, especially in the area of property, i.e., Land Rights, Marriage, and Succession Laws (e.g., *Malawi's Wills and Inheritance Act of 1967*). The 1986 *African Charter on Human and Peoples Rights* (adopted by the Organization of African Unity), which aligns itself with the *Universal Declaration of Human Rights* (1948) and other international covenants and conventions, attests to "the virtues of historical tradition and values of African civilization . . . which should inspire their reflection on the concept of human and peoples rights," together with elimination of "colonialism, neo-colonialism, apartheid and Zionism." *The International Law of Human Rights in Africa: Basic Documents and Annotated Bibliography*, compiled by M. Hamalengwa et al. (Dordrecht/Netherlands, 1988) provides a good overview on de-colonization, territorial independence, and human rights.

The steadily growing collection on Customary Law in the Library includes standard works on the subject, such as *The principles of African Customary Law* (Ogbomoso/Nigeria, 1997) by Akintunde Emiola; the basic text, *The Nature of African Customary Law* (Manchester, 1956) by Taslim Olawale Elias, a prolific writer on all aspects of Nigerian Law and International Law; and a collection of essays on *African Law and Legal Theory* (Gordon R. Woodman and A. O. Obilade, editors, New York, 1995). This work is volume 8 in the series *International Library of Essays in Law and Legal Theory*. Besides such works of general nature, there are also works

OPPOSITE: *News from Africa. A Collection of Facts, Relating to the Colony in Liberia, for the Information of the Free People of Colour in Maryland* (Baltimore, 1832). This booklet's description of life in the newly established State of Liberia was intended to entice "free people of colour in the United States" to emigrate there. It contains an "abstract of the examination of Mr. Francis Devany, High Sheriff of the Colony of Liberia, before a Committee of Congress, on the 26th and 27th of May, 1830." After being freed by his master, Devany, a former South Carolina slave, became a wealthy sailmaker and emigrated to Liberia. (*Rare Book and Special Collections Division; LCCN 11008725*)

on particular jurisdictions, e.g., *Report of the Native Courts* (Nigeria. Northern Provinces. London, 1952); and *A Report on the Administration of Justice in the Magistrates and Customary Courts of Southern Nigeria* (Lagos, Nigeria, 1996); as well as works on various individual ethnic groups, such as *The Judicial Process Among the Barotse of Northern Rhodesia* by Max Gluckman (Manchester, 1967); *Fanti Customary Laws* (London, 1968) by John Mensah Sarbah; the *Justice and Judgment Among the Tiv* (Prospects Heights, Illinois, 1989) by Paul Bohannan; and *Beduin Justice: Laws and Customs Among the Egyptian Bedouin* by Austin Kennett (London, 2000). The reader will find works on Customary Law of many more African countries in the Library's online catalog, e.g., Chad, Cote d'Ivoire, Botswana, Eritrea, Belgian Congo, the Democratic Republic of the Congo, Rwanda, and others. A very valuable work is *Droit coutumier africain: proverbs judiciaires kongo (Zaire)* by André Ryckmans (Paris, 1992); it is of humanistic importance as well since the legal maxims capture oral folk traditions which might get lost in "modern" civil life.

A host of comparative literature and works on a multiplicity of law conflicts and issues of the harmonization of laws, arising in multicultural countries with two or more co-existing legal systems in operation (such as Civil and Customary or Religious Law), can be of a general nature, such as *Law, Society, and National Identity in Africa* (Jamil M. Abun-Nasr et al., editors; Hamburg, 1990); *Afrikanisches Gewohnheitsrecht und "modernes" staatliches Recht* (Frankfurt, 1999) by Peter Hazdra; and *Harmonisation of Laws in Africa* (Ikeja/Nigeria, 1999) by Ademola Yakubu. However, comparative works specifically on Civil and Religious Law are found mostly in the collection of such countries where (British) Common Law intersects with both Customary and Religious Law, i.e., Hindu or Islamic Law, or where European Civil Law has a strong presence beside Islamic Law. The focus here is on the traditional areas of Family Law (marriage and multiple marriage, consanguinity, and kinship), the status of women, inheritance, and succession. An instructive work on Family Law in the Arabic states of North Africa is *Le leggi del diritto di famiglia negli stati arabi del Nord-Africa* (ed. Roberta Aluffi Beck-Peccoz; Torino, 1997). Probably the most complex legal issues for many jurisdictions arise from real property and land laws (with native/customary land rights, customary co-ownership, grazing and hunting rights, etc.) and modern public land legislation. Post-colonial national legislation often welds concepts stemming from indigenous land rights and public land-system policies together in an attempt to re-structure the system of land holding, land use, and land resettlement—e.g., *Rhodesia Customary Land (Development) Act*, 1967, and *Tribal Trustland Act*, 1967, which restores chiefs' control of occupation and use of tribal trust land; or the *Kenya Land Control Act*, 1967. Recent comparative-historic research on Customary and Colonial Law has taken issue with the super-imposition of Colonial Law on Customary Law —e.g., *Les conventions indigènes et la legislation coloniale: 1893–1946: essai d'anthropologie juridique* (Abidjan/R. I. C., 1994) by Henri Legré Okou—and court and procedure rules that provided tools for the colonizers to safeguard and stabilize colonial rule. The laws in force, for example French and British Procedure Law, recognize Customary/Indigenous Law in principle—when presented in court—as a valid source of law. However, the Civil Law limits application of Customary Law if "certainty" is an issue: is unwritten law certain enough to be recognized by a colonial court, and how credible is the party? English rule, in contrast, tests the general compatibility of Customary Law with the concept of European ethics and morality by the introduction of the highly selective repugnancy clause into procedure that conditionally limits the application of Customary Law in a colonial court if found "repugnant" to "natural," i.e., British, justice.

The collections on African regional integration and organizations contain official gazettes, the establishing treaties or literature on such bodies as the Organization of African Unity (*Organisation de l'Unité Africaine.* 1963); the Economic Community of West African States (*Communauté économique des Etats de l'Afrique de l'Ouest.* 1993); East African Community (1967–77); Common Market for Eastern and Southern Africa (1993); Economic Community of Central African States (*Communauté Economique des Etats de l'Afrique Centrale.* 1983); and the Arab Maghreb Union (1989).

For the literature on conflicts in current history, such as civil wars, inter-tribal hostilities, and ethnic cleansing, accompanied by the mass refugee movements, forced migration and displacement of whole populations, and a host of other humanitarian problems in certain regions of the continent, several collections have to be consulted. Some will be in the African Regional Collection; the majority, however, are housed in the collection on International Law (Law of Nations). The documents of intergovernmental organizations, e.g., the League of Nations and the United Nations and their organs concerned with these subjects, are part of the International Relations Document Collection.

Among the individual national collections in the Law Library, the collections of Egypt, Morocco, Nigeria, and South Africa are the largest, with long runs of official gazettes and court reports, but also codes and modern secondary literature. Much of the literature of countries with a strong presence of Islam and Islamic Law is in the Arabic language. South African collections, consisting to a large extent of older materials of the different provinces and regions, are mostly in Afrikaans.

International Law

The term "International Law" was coined by the English philosopher Jeremy Bentham in 1780 in his *An Introduction to the Principles of Morals and Legislation*. Before then, jurists commonly referred to "the law of nations," a term echoing the Roman category of *jus gentium*, a universal law that could be applied to foreigners by Roman courts when Roman Law was not appropriate. By the seventeenth century that meaning had become secondary to a focus on the relations between sovereign nation states, as expressed in treaties. The distinction survives in the common term "Public International Law," referring to state-to-state relations and obligations.

The Library's collection on the subject International Law—or the Law of Nations, with approximately eighty thousand titles—is the largest of specialized law collections. It is also one of the oldest and most arresting collections for both the historic intellectual content of what was written in the field and of what was collected. Both reflect in an interesting way how contemporary political orientation of the times formed the Library's collection policies.

Chancellor James Kent (1763–1847), author of the first great U.S. legal treatise, the four-volume *Commentaries on American Law* (1826–30), began his work with two hundred pages on the law of nations. There he noted that:

A comprehensive and scientific knowledge of international law is highly necessary, not only to lawyers practicing in our commercial ports, but to every [one] who is animated by liberal views, and a generous ambition to assume stations of high public trust. It would be exceedingly to the discredit of any person who should be called to take a share in the councils of the nation, if [that person] should be found deficient in the great leading principles of this law.

The first and subsequent editions of the Commentaries are also in the Law Library collection. Chancellor Kent's opinion was shared by those who selected the books for the Library of Congress in its first decade. Law books, primarily British, constituted some 20 percent of the two hundred forty-three volumes listed in the 1802 catalog. International law was represented by George Chalmers's *A Collection of Treaties Between Great Britain and Other Powers* (London, 1790) and the standard eighteenth-century treatise written by the Swiss jurist Emer de Vattel (1714–67), *Droit des Gens* (London, 1758), with an English edition (London, 1760) and the first American edition (New York, 1796). In that period it was probably the most commonly read and cited authority on International Law. On March 10, 1794, before the 1800 establishment of the Library of Congress, the U.S. Senate ordered the Secretary to purchase Vattel's *Law of*

OPPOSITE: *L'arbre des batailles: autreme[n]t dit L'arbre de douleur*, Honoré Bonet (fl. 1378–98) (The tree of battles: also called The tree of sadness). This fourteenth-century manuscript is one of the most important early treatises on the law of war; it includes rules of military ethics, honor, and chivalry, and was probably produced in France by the hand of a single professional scribe. (*Law Library Rare Book Collection*; LCCN 95125943)

al saincte couronne de france, en laquelle aujourdhui
par lordonnance de dieu Regne, Charles le .vie.me
en son nom tresbien ame et partout le monde Re=
doubte. Soit donne los et gloure sur toutes seigno=ries
terriennes. ☙ Je Jeshault prince Jesus appellez par
mon droit nom honore bonnet prieur de salon docteur en decret
souvent et maint ay eu en voulente de faire aucun liure p̃mierement

Nature and Nations for the use of the Senate. The Library holds over thirty-five titles of this work in several European languages.

Thomas Jefferson's library, since 1815 part of the Library of Congress collections, contained five hundred ten law titles. His category The Law of Nature and Nations included forty-seven titles, twenty-nine of which were written in French. Reflecting Jefferson's experience as Secretary of State and President, this section included collections of treaties and many works of diplomatic history and accounts of negotiations. His category labeled Law-Maritime included sixteen titles, most of which would now be regarded as belonging to International Law (Law of the Sea). The numerous titles on the rights of neutral shipping may reflect the tribulations of the American merchant marine during the Napoleonic Wars.

Various accounts, such as annual reports, memoranda, etc., allow insight into the Library of Congress's early collecting in this field. From 1808 on, the focus was mainly on treaties, official/diplomatic correspondence, and congressional papers; between 1867 and 1875, the exchange of foreign government documents was formalized. In the latter part of the nineteenth-century, the cultural and scholarly exchange between the United States and Europe kindled and deepened the interest in sciences, philosophy, and above all, in antiquity and history. The same held true for the field of International Law. Thus, the pre—World War I collections of treaties and treatises reach far back into history and antiquity, tracing the roots of International Law for the modern reader. Comparative works analyze the development of this branch of law on both continents, such as the *Histoire des progrès du droit des gens en Europe et en Amérique depuis la paix de Westphalie jusqu' à nos jours* [i.e., to the Treaty of Washington in 1871], *avec une introduction sur les progrès du droit des gens en Europe avant la paix de Westphalie* by Henry Wheaton (1785—1848). This work is represented in the Law Library in several languages. All in all, the original collection was a hybrid of nineteenth-century comprehension of International Law and international relations and slipped in and out of political and diplomatic history.

Fontes juris gentium, the source collection and the core of any collection on International Law, holds thus in descending order of authority: treaties (international legislation) and other international agreements on a broad spectrum of topics; international arbitral awards by arbitration commissions, and decisions by international tribunals or courts; official documents and proceedings generated by intergovernmental congresses; and the various codifications of International Law, mostly private works, e.g., David Dudley Field (1805—94), *Draft outline of an Inter-*

national Code (1872); or Alfons Emrich von Domin-Petrushevecz (1835–71), *Précise d'un code du droit international* (1861).

One traditional source of International Law is Customary Law and the *principés généraux*, which guide the interpretation of treaties or serve as general rules in the absence of an explicit treaty. A frequently cited source on the determination of Customary International Law is the *Paquete Habana Case*, decided by the U.S. Supreme Court in 1900 (175 U.S. 677). This concerned the legality of the U.S. Navy's capture of Cuban fishing boats and their subsequent sale as prizes of war during the Spanish-American War of 1898. Justice Gray, after noting that "international law is part of our law and must be ascertained and administered by the courts of justice," stated that, where there is no treaty, "resort must be had to the customs and usages of civilized nations … and to the works of jurists and commentators." On a side note, Justice Gray and his clerks resorted to the collection of the Law Library of Congress, which in 1900 was housed in the Capitol Building, one floor directly below the Supreme Court chamber. (The books cited in the decision are still in the collection and may still be consulted by readers today.) Justice Gray began his decision by citing four nineteenth-century treatises on International and Maritime Law, three written in French and published in Paris and one by an American scholar: Jean-Felicité Théodore Ortolan (1808–74), *Règles Internationales et Diplomatie de la Mer* (1845); Carlos Calvo (1822–1906), *Le droit international theorique et pratique* (Paris, 1896); Charles de Boeck (b. 1856), *De la propriété privée ennemie sous pavillon ennemi* (Paris, 1882); and William Edward Hall (1836–94), *A treatise on international law* (Oxford, 1880). The earliest precedent cited was a set of orders that the English King Henry IV had issued to his admirals in 1403 and 1406. These prohibited them from interfering with French fishing boats. The texts, one in Latin and one in Norman French, are contained in Thomas Rymer's (1641–1713) *Foedera, conventiones, literae … inter reges Angliae et alios quosvis imperatores* (London, 1704–17), the first collection of the diplomatic correspondence and treaties of the English kings from the year 1101 to the late 1600s. The Law Library has two original editions of this work, the first published in London in seventeen volumes between 1704 and 1717, and the second in twenty volumes from 1727 to 1735. It also holds a French translation from 1745; a modern reprint in ten volumes (1967); a digest of the work by the French historian Paul Rapin de Thoyras (1661–1725), *Acta regia; or, An account of the treaties, letters and instruments between the monarchs of England and foreign powers* (London, 1726–27); and an English translation of that digest by Stephen Whatley published in London under the same title in 1727. Equivalent publications for other major European states, historic and current, as well as named treaty collections and prestigious compilations are in the extremely rich collection of the Law Library.

Some examples of such compilations include: *Recueil international des traités du XXe siècle* (Paris, 1904–21) by Éduard Eugène François Descamps (1847–1933); Georg Friedrich von Martens (1756–1821), *Recueil des traités d'alliance, de paix, de trêve . . .* , updated and printed several times between 1817 and 1908; Fred L. Israel, *Major Peace Treaties of Modern History, 1648–2002* (Philadelphia, 2002); and the treaty sets of the two universal international organizations—the League of Nations and the United Nations—and *Parry's Consolidated Treaty* series; all of the above supported by historic and modern bibliographic aids.

Though multi-national cooperation in the field of law is seen as an ideal, the use of treaties oftentimes in history has been used to coerce a weaker party into signing an unfavorable treaty in the name, but not in the spirit, of the law or as merely a pro forma act to give a legal veneer to imperialist designs. The resulting provisions of such treaties can have long-lasting, disastrous political and social effects. One such treaty was the Molotov-Ribbentrop Pact signed on the eve of World War II between Germany and Russia. Secret protocols to the treaty divided territories and spheres of influence between the two powers, resulting in Soviet domination over Latvia, Estonia, and Finland; German domination over Lithuania and Danzig, as well as the partition of Poland with the partitions divided between the two powers; and the mass displacement of peoples from their homelands. On September 1, 1939, Hitler invaded Poland from the west and on September 17, the Soviets invaded Poland from the east, taking over lands that were predominantly populated by Ukrainians. Ignoring the treaty, Hitler invaded the Soviet Union on June 22, 1941.

The Hague Peace System, the twentieth-century European War theaters, the Geneva Law, and the decisions of a line of international courts, such as the Permanent Court of Arbitration (1900–), Permanent Court of Justice (PCIJ, 1920–46), and International Court of Justice (ICJ, 1946–), have contributed over the years to the enormous volume of the source collection. Tied to international conflicts are the tribunals instituted on an ad hoc basis to deal with war crimes, mostly crimes against humanity. The Law Library has a complete collection (on microfilm) of the Nuremberg trials, as well as materials on the Tokyo and Manila trials. The collections—reflecting current conflicts—are growing at a steady rate.

The monographic collection on International Law, an exhaustive list of illustrious philosophers and thinkers, the publicists, and their theoretical-authoritative

OPPOSITE: The signing of the *Berlin-Moscow Non-Aggression Pact* took place on August 23, 1939, in Moscow, days before the onset of World War II. Standing in the rear are German Foreign Minister Joachim von Ribbentrop and Soviet leader Josef Stalin, looking on as the treaty is signed by Russian Foreign Minister Viacheslav Molotov (seated). (*Prints and Photographs Division; LC-USZ62-101607*)

This well-known portrait of the famous Dutch jurist Hugo Grotius appears in the 1651 edition of *De juri belli ac pacis libri tres* (Of war and peace. *Law Library Rare Book Collection;* LCCN 10016923). The first edition of 1625 is held in the Rare Book and Special Collections Division of the Library. (*Rare Book and Special Collections Division;* LCCN 37039658)

RVIT   HORA.

HUGO GROTIUS,

Reginæ Regnique Suedici Consiliarius, eorundemque ad Regem Christianissimum Legatus ordinarius. quondam Syndicus Roterodamensis. ejusdemque Urbis in Conventu Ordinum Hollandiæ & Westfrisiæ Delegatus.

works on all things public and international, is not less remarkable. Over the course of four centuries, they explored the wide field of religion and Natural Law, sovereignty over land and sea, war and peace, folding in Humanitarian Law—viewed all together up until the twentieth century by many as inseparable subjects. From the large number of writers and subjects, only those can be quoted here who have significantly contributed to the development of the science of International Law. Francisco de Vitoria (c. 1486–1546), the most outstanding among a group of noted Dominican theologians educated at the University of Salamanca, Spain, had specialized in international law, and is now commonly invoked as "The Father of International Law." His statue stands today outside the United Nations building in New York City. Most noteworthy are Samuel Pufendorf (1632–94) with his *De jure naturae et gentium* (Law of Nature and Nations; first published in Latin in 1672 with several French and English translations); Christian Thomasius (1655–1728), *Fundamenta juris naturae et gentium* (Halle, 1718); Cornelis van Bijnkershoek (1673–1743), *Quaestionum juris publici libri duo* (Leiden, 1737); Giovanni Maria Lampredi (1732–93), *Juris publici universalis, sive juris naturae et gentium theoremata* (1776–78); and Gabriel Bonnot de Mably (1709–85), *Le droit public de l'Europe* (Geneva, 1748). And on the subject of war and peace, the following names stand out: Alberico Gentili (1552–1608), *De jure belli libri tres* (Hanau, 1598); and Charles Molloy (1646–90), *De jure maritimo et navali, or, A treatise of affairs maritime* (London, 1676). Not even the most thoughtful selection can do justice to the steadily growing pool of the "noted and famous" in the field of International Law of the nineteenth and twentieth centuries; thus, three names will stand for the many: Johann Kaspar Bluntschli (1808–81), Lassa Oppenheim (1858–1919), and Hans Kelsen (1881–1973).

One man, though, stands out among all: Hugo Grotius (1583–1645) of the Netherlands. His work is represented in the Library's collections by over two hundred twenty-five titles in all, including first and subsequent editions, as well as translations and commentaries on his work, past and present. *De juri belli ac pacis libri tres* (Of war and peace) is considered the first modern statement of International Law, including the doctrine of the "just war" which recurs in many conflicts in the name of religion over the centuries. Numerous earlier and subsequent editions (including translations) are housed in the Law Library's Rare Book Collection. A very important commentary on Grotius's work, *Grotius illustratus: seu, commentarii ad Hugonis Grotii De jure belli ac pacis . . . in quibus jus naturae et gentium . . . explicantur*, was written by Heinrich von Cocceji (1644–1719), with extensive annotations of Samuel von Cocceji (1679–1755), published in 1744 to 1752.

Grotius's writings were not limited, though, to International Law. He wrote extensively on the Civil Law of the Netherlands, and just as his contemporary John Selden, Grotius wrote tractates on Natural Law, theology, and Roman Law. The cardinal work of this Continental humanist, however, with long-lasting effect on the development of legal doctrine was the celebrated *De Mari libero* (On the freedom of the High Seas. Leiden, 1633). If nothing else, it challenged England's claim at that time to the high seas south and east of the British Isles. The response by the Englishman John Selden (1584–1654), *Mare clausum, seu, De dominio maris* (National claim to marine areas, or Ownership of the sea. Lund/Amsterdam?, 1636), representing British seafaring imperialism, became equally famous. In this treatise, Selden established the theory that the sea, by the law of nature or of nations, is not common to all men "but capable of private dominion or proprietie as well as the land. Further, that the dominion of the British sea was always a part or appendant of the empire of that island."—cited from the English translation of Marchamont Nedham (1620–178), *Of the dominion, or, Ownership of the sea* (London, 1652 and 1663. Rare Book and Special Collections; LCCN 33025130).

These two works surface again in contemporary history as the two hinges on which the contentious deliberations swung back and forth during the three UN Conferences on the Law of the Sea between 1958 and 1982. The Law Library holds many editions of Grotius's and Selden's works side by side with numerous editions of the *UN Convention on the Law of the Sea* (1982) and the documents of the preceding conferences. The High Seas, in modern doctrine one of the global commons, are free and exempt from the jurisdiction of any single state in the interest of all. However, the impact areas of the *dominium maris* doctrine remain the territorial sea, with exclusive fishery and economic zones, and the continental and outer-continental shelf, all delimited sea areas under the sovereignty (authority) of coastal and port states.

The fallout from the Law of the Sea deliberations—in addition to subsequent treaties and an enormous volume of monographic literature now in the Law Library—was a host of new complex doctrines that had been developed and shaped over time by political and ideological forces in the international community. One led to the recognition of the global commons, i.e., resources or areas of the world shared by all nations commonly, which include the High Seas, Space, the Moon, and other Celestial Bodies under highly politicized administrative regimes for access, exploration, and resources exploitation. Another category of global commons with yet broader political implications for the international

OPPOSITE: John Selden. *Mare clausum, seu, De dominio maris* (Lund/Amsterdam?, 1636). Selden established the theoretical precedent for the dominion of the sea by the British Empire. (*Rare Book and Special Collections Division; LCCN 28003354*)

our and furnsue all merchants
that shall fall within the
any such as shall attain
us in so neer plats to the
of trade and trasique out
homeward from and to
gainers / It eſt , Placuit noẛe
damus omnibus Maginss noẛo
Mare & per Terram,ṕg quar-
ipſos prohibere cunctis racos orna-
dorum parte ita immmmmum
alcujus portuum noſtrorum̂n̂
atque at tutelam præ̃ſtent ju-
merc̃atoribus alijśque qũ
quorumcumque imminentia
adeu propinquis, unde impedi-
& negotiatio extrorsus &
mꝛa noṛ́& ab eis. Præliim
limmestabulæ typis ance-
Regio in publicum noẛe
arum ratio ita ſe habitiiner
momorio aut adjacen̄b̄al̄ ad
in litore Anglican̄promonto-
fuam ductæ deſeruere tam ſe-
Mare quâipſosipras hnuj.ce.

SCOTIÆ PARS.

ANGLIA

Scala Leucarum

ANTARCTIC REGION

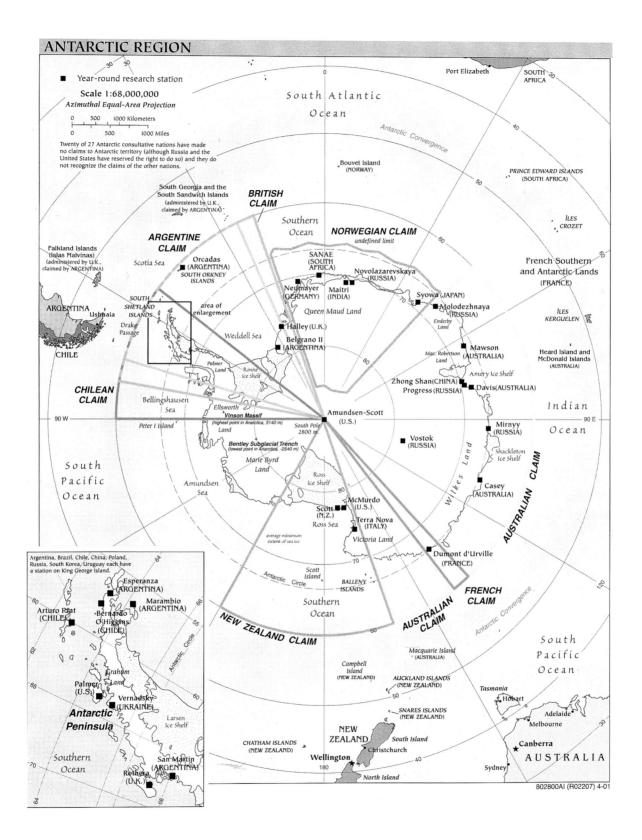

- ■ Year-round research station

Scale 1:68,000,000
Azimuthal Equal-Area Projection

0   500   1000 Kilometers
0   500   1000 Miles

Twenty of 27 Antarctic consultative nations have made
no claims to Antarctic territory (although Russia and the
United States have reserved the right to do so) and they do
not recognize the claims of the other nations.

South Atlantic Ocean

Port Elizabeth
SOUTH AFRICA

Antarctic Convergence

Bouvet Island (NORWAY)

PRINCE EDWARD ISLANDS (SOUTH AFRICA)

ÎLES CROZET

South Georgia and the South Sandwich Islands (administered by U.K. claimed by ARGENTINA)

BRITISH CLAIM

Southern Ocean

NORWEGIAN CLAIM
undefined limit

French Southern and Antarctic Lands (FRANCE)

ARGENTINE CLAIM

Falkland Islands (Islas Malvinas) (administered by U.K., claimed by ARGENTINA)

Scotia Sea

Orcadas (ARGENTINA) SOUTH ORKNEY ISLANDS

SANAE (SOUTH AFRICA)

Novolazarevskaya (RUSSIA)

ÎLES KERGUELEN

ARGENTINA
Ushuaia

SOUTH SHETLAND ISLANDS

area of enlargement

Neumayer (GERMANY) Maitri (INDIA)

Syowa (JAPAN)

Molodezhnaya (RUSSIA)

Queen Maud Land

Enderby Land

Heard Island and McDonald Islands (AUSTRALIA)

CHILE

Drake Passage

Weddell Sea

Halley (U.K.)

Belgrano II (ARGENTINA)

Mac. Robertson Land

Mawson (AUSTRALIA)

Palmer Land

Ronne Ice Shelf

Amery Ice Shelf

CHILEAN CLAIM

Bellingshausen Sea

Ellsworth Land

Zhong Shan (CHINA) Progress (RUSSIA)

Davis (AUSTRALIA)

Indian Ocean

90 W

Peter I Island

Vinson Massif (highest point in Antarctica, 5140 m)

South Pole 2800 m.

Amundsen-Scott (U.S.)

90 E

Mirnyy (RUSSIA)

Shackleton Ice Shelf

South Pacific Ocean

Bentley Subglacial Trench (lowest point in Antarctica, -2540 m)

Marie Byrd Land

Vostok (RUSSIA)

Wilkes Land

Casey (AUSTRALIA)

AUSTRALIAN CLAIM

Amundsen Sea

Ross Ice Shelf

McMurdo (U.S.)

Scott (N.Z.)

Terra Nova (ITALY)

Dumont d'Urville (FRANCE)

Ross Sea

Victoria Land

average minimum extent of sea ice

NEW ZEALAND CLAIM

Scott Island

Antarctic Circle

BALLENY ISLANDS

FRENCH CLAIM

AUSTRALIAN CLAIM

Southern Ocean

Antarctic Convergence

South Pacific Ocean

Macquarie Island (AUSTRALIA)

Campbell Island (NEW ZEALAND)

AUCKLAND ISLANDS (NEW ZEALAND)

Tasmania

Hobart

Canberra

AUSTRALIA

Adelaide

Melbourne

SNARES ISLANDS (NEW ZEALAND)

NEW ZEALAND

CHATHAM ISLANDS (NEW ZEALAND)

South Island

Christchurch

Wellington

North Island

Sydney

Argentina, Brazil, Chile, China, Poland, Russia, South Korea, Uruguay each have a station on King George Island.

Esperanza (ARGENTINA)

Marambio (ARGENTINA)

Arturo Prat (CHILE)

Bernardo O'Higgins (CHILE)

Palmer (U.S.)

Graham Land

Vernadsky (UKRAINE)

Antarctic Peninsula

Larsen Ice Shelf

Antarctic Circle

Southern Ocean

San Martin (ARGENTINA)

Rothera (U.K.)

802800AI (R02207) 4-01

community were those recognized as the common heritage of mankind. They are certain areas of the world, beyond any jurisdiction, protected and preserved as the patrimony of future generations. The ocean bottom, its subsoil, and, most importantly, the pristine Antarctica fall within this category.

In the Library's collections, the conflicting claims surrounding Antarctica are reflected in titles which are among some of the best that were ever derived from legal thought. The terms *Territorial Division (Sectors)* and *Territorial Claims* throw the complex issues open. Seven nations (Great Britain, Chile, France, New Zealand, Norway, Argentina, and Australia) out of the twelve original signatories of the *Antarctic Treaty* (1959) have laid claims to the continent, none of which is recognized by the others (Belgium, Japan, Russia, South Africa, and the United States). At least two parties have based their claims on geographical contiguity, proximity, or territorial extension from the national territory into the Antarctic; others base their claim on the "sector theory," on occupation, or simply on some historic facts seasoned by the passage of time. Elegant legal constructs seem to aim at establishing sovereignty over a piece (sector) of Antarctica, with rights to exploit resources locked in the lands under the ice, in the Continental Shelf, and in the surrounding seas.

Still, the political and legal acts contesting the sole jurisdiction of the seven claimant nations, and the maneuvers of the international entrepreneurdom, preserved in the Library of Congress's collections, do not appear much different from those international quests mounted on ideologies in pursuit of treasure and real estate at other times in history. So far, by virtue of treaties of accession and association, twenty-seven nations have been added to the original "club," making up the thirty-nine treaty parties.

The growing human impact on the Antarctic ecosystem did not drop from the international agenda for years and led to a number of interesting treaties and conventions supplementing the *Antarctic Treaty*. Grave concerns focused on pollution of the pristine environment, after twentieth-century science established evidence of Antarctica's importance for the geo-climatic health. This brought forth a *Code of Environmental Conduct* concerned with pollution and wilderness preservation in an *Antarctic Protected Area System* and two major treaties targeting fishers and hunters whose killings and massive commercial harvesting threatened the fragile Antarctic marine ecosystem (*Convention on the Conservation of Antarctic Seals*, 1972, and *Convention of the Conservation of Antarctic Marine Living Resources*, 1980).

The "Antarctic mineral resources" competition in the wake of energy shortages provoked widespread protest against Antarctic exploitation and pollution in

OPPOSITE: *Antarctica*. This modern map of Antarctica produced by the Central Intelligence Agency shows the Sectors, based on competing legal claims to Antarctic territory. By researching maps from the rare map collection of the Library's Geography and Map Division, one can trace the history of various countries' explorations and mapping of the regions that support their claims, such as the southern polar region shown here. (*Geography and Map Division; LCCN 2003629181*)

an atmosphere of rising global anxiety over ecological implications. Beginning in 1983, a number of high-profile environmental pressure groups mounted their political campaigns in defense of Antarctica under the slogan "World Park Antarctica," which ended up at the United Nations. As documented in the collections of the Library, this call eventually lead in 1991 to the *Protocol to the Antarctic Treaty*, which designated Antarctica as *Heritage of Mankind*, a natural reserve devoted to peace and science, with its resources as commons for generations to come.

THE UNITED NATIONS AND OTHER INTERNATIONAL ORGANIZATIONS

Law touches on most aspects of social life, and International Law and war are no exception. The scope of contemporary International Law had broadened dramatically over the past century, mostly as a consequence of wars. Both the need to understand the legal systems of allied or opposed nations and the long-standing attempts to mitigate some of the horrors of war through international conventions began to be explored more systematically in the nineteenth century.

Humanitarian Law had its start in 1859, when, viewing the helpless wounded lying on an open field after the battle of Solferino, Italy, a merchant named Henry Dunant solicited the help of local villagers to assist the combatants of both sides in the conflict. He later wrote a book, *Un Souvenir de Solferino* (Memory of Solferino), which started a movement that eventually resulted in the founding of a committee that was to become the International Red Cross. Responding to the appeals of Dunant and his supporters, the Swiss government agreed to convene the first Geneva Convention in 1864. The multi-national body of participants at that meeting prepared and adopted a document known as the Geneva Convention for the Amelioration of the Condition of the Wounded in Armies in the Field. Subsequent conventions and protocols have expanded coverage of the initial protection to include prisoners of war, refugees, and other non-combatants.

The inhuman force of the two World Wars had also brought about a line of inter-governmental organizations for cooperation and dialogue among nations, the most important of all being the League of Nations (1925–45) and the United Nations (1945–), followed by scores of regional inter-governmental organizations in Europe, Africa, Asia, and in the Pacific Area. The Law Library holds the full set of documents and publications of the League of Nations and the United Nations (including the treaty set) as well as of regional bodies, in particular the European Community/European Union. Researchers will find an intriguing collection of works on the genesis of the UN. Among them are the papers of the so-called *Dumbarton Oaks Conversations*, the conference held 1945 at Dumbarton Oaks in Washington, D.C. The principles for the new international organization formulated during the Dumbarton Oaks Conference were introduced into the charter of the UN later that year during the San Francisco conference.

Since its inception, the United Nations has become a major publisher not only of the large document sets produced by its individual organs, but of monographic literature relating to its many functions and missions, in particular in the area of human rights (with special focus on women, children, international ethnic rights, right to food, and famine relief). The Humanitarian Law which has its roots in the nineteenth-century Hague Peace System, followed by the twentieth-century Geneva Law, has been recently expanded to encompass the concerns of refugees and mass displacement of peoples, environmental protection, and, of great current urgency, the UN disarmament and peace enforcement machinery.

One of the UN commissions is the International Law Commission, which is continuing the work begun under the League of Nations on the codification of International Law. The Law Library houses its multi-volume, continuing publication (from 1948 forward). The organization is the subject of a watershed of literature as well, including analyses such as Hans Kelsen's work *The Law of the United Nations: A Critical Analysis of Its Fundamental Problems* (New York, 1950) and *International Law on the Eve of the Twenty-first Century: Views from the International Law Commission* (1997).

Although there are multitudinous topics in the collections of the Library that intersect with law, it seems fitting to conclude this overview with a mention of the subject of justice. From such earlier works as *De iure et aequitate forensis disputatio* written in 1541 (LCCN 36024009) by Johann Oldendorp (ca. 1480–1567), to recent works on "organizational justice," the Library contains substantial collections of analytical and comparative treatises on the many facets of justice. Cartoons, posters, and photographs also explore, and in many cases deplore, the vagaries of humankind's pursuit of this most elusive goal.

A Note to Researchers

GENERALLY SPEAKING, the Law Library of Congress is the principal contact point for the study of law materials in the Library of Congress. Researchers are asked to first consult their local, university, county, and state law libraries before using the Law Library's facilities. Remote access is available through the Law Library's home page and reading room sites:

http://www.loc.gov/law/public and http://www.loc.gov/rr/law

The Law Library is located in the James Madison Memorial Building. The Law Library Reading Room is located in room 201 and is open, except for holidays, from Monday through Saturday from 8:30 A.M. to 5:00 P.M. Researchers needing to consult rare law books are invited to call the Law Library at (202) 707–8249 to make an appointment.

Jus est ars boni et aequi.

(Law is the art of the good and the just. Celsus, quoted in Justinian's Digest.)

Contemplation of Justice is one of a pair of heroic statues sculpted by James Earle Fraser in 1935 that flank the main steps of the U.S. Supreme Court (photograph by Hirst Dillow Milhollen, 1940s). (*Prints and Photographs Division; LC-USZ62-104102*)